AF522414

OBJECT ORIENTED PROGRAMMING WITH C++

OBJECT ORIENTED PROGRAMMING WITH C++

Manoj Bhatia

ANMOL PUBLICATIONS PVT. LTD.
NEW DELHI-110 002 (INDIA)

ANMOL PUBLICATIONS PVT. LTD.
Regd. Office: 4360/4, Ansari Road, Daryaganj,
New Delhi-110002 (India)
Tel.: 23278000, 23261597, 23286875, 23255577
Fax: 91-11-23280289
Email: anmolpub@gmail.com
Visit us at: www.anmolpublications.com

Branch Office: No. 1015, Ist Main Road, BSK IIIrd Stage
IIIrd Phase, IIIrd Block, Bangalore-560 085 (India)
Tel.: 080-41723429 • Fax: 080-26723604
Email: anmolpublicationsbangalore@gmail.com

Object Oriented Programming with C++

First Edition, 2010

ISBN 978-81-261-4398-6

PRINTED IN INDIA

Printed at Mehra Offset Press, Delhi.

Contents

Preface

Object Oriented Programming using C++ is now established as one of the leading textbook which highlights on programming languages for object-oriented software development. Its advantages over other languages include speed and flexibility. It is used as the base for many commercial software products and for performance solutions to complex problems. Not often taught as the primary programming language, students are frequently expected to pick up the language for themselves. This book is an ideal student self-learning guide.

The book is designed as a step-by-step, which covers all language features and explains their practical usage. Intuitive examples are used that are neither too complex to distract, nor oversimplified. A key concept in C++ is programming with templates, which can help to program generic solutions - for example implementing polymorphism. It is a book that goes well beyond the basics.

Author

Chapter 1

Object Modelling

REAL TOOL

A type of programming in which programmers define not only the data type of a data structure, but also the types of operations (functions) that can be applied to the data structure. In this way, the data structure becomes an object that includes both data and functions. In addition, programmers can create relationships between one object and another.

For example, objects can inherit characteristics from other objects. One of the principal advantages of object-oriented programming techniques over procedural programming techniques is that they enable programmers to create modules that do not need to be changed when a new type of object is added. A programmer can simply create a new object that inherits many of its features from existing objects.

This makes object-oriented programmes easier to modify. To perform object-oriented programming, one needs an object-oriented programming language (OOPL). Java, C++ and Smalltalk are three of the more popular languages, and there are also object-oriented versions of Pascal.

OBJECTS

An object is a software bundle of related state and behaviour. Software objects are often used to model the real-world objects that you find in everyday life. This lesson explains how state and behaviour are represented within an object, introduces the concept of data encapsulation, and explains the benefits of designing your software in this manner.

CLASS

A class is a blueprint or prototype from which objects are created. This section defines a class that models the state and behaviour of a real-world object. It intentionally focuses on the basics, showing how even a simple class can cleanly model state and behaviour.

INHERITANCE

Inheritance provides a powerful and natural mechanism for organizing and structuring your software. This section explains how classes inherit state and behaviour from their superclasses, and explains how to derive one class from another using the simple syntax provided by the Java programming language.

INTERFACE

An interface is a contract between a class and the outside world. When a class implements an interface, it promises to provide the behaviour published by that interface. This section defines a simple interface and explains the necessary changes for any class that implements it.

PACKAGE

A package is a namespace for organizing classes and interfaces in a logical manner. Placing your code into packages makes large software projects easier to manage. This section explains why this is useful, and introduces you to the Application Programming Interface (API) provided by the Java platform. Object-oriented programming (OOP) is a programming language model organized around "objects" rather than "actions" and data rather than logic. Historically, a programme has been viewed as a logical procedure that takes input data, processes it, and produces output data.

The programming challenge was seen as how to write the logic, not how to define the data. Object-oriented programming takes the view that what we really care about are the objects we want to manipulate rather than the logic required to manipulate them. Examples of objects range from human beings (described by name, address, and so forth) to buildings and floors (whose properties can be described and managed) down to the little widgets on your computer desktop (such as buttons and scroll bars).

The first step in OOP is to identify all the objects you want to manipulate and how they relate to each other, an exercise often known as data modeling. Once you've identified an object, you generalize it as a class of objects (think of Plato's concept of the "ideal" chair that stands for all chairs) and define the kind of data it contains and any logic sequences that can manipulate it. Each distinct logic sequence is known as a method. A real instance of a class is called (no surprise here) an "object" or, in some environments, an "instance of a class." The object or class instance is what you run in the computer. Its methods provide computer instructions and the class object characteristics provide relevant data. You communicate with objects - and they communicate with each other - with well-defined interfaces called messages.

The concepts and rules used in object-oriented programming provide these important benefits: The concept of a data class makes it possible to define subclasses of data objects that share some or all of the main class characteristics. Called inheritance, this property of OOP forces a more thorough data analysis, reduces development time, and ensures more accurate coding. Since a class defines only the data it needs to be concerned with, when an instance of that class (an object) is run, the code will not be able to accidentally access other programme data. This characteristic of data hiding provides greater system security

DEFINITION

The demand for businesses to deploy solutions across multiplc servers is bound to increase. With the growth and acceptance of the Internet, businesses have come to think of their applications and information be connected and distributed across multiple servers from remote locations. Also data can be processed and accessed through the use of Web browsers and by user interfaces. But a number of problems stands on the way towards developing and deploying mission-critical business applications on several server systems. These applications are named as distributed software applications. They are communication issues among different programming languages and platforms and security. There are a few promising technologies for promoting these critical applications.. Microsoft has come out with a new technology called as Component Object Model (COM) that addresses these problems towards the goal of design of distributed software components.

COM

COM is an outgrowth of the OO technology. It is a specification that is based on a binary standard for reuse through interfaces. That is, components, which are pre-compiled blocks of code, written for COM can be reused without any dependencies on the language in which they are coded. The programming language may be Visual Basic, C++ etc. COM uses system-level code that is implemented in the form of dynamic link libraries, which are collectively called COM library.

The COM library consists of several application programming interface (API) functions that are necessary for COM components to do various tasks. COM library is responsible for locating and activating server applications. With client applications, COM APIs contains the necessary functions for instantiating objects that the client want to use. Also the COM library provides locator services using the System Control Manager (SCM), which also provides transparent remote procedure calls when an object is executing out-of-process in a local or remote server.

COMPONENT-BASED DEVELOPMENT (CBD)

CBD came from OO software development methodology towards facilitating software reusability in larger scale. Suppose there is an object and we want to use that in an application. For that, we have to cut and paste the code in the application. If there is any changes made in the object, we have to search for all the object copies in the application to insert the relevant changes. This becomes cumbersome when there are more applications with more copies of the same object. Here comes the idea of designing components as a robust solution. A component can be technically defined as a coarse-grained object.

It is also defined as a reusable software module, which displays its services through interfaces for use by client· software. On using a component, which is stored in a single place, applications can use the object directly from the component and get the same functionality. Thus both classes, where objects get derived from and components provide same type of services. Classes pro! vide services to single applications because they can not communicate with other applications due to the differences in language and platform, while components provide services to numerous applications irrespective of the languages used. There came a number of architecture for developing both client-side and server-side components. They are OMG's CORBA, Sun's JaveBeans and Enterprise JavaBeans and Microsoft's COM. Thus the world is full of software components, which in turn can be of greater use for hundreds of different applications. As both CORBA and COM supports language independence, a different software vendor can create components using different programming languages without any integration problems.

ADVANTAGES OF COM

- COM promotes component-based software development - before component-based development came, software programmes have been coded using procedural programming paradigm, which supports linear form of programme execution. But component-based programme development comes with a number of advantages, such as the ability to use pre-packaged components and tools from third party vendors into an application and support for code reusability in other parts of the same application.
- COM promotes code reusability - standard classes

are normally reused in the same application but not to be used easily in other applications. But COM components are designed to separate themselves from single applications and hence can be accessed and used by several different applications without any hassle.

- COM promotes Object-oriented programming (OOP) - The primary characteristics of OOP are encapsulation, which allows the implementation details of an object to be hidden, polymorphism, which is the ability to exhibit multiple behaviours, and inheritance, which allows for the reuse of existing classes in order to design new and more specialized classes. Among these, encapsulation is one of COM's most important characteristics. Encapsulation helps to hide how an object has implemented a method internally. This ultimately helps to incorporate more vigorously implemented or advanced implementation into an object at later time without affecting the client which uses it.
- COM comprises the necessary mechanisms for COM components to communicate with each other - In the normal case, two components coded using two different programming languages can not communicate with each other. But COM can make it possible for different language components, which adhere to the COM specification, to interact with each other and hence COM is language-independent.
- COM helps to access components loaded in different machines on the network - COM component can reside anywhere on our computer or even on another computer connected to a network. That is, applications using COM can access and share COM components regardless of their locations. Thus COM abstracts away the nitty-gritty of clients to locate COM components anywhere in the network. Thus COM provides location transparency and COM components are location independent.

COM INTERFACES

Components, especially server-side ones, are bound to have their own interfaces. An interface is simply a list of methods a COM component implements and makes them available to consumers. COM interface are immutable. That is, once a COM component has been released with an interface, this interface must never be manipulated. COM interfaces are the mechanisms by which a client contacts, connects and use components. If the client component is using a different language from the one a server component is coded, there will be language problem for interactions. In order to remove this barrier, COM interfaces provide an universal way so that components coded in different languages can communicate with each other. Thus every interface constitutes a binding contract between a COM object (no interface is attached with this) and a COM component with an interface. COM specification makes life easier by allowing a component to publish more than one interface at a time. New interfaces can! be incorporated to support new features of the components while keeping the original interface intact. We have to increment a version number for the new interface. A class module then would need to be implemented for both old and new interfaces in order to support both old clients that rely on the old interface and new clients that can take advantage of the new interface. Thus the immutability factor of COM interfaces can be overcome.

INTERFACE DEFINITION LANGUAGE (IDL)

To successfully make COM language-independent, the COM interfaces have to coded using IDL. IDL is just a declaration language, not a programming language. The syntax for IDL is almost similar to C++ language. But IDL goes beyond what C++ can offer by being able to define functions that extend process boundaries. IDL provides many vital extensions that allow attributes such as type libraries, co-classes, interfaces, and method parameters to be specified quite elegantly. But if there is no language problem, it is not mandatory to use IDL for defining COM interfaces.

Here comes an model interface definition for a COM component coded using Microsoft IDL.

```
[ object,
  uuid (122323FAGAd098776)
]
  interface IFindSum : IUnknown
{
  import "unknown.idl"
  HRESULT SumOfNumbers ([in] long lnum1,
  [in] long lnum2, [out, retval] long*
  sum);
}
```

The interface definition begins with an object attribute. The object attribute is used to identify a COM interface. Then a UUID (universally unique identifier), which provides an unique identifying number (a string of hexadecimal digits) for each interface and this number is being generated by an algorithm, which takes into account the unique value from the network card on the programmer's PC and the current system date and time, follows that. The interface keyword is followed by the name of the interface (IFindSum). The letter I in the interface name helps to identify that this is an interface. Following IFindSum is a colon and then the interface name IUnknown, the base interface and every COM object has to have this interface. IUnknown has three methods that a client can invoke: QueryInterface, AddRef, and Release.

The QueryInterface method is the mechanism that a client uses to discover and navigate the interfaces of a component dynamically. It is the most significant method of all COM interfaces available for a component since this method allows run-time checking of all of these interfaces. When the QueryInterface method provides an interface pointer to a client, the QueryInterface calls the method AddRef. The only way to access a COM object is through a pointer to an interface.

An interface pointer is actually a pointer to a pointer in a virtual table that is implemented in memory. That is, for every class that contains public methods, a virtual table will be created and placed in memory at run time. Virtual tables are generated for each class and not for objects of that class. Each virtual table contains an array of function pointers whose elements contain the address of each specific function that an object can implement. At the top of every virtual table array will be three fundamental methods that make up this IUnknown interface. The methods AddRef and Release manage reference counting. This reference count is an internal count of the number of clients using a particular COM object . It is possible for several clients to invoke the services available with a COM object at the same time. When a client begins a session with an object, it calls the AddRef method, which increments one to the existing count. Once the session is over, the corresponding Release method gets invoked to decrement one from the existing count. The next line down is used to locate the definition for the base interface IUnknown The next line identifies the interface method "SumofNumbers". This interface method is designed to return an HRESULT value.

An HRESULT is used with COM to indicate whether a method call is successfully accomplished or not. Almost all COM interfaces return a special 32-bit code, called as HRESULT, from their methods to return status information. It is actually the method COM utilizes to return errors to the caller of the method. The reason for this mechanism is due to the inability of COM to transmit error messages back to the client if there is anything wrong on the server side or on the way to the server. As components are being written using different programming languages and each language follows its own exception mechanisms, COM can not correctly pass on the error messages and hence HRESULT. Following the HRESULT are three parameters for the interface method SumOfNumbers. The [in] in the first two parameters specifies that these parameters are input values to be passed to the interface method and the [out, retval] in the last parameter indicates that this parameter returns a value that will be ultimately passed to back to the client.

WINDOWS REGISTRY AND COMPONENTS

COM components may be loaded in different address

spaces in the same machine or machine connected with the network. Before an object can be created, the COM runtime must first locate the COM components. The COM runtime is able to locate COM components through the use of Windows registry.

COM components may be out-of-process or in-process. An out-of-process component can effectively be a separate programme containing objects. This type runs in its own process space and will thus be largely independent from any client programmes.

These components are often large applications themselves, and provide access to their objects to make it easy for other programmes to create macros or otherwise make use of existing functionality. This can be very beneficial, because the component developer can choose his own threading models. The drawback here is that the developer has to write the code for threading.

This work can be handled by automatically COM+ , the latest one from the COM family. There is also a performance issue. Because the client application is communicating with objects which are in an entirely different process there is quite a bit of overhead.

COM steps in between the client and the server and handles all the communication between them. Mainly out-of-process components are useful if we are trying to make use of the objects in a pre-existing application. An in-process component is one where the objects run inside the client's process. Each client gets its own private copy of the component and hence a copy of all the objects in that component. An in-process component is often called COM DLLs or ActiveX DLLs. In-process component does not have a process of its own and it always runs within the context of another process. Often this other process is the client application itself but may be run within the context of a different process entirely.

In this case, we can get performance boost as the component is loaded in the client application itself. There is almost no overhead when client interacts with an object that is running in the same process. The major advantages of having in-process components are stability and increased manageability

CREATING A COM OBJECT

There is a lot of communication that must occur behind the scenes in order for a COM object to be created. First of all, a client looking for an object has to make a call to an API function called CoCreate Instance with the CLSID for the class, which comprises the particular object. The prefix Co in this function is a typical naming convention for COM runtime API functions. Co Create Instance in turn as a second step calls another API function called Co Get Class Object. Basically the function Co Create Instance asks the SCM to search the Windows registry location, which is HKEY_CLASSES _ROOT\ CLSID. The function of SCM is to locate the requested class object by using the specified CLSID. The first place the SCM looks to locate the class object is within its own internal database. If the class is not located inside its database, the SCM turns to the system registry as a third step. As soon as the class object is found, the SCM immediately returns to COM an interface pointer referred to as IClass Factory.

Every COM class must have a factory object associated with it. The main purpose of these class objects is to implement the IClass Factory interface. Once the client gets the IClass Factory pointer, two things happen. One, by obtaining a pointer to the IClass Factory, Co Create Instance can call IClass Factory:: Create Instance in order to create the requested COM object. Once the object is created, a second step occurs: the interface pointer to the IClass Factory gets released.

The interface called IClass Factory's job is to talk to other class objects. Further, Co Get Class Object is a COM class object whose sole purpose is to create a new instance of a different class. Because this COM class creates class objects by implementing the IClass Factory interface, CoGet Class Object is referred to as a class factory.

LOCKSERVER

When an object is created it resides in memory. It is the

client's job to notify the object when it is no longer needed. The Release method told above can decrement the reference count for the interface. If there are several interfaces for an object, it is possible that the object is still being accessed somewhere else. The idea is that the reference count has to reach zero before the object is to be released from the memory. Releasing objects from memory usually improves performance. Some special clients constantly create and destroy objects, which normally affects the application's performance. The Lock Server method allows components to remain in memory by incrementing the reference count by one. Because LockServer keeps a count of one in the reference counter, the object will stay in memory even if it is not being accessed currently. Having the component reside in memory has the advantage of allowing the object to be called without having to go through the process of recre! ating it. But on the other hand, if objects are not destroyed when they are not in use, there will be reduction of system memory resources.

Chapter 2

C-Language

HIGH LEVEL LANGUAGE

C is a relatively small language, but one which wears well. C's small, unambitious feature set is a real advantage: there's less to learn; there isn't excess baggage in the way when you don't need it. It can also be a disadvantage: since it doesn't do everything for you, there's a lot you have to do yourself. C is sometimes referred to as a "high-level assembly language." Some people think that's an insult, but it's actually a deliberate and significant aspect of the language.

If you have programmed in assembly language, you'll probably find C very natural and comfortable (although if you continue to focus too heavily on machine-level details, you'll probably end up with unnecessarily nonportable programmes). If you haven't programmed in assembly language, you may be frustrated by C's lack of certain higher-level features. In either case, you should understand why C was designed this way: so that seemingly-simple constructions expressed in C would not expand to arbitrarily expensive (in time or space) machine language constructions when compiled.

If you write a C programme simply and succinctly, it is likely to result in a succinct, efficient machine language executable. If you find that the executable programme resulting from a C programme is not efficient, it's probably because of something silly you did, not because of something the compiler did behind your back which you have no control over. In any case, there's no point in complaining about C's low-level flavour: C is what it is. A programming language is a tool, and no tool can perform every task unaided. If you're building a house, and I'm teaching you how to use a hammer, and you ask how to assemble rafters and trusses into gables, that's a legitimate question, but the answer has fallen out of the realm of "How do I use a hammer?" and into "How do I build a house?". In the same way, we'll see that C does not have built-in features to perform every function that we might ever need to do while programming.

As mentioned above, C imposes relatively few built-in ways of doing things on the programmer. Some common tasks, such as manipulating strings, allocating memory, and doing input/output (I/O), are performed by calling on library functions. Other tasks which you might want to do, such as creating or listing directories, or interacting with a mouse, or displaying windows or other user-interface elements, or doing colour graphics, are not defined by the C language at all.

You can do these things from a C programme, of course, but you will be calling on services which are peculiar to your programming environment (compiler, processor, and operating system) and which are not defined by the C standard. Since this course is about portable C programming, it will also be steering clear of facilities not provided in all C environments. Another aspect of C that's worth mentioning here is that it is, to put it bluntly, a bit dangerous.

C does not, in general, try hard to protect a programmer from mistakes. If you write a piece of code which will (through some oversight of yours) do something wildly different from what you intended it to do, up to and including deleting your data or trashing your disk, and if it is possible for the compiler to compile it, it generally will. You won't get warnings of the form "Do you really mean to...?" or "Are you sure you really want to...?". C is often compared to a sharp knife: it can do a surgically precise job on some exacting task you have in mind, but it can also do a surgically precise job of cutting off your finger. It's up to you to use it carefully.

This aspect of C is very widely criticized; it is also used (justifiably) to argue that C is not a good teaching language. C aficionados love this aspect of C because it means that C does not try to protect them from themselves: when they know what they're doing, even if it's risky or obscure, they can do it. Students of C hate this aspect of C because it often seems as if the language is some kind of a conspiracy specifically designed to lead them into booby traps.

This is another aspect of the language which it's fairly pointless to complain about. If you take care and pay attention, you can avoid many of the pitfalls. These notes will point out many of the obvious (and not so obvious) trouble spots.

The first example programme is the first example programme in any language: print or display a simple string, and exit. Here is "hello, world" programme:

```
#include <stdio.h>
main()
{
  printf("Hello, world!\n");
  return 0;
}
```

If you have a C compiler, the first thing to do is figure out how to type this programme in and compile it and run it and see where its output went.The first line is practically boilerplate; it will appear in almost all programmes we write. It asks that some definitions having to do with the "Standard I/O Library" be included in our programme; these definitions are needed if we are to call the library function printf correctly.

The second line says that we are defining a function named main. Most of the time, we can name our functions anything we want, but the function name main is special: it is the function that will be "called" first when our programme starts running. The empty pair of parentheses indicates that our main function accepts no*arguments*, that is, there isn't any information which needs to be passed in when the function is called. The braces { and } surround a list of statements in C. Here, they surround the list of statements making up the function main.

The line

```
printf("Hello, world!\n");
```

is the first statement in the programme. It asks that the

function printf be called; printf is a library function which prints formatted output. The parentheses surroundprintf's argument list: the information which is handed to it which it should act on. The semicolon at the end of the line terminates the statement (printf's name reflects the fact that C was first developed when Teletypes and other printing terminals were still in widespread use. Today, of course, video displays are far more common. printf's "prints" to the *standard output,* that is, to the default location for programme output to go. Nowadays, that's almost always a video screen or a window on that screen.

If you do have a printer, you'll typically have to do something extra to get a programme to print to it.) printf's first (and, in this case, only) argument is the string which it should print. The string, enclosed in double quotes "", consists of the words "Hello, world!" followed by a special sequence: \n. In strings, any two-character sequence beginning with the backslash \ represents a single special character. The sequence \nrepresents the "new line" character, which prints a carriage return or line feed or whatever it takes to end one line of output and move down to the next. (This programme only prints one line of output, but it's still important to terminate it.)

The second line in the main function is

```
return 0;
```

In general, a function may return a value to its caller, and main is no exception. When main returns (that is, reaches its end and stops functioning), the programme is at its end, and the return value from main tells the operating system (or whatever invoked the programme that main is the main function of) whether it succeeded or not. By convention, a return value of 0 indicates success.

This programme may look so absolutely trivial that it seems as if it's not even worth typing it in and trying to run it, but doing so may be a big (and is certainly a vital) first hurdle. On an unfamiliar computer, it can be arbitrarily difficult to figure out how to enter a text file containing programme source, or how to compile and link it, or how to invoke it, or what happened after (if?) it ran. The most experienced C programmers immediately go back to this one, simple programme whenever they're trying out a new system or a new way of entering or building programmes or a new way of printing output from within programmes. As Kernighan and Ritchie say, everything else is comparatively easy.

How *you* compile and run this (or any) programme is a function of the compiler and operating system you're using. The first step is to type it in, exactly as shown; this may involve using a text editor to create a file containing the programme text. You'll have to give the file a name, and all C compilers require that files containing C source end with the extension .c. So you might place the programme text in a file called hello.c.

The second step is to compile the programme. (Strictly speaking, compilation consists of two steps, compilation proper followed by linking, but we can overlook this distinction at first, especially because the compiler often takes care of initiating the linking step automatically.) On many Unix systems, the command to compile a C programme from a source file hello.c is

```
cc -o hello hello.c
```

You would type this command at the Unix shell prompt, and it requests that the cc (C compiler) programme be run, placing its output (i.e. the new executable programme it creates) in the file hello, and taking its input (i.e. the source code to be compiled) from the file hello.c.

The third step is to run (execute, invoke) the newly-built hello programme. Again on a Unix system, this is done simply by typing the program's name:

```
hello
```

Depending on how your system is set up (in particular, on whether the current directory is searched for executables, based on the PATH variable), you may have to type

```
./hello
```

to indicate that the hello programme is in the current directory (as opposed to some "bin" directory full of executable programmes, elsewhere). You may also have your choice of C compilers. On many Unix machines, the cc command is an older compiler which does not recognize modern, ANSI Standard C syntax. An old compiler will accept the simple programmes we'll be starting with, but it will not accept most of our later programmes. If you find yourself getting baffling compilation errors on programmes which you've typed in exactly as they're shown, it probably indicates that you're using an older compiler.

On many machines, another compiler called acc or gcc is available, and you'll want to use it, instead. (Both acc and gcc are typically invoked the same as cc; that is, the above cc command would instead be typed, say, gcc -o hello hello.c .)

In an integrated or "visual" progamming environment, such as those on the Macintosh or under various versions of Microsoft Windows, the steps you take to enter, compile, and run a programme are somewhat different (and, theoretically, simpler). Typically, there is a way to open a new source window, type source code into it, give it a file name, and add it to the programme (or "project") you're building.

If necessary, there will be a way to specify what other source files (or "modules") make up the programme. Then, there's a button or menu selection which compiles and runs the programme, all from within the programming environment.

(There will also be a way to create a standalone executable file which you can run from outside the environment.) In a PC-compatible environment, you may have to choose between creating DOS programmes or Windows programmes. (If you have troubles pertaining to the printf function, try specifying a target environment of MS-DOS.

Supposedly, some compilers which are targeted at Windows environments won't let you call printf, because until you call some fancier functions to request that a window be created, there's no window for printf to print to.)

Again, check the introductory or tutorial manual that came with the programming package; it should walk you through the steps necessary to get your first programme running. Our second example is of little more practical use than the first, but it introduces a few more programming language elements:

```
#include <stdio.h>
/* print a few numbers, to illustrate a
 simple loop */
main()
{
  int i;
  for(i = 0; i < 10; i = i + 1)
  printf("i is %d\n", i);
  return 0;
}
```

As before, the line #include <stdio.h> is boilerplate which is necessary since we're calling the printf function, and main() and the pair of braces {} indicate and delineate the function named main we're (again) writing.

The first new line is the line

```
/* print a few numbers, to illustrate a
 simple loop */
```

which is a *comment*. Anything between the characters /* and */ is ignored by the compiler, but may be useful to a person trying to read and understand the programme. You can add comments anywhere you want to in the programme, to document what the programme is, what it does, who wrote it, how it works, what the various functions are for and how *they* work, what the various variables are for, etc.

The second new line, down within the function main, is

```
int i;
```

which *declares* that our function will use a variable named i. The variable's type is int, which is a plain integer.

Next, we set up a *loop*:

```
for(i = 0; i < 10; i = i + 1)
```

The keyword for indicates that we are setting up a "for loop." A for loop is controlled by three expressions, enclosed in parentheses and separated by semicolons. These expressions say that, in this case, the loop starts by setting i to 0, that it continues as long as i is less than 10, and that after each iteration of the loop, i should be incremented by 1 (that is, have 1 added to its value). Finally, we have a call to the printf function, as before, but with several differences. First, the call to printf is within the *body* of the for loop. This means that control flow does not pass once through the printf call, but instead that the call is performed as many times as are dictated by the for loop. In this case, printfwill be called several times: once when i is 0, once when i is 1, once when i is 2, and so on until i is 9, for a total of 10 times.

A second difference in the printf call is that the string to be printed, "i is %d", contains a per cent sign. When ever printf sees a per cent sign, it indicates thatprintf is not supposed to print the exact text of the string, but is instead supposed to read another one of its arguments to decide what to print. The letter after the per cent sign tells it what type of argument to expect and how to print it. In this case, the letter d indicates that printf is to expect an int, and to print it in decimal. Finally, we see that printf is in fact being called with another argument, for a total of two, separated by commas. The second argument is the variable i, which is in fact an int, as required by %d. The effect of all of this is that each time it is called, printf will print a line containing the current value of the variable i:

```
i is 0
i is 1
i is 2
...
```

After several trips through the loop, i will eventually equal 9. After that trip through the loop, the third control expression i = i + 1 will increment its value to 10. The condition i < 10 is no longer true, so no more trips through the loop are taken. Instead, control flow jumps down to the statement following the for loop, which is the return statement. The main function returns, and the programme is finished.

PROGRAMME STRUCTURE

We'll have more to say later about programme structure, but for now let's observe a few basics. A programme consists of one or more functions; it may also contain global variables.

(Our two example programmes so far have contained one function apiece, and no global variables.) At the top of a source file are typically a few boilerplate lines such as #include <stdio.h>, followed by the definitions (i.e. code) for the functions. (It's also possible to split up the several functions making up a larger programme into several source files, as we'll see in a later chapter.)

Each function is further composed of *declarations* and *statements*, in that order. When a sequence of statements should act as one (for example, when they should all serve together as the body of a loop) they can be enclosed in braces (just as for the outer body of the entire function). The simplest kind of statement is an *expression statement*, which is an expression (presumably performing some useful operation) followed by a semicolon. Expressions are further composed of *operators*, *objects*(variables), and *constants*.

C source code consists of several *lexical elements*. Some are words, such as for, return, main, and i, which are either *keywords* of the language (for, return) or *identifiers* (names) we've chosen for our own functions and variables (main, i). There are *constants* such as 1 and 10 which introduce new values into the programme. There are *operators* such as =, +, and >, which manipulate variables and values. There are other punctuation characters (often called *delimiters*), such as parentheses and squiggly braces {}, which indicate how the other elements of the programme are grouped. Finally, all of the preceding elements can be separated by*whitespace*: spaces, tabs, and the "carriage returns" between lines.

The source code for a C programme is, for the most part, "free form." This means that the compiler does not care how the code is arranged: how it is broken into lines, how the lines are indented, or whether whitespace is used between things like variable names and other punctuation. (Lines like #include <stdio.h> are an exception; they must appear alone on their own lines, generally unbroken. Only lines beginning with # are affected by this rule; we'll see other examples later.) You can use whitespace, indentation, and appropriate line breaks to make your programmes more readable for yourself and other people (even though the compiler doesn't care). You can place explanatory *comments* anywhere in your programme—any text between the characters /* and */ is ignored by the compiler. (In fact, the compiler pretends that all it saw was whitespace.) Though comments are ignored by the compiler, well-chosen comments can make a programme *much* easier to read. The usage of whitespace is our first *style* issue.

It's typical to leave a blank line between different parts of the programme, to leave a space on either side of operators such as + and =, and to *indent* the bodies of loops and other control flow constructs. Typically, we arrange the indentation so that the subsidiary statements controlled by a loop statement (the "loop body," such as the printf call in our second example programme) are all aligned with each other and placed one tab stop (or some consistent number of spaces) to the right of the controlling statement.

This indentation (like all whitespace) is not required by the compiler, but it makes programs*much* easier to read. (However, it can also be misleading, if used incorrectly or in the face of inadvertent mistakes. The compiler will decide what "the body of the loop" is based on its own rules, not the indentation, so if the indentation does not match the compiler's interpretation, confusion is inevitable.)

To drive home the point that the compiler doesn't care about indentation, line breaks, or other whitespace, here are a few (extreme) examples: The fragments

```
for(i = 0; i < 10; i = i + 1)
printf("%d\n", i);
```

and

```
for(i = 0; i < 10; i = i + 1) printf("%d\n",
 i);
```

and

```
for(i=0;i<10;i=i+1)printf("%d\n",i);
```

and

```
for(i = 0; i < 10; i = i + 1)
printf("%d\n", i);
```

and

```
for ( i
```

```
= 0 ;
i < 10
; i =
i + 1
) printf (
"%d\n"    ,   i
) ;
and
for
(i=0;
i<10;i=
i+1)printf
("%d\n", i);
```

are all treated exactly the same way by the compiler. Some programmers argue forever over the best set of "rules" for indentation and other aspects of programming style, calling to mind the old philosopher's debates about the number of angels that could dance on the head of a pin. Style issues (such as how a programme is laid out) *are* important, but they're not something to be too dogmatic about, and there are also other, deeper style issues besides mere layout and typography:

Although C compilers do not care about how a programme looks, proper indentation and spacing are critical in making programmes easy for people to read. We recommend writing only one statement per line, and using blanks around operators to clarify grouping. The position of braces is less important, although people hold passionate beliefs. We have chosen one of several popular styles. Pick a style that suits you, then use it consistently.

Chapter 3

Data Types and Operators

TYPES

There are only a few basic data types in C. The first ones we'll be encountering and using are:

- Char a character
- Int an integer, in the range -32,767 to 32,767
- Long int a larger integer (up to +-2,147,483,647)
- Float a floating-point number
- Double a floating-point number, with more precision and perhaps greater range than float

If you can look at this list of basic types and say to yourself, "Oh, how simple, there are only a few types, I won't have to worry much about choosing among them," you'll have an easy time with declarations. (Some masochists wish that the type system were more complicated so that they could specify more things about each variable, but those of us who would rather not have to specify these extra things each time are glad that we don't have to.)

The ranges listed above for types int and long int are the guaranteed minimum ranges. On some systems, either of these types (or, indeed, any C type) may be able to hold larger values, but a programme that depends on extended ranges will not be as portable. Some programmers become obsessed with knowing exactly what the sizes of data objects will be in various situations, and go on to write programmes which depend on these exact sizes. Determining or controlling the size of an object is occasionally important, but most of the time we can sidestep size issues and let the compiler do most of the worrying. (From the ranges listed above, we can determine that type int must be at least 16 bits, and that type long int must be at least 32 bits.

But neither of these sizes is exact; many systens have 32-bit ints, and some systems have 64-bit long ints.) You might wonder how the computer stores characters. The answer involves a *character set,* which is simply a mapping between some set of characters and some set of small numeric codes. Most machines today use the ASCII character set, in which the letter A is represented by the code 65, the ampersand & is represented by the code 38, the digit 1 is represented by the code 49, the space character is represented by the code 32, etc. (Most of the time, of course, you have *no* need to know or even worry about these particular code values; they're automatically translated into the right shapes on the screen or printer when characters are printed out, and they're automatically generated when you type characters on the keyboard.

Eventually, though, we'll appreciate, and even take some control over, exactly when these translations—from characters to their numeric codes—are performed.) Character codes are usually small—the largest code value in ASCII is 126, which is the ~ (tilde or circumflex) character. Characters usually fit in a byte, which is usually 8 bits. In C, type char is defined as occupying one byte, so it is usually 8 bits. Most of the simple variables in most programmes are of types int, long int, or double.

Typically, we'll use int anddouble for most purposes, and long int any time we need to hold integer values greater than 32,767. As we'll see, even when we're manipulating individual characters, we'll usually use an int variable, for reasons to be discussed later. Therefore, we'll rarely use individual variables of type char; although we'll use plenty of arrays of char.

CONSTANTS

A constant is just an immediate, absolute value found in an expression. The simplest constants are decimal integers, e.g. 0,1, 2, 123 . Occasionally it is useful to specify constants in base 8 or base 16 (octal or hexadecimal); this is done by prefixing an extra 0 (zero) for octal, or 0x for hexadecimal: the constants 100, 0144, and 0x64 all represent the same number. (If you're not using these non-decimal constants, just remember not to use any leading zeroes. If you accidentally write 0123 intending to get one hundred and twenty three, you'll get 83 instead, which is 123 base 8.)

We write constants in decimal, octal, or hexadecimal for our convenience, not the compiler's. The compiler doesn't care; it always converts everything into binary internally, anyway. (There is, however, no good way to specify constants in source code in binary.)

A constant can be forced to be of type long int by suffixing it with the letter L (in upper or lower case, although upper case is strongly recommended, because a lower case l looks too much like the digit 1). A constant that contains a decimal point or the letter e (or both) is a floating-point constant: 3.14, 10., .01, 123e4, 123.456e7 . The e indicates multiplication by a power of 10; 123.456e7 is 123.456 times 10 to the 7th, or 1,234,560,000. (Floating-point constants are of type double by default.)

We also have constants for specifying characters and strings. (Make sure you understand the difference between a character and a string: a character is exactly one character; a string is a set of zero or more characters; a string containing one character is distinct from a lone character.) A character constant is simply a single character between single quotes:'A', '.', '%'. The numeric value of a character constant is, naturally enough, that character's value in the machine's character set. (In ASCII, for example, 'A' has the value 65.)

A *string* is represented in C as a sequence or array of characters. (We'll have more to say about arrays in general, and strings in particular, later.) A string constant is a sequence of zero or more characters enclosed in double quotes: "apple" ,"hello, world", "this is a test". Within character and string constants, the backslash character \ is special, and is used to represent characters not easily typed on the keyboard or for various reasons not easily typed in constants.

The most common of these "character escapes" are:

```
\n  a "newline" character
\b  a backspace
\r  a carriage return (without a line feed)
\'  a single quote (e.g. in a character
    constant)
\"  a double quote (e.g. in a string
    constant)
\\  a single backslash
```

For example, "he said \"hi\"" is a string constant which contains two double quotes, and '\'' is a character constant consisting of a (single) single quote. Notice once again that the character constant 'A' is very different from the string constant "A".

DECLARATIONS

Informally, a *variable* (also called an *object*) is a place you can store a value. So that you can refer to it unambiguously, a variable needs a name. You can think of the variables in your programme as a set of boxes or cubbyholes, each with a label giving its name; you might imagine that storing a value "in" a variable consists of writing the value on a slip of paper and placing it in the cubbyhole. A *declaration* tells the compiler the name and type of a variable you'll be using in your programme. In its simplest form, a declaration consists of the type, the name of the variable, and a terminating semicolon:

```
char c;
int i;
float f;
```

You can also declare several variables of the same type in one declaration, separating them with commas:

```
int i1, i2;
```

Later we'll see that declarations may also contain initializers, qualifiers and storage classes, and that we can declare arrays,functions, pointers, and other kinds of data structures. The placement of declarations is significant. You can't place them just anywhere (i.e. they cannot be interspersed with the other statements in your programme). They must either be placed at the beginning of a function, or at the beginning of a brace-enclosed block of statements (which we'll learn about in the next chapter), or outside of any function. Furthermore, the placement of a declaration, as well as its storage class, controls several things about its visibility and lifetime.

You may wonder why variables must be declared before use. There are two reasons:

- It makes things somewhat easier on the compiler; it knows right away what kind of storage to allocate and what code to emit to store and manipulate each variable; it doesn't have to try to intuit the programmer's intentions.
- It forces a bit of useful discipline on the programmer: you cannot introduce variables willy-nilly; you must think about them enough to pick appropriate types for them. (The compiler's error messages to you, telling you that you apparently forgot to declare a variable, are as often helpful as they are a nuisance: they're helpful when they tell you that you misspelled a variable, or forgot to think about exactly how you were going to use it.)

Although there are a few places where declarations can be omitted making use of these removes the advantages of reason 2 above, so I recommend always declaring everything explicitly. Most of the time, I recommend writing one declaration per line. For the most part, the compiler doesn't care what order declarations are in. You can order the declarations alphabetically, or in the order that they're used, or to put related declarations next to each other. Collecting all variables of the same type together on one line essentially orders declarations by type, which isn't a very useful order (it's only slightly more useful than random order).A declaration for a variable can also contain an initial value.

This initializer consists of an equals sign and an expression, which is usually a single constant:

```
int i = 1;
int i1 = 10, i2 = 20;
```

VARIABLE NAMES

Within limits, you can give your variables and functions any names you want. These names (the formal term is "identifiers") consist of letters, numbers, and underscores. For our purposes, names must begin with a letter.

Theoretically, names can be as long as you want, but extremely long ones get tedious to type after a while, and the compiler is not required to keep track of extremely long ones perfectly. (What this means is that if you were to name a variable, say, supercalafragalisticespialidocious, the compiler might get lazy and pretend that you had named it super calafragalisticespialidocio, such that if you later misspelled itsupercalafragalisticespialidociouz, the compiler wouldn't catch your mistake. Nor would the compiler necessarily be able to tell the difference if for some perverse reason you *deliberately* declared a second variable named super calafragalisticespialidociouz.)

The capitalization of names in C is significant: the variable names variable, Variable, and VARIABLE (as well as silly combinations like variAble) are all distinct. A final restriction on names is that you may not use *keywords* (the words such as int and for which are part of the syntax of the language) as the names of variables or functions (or as identifiers of any kind).

ARITHMETIC OPERATORS

The basic operators for performing arithmetic are the same in many computer languages:

```
+ addition
- subtraction
* multiplication
/ division
% modulus (remainder)
```

The - operator can be used in two ways: to subtract two numbers (as in a - b), or to negate one number (as in -a + bor a + -b). When applied to integers, the division operator / discards any remainder, so 1 / 2 is 0 and 7 / 4 is 1. But when either operand is a floating-point quantity (type float or double), the division operator yields a floating-point result, with a potentially nonzero fractional part. So 1 / 2.0 is 0.5, and 7.0 / 4.0 is 1.75. The *modulus* operator % gives you the remainder when two integers are divided: 1 % 2 is 1; 7 % 4 is 3. (The modulus operator can only be applied to integers.) An additional arithmetic operation you might be wondering about is exponentiation. Some languages have an exponentiation operator (typically ^ or **), but C doesn't. (To square or cube a number, just multiply it by itself.) Multiplication, division, and modulus all have higher *precedence* than addition and subtraction. The term "precedence" refers to how "tightly" operators bind to their operands (that is, to the things they operate on). In mathematics, multiplication has higher precedence than addition, so 1 + 2 * 3 is 7, not 9.

In other words, 1 + 2 * 3 is equivalent to1 + (2 * 3). C is the same way. All of these operators "group" from left to right, which means that when two or more of them have the same precedence and participate next to each other in an expression, the evaluation conceptually proceeds from left to right. For example, 1 - 2 - 3 is equivalent to (1 - 2) - 3 and gives -4, not +2. ("Grouping" is sometimes called *associativity*, although the term is used somewhat differently in programming than it is in mathematics.

Not all C operators group from left to right; a few group from right to left.) Whenever the default precedence or associativity doesn't give you the grouping you want, you can always use explicit parentheses. For example, if you wanted to add 1 to 2 and then multiply the result by 3, you could write (1 + 2) * 3. By the way, the word "arithmetic" as used in the title of this section is an adjective, not a noun, and it's pronounced differently than the noun: the accent is on the third syllable.

ASSIGNMENT OPERATORS

The assignment operator = assigns a value to a variable. *For example*:

```
x = 1
sets x to 1, and
```

```
a = b
sets a to whatever b's value is. The
expression
i = i + 1
```

is, as we've mentioned elsewhere, the standard programming idiom for increasing a variable's value by 1: this expression takes i's old value, adds 1 to it, and stores it back into i. (C provides several "shortcut" operators for modifying variables in this and similar ways, which we'll meet later.)

We've called the = sign the "assignment operator" and referred to "assignment expressions" because, in fact, = *is* an operator just like + or -. C does not have "assignment statements"; instead, an assignment like a = b is an expression and can be used wherever any expression can appear. Since it's an expression, the assignment a = b has a value, namely, the same value that's assigned to a. This value can then be used in a larger expression; for example, we might write

```
c = a = b
which is equivalent to
c = (a = b)
```

and assigns b's value to both a and c. (The assignment operator, therefore, groups from right to left.). It's usually a matter of style whether you initialize a variable with an initializer in its declaration or with an assignment expression near where you first use it. That is, there's no particular difference between

```
int a = 10;
and
int a;
/* later... */
a = 10;
```

FUNCTION CALLS

We'll have much more to say about functions in a later chapter, but for now let's just look at how they're called.You call a function by mentioning its name followed by a pair of parentheses. If the function takes any arguments, you place the arguments between the parentheses, separated by commas.

These are all function calls:

```
printf("Hello, world!\n")
printf("%d\n", i)
sqrt(144.)
getchar()
```

The arguments to a function can be arbitrary expressions. Therefore, you don't have to say things like

```
int sum = a + b + c;
printf("sum = %d\n", sum);
```

if you don't want to; you can instead collapse it to

```
printf("sum = %d\n", a + b + c);
```

Many functions return values, and when they do, you can embed calls to these functions within larger expressions:

```
c = sqrt(a * a + b * b)
x = r * cos(theta)
i = f1(f2(j))
```

The first expression squares a and b, computes the square root of the sum of the squares, and assigns the result to c. (In other words, it computes a * a + b * b, passes that number to the sqrt function, and assigns sqrt's return value toc.) The second expression passes the value of the variable theta to the cos (cosine) function, multiplies the result by r, and assigns the result to x. The third expression passes the value of the variable j to the function f2, passes the return value of f2 immediately to the function f1, and finally assigns f1's return value to the variable i.

Chapter 4

Statements and Control

EXPRESSION STATEMENTS

Most of the statements in a C programme are *expression statements*. An expression statement is simply an expression followed by a semicolon.

```
i = 0;
i = i + 1;
and
printf("Hello, world!\n");
```

The lines are all expression statements. (In some languages, such as Pascal, the semicolon separates statements, such that the last statement is not followed by a semicolon. In C, however, the semicolon is a statement terminator; all simple statements are followed by semicolons. The semicolon is also used for a few other things in C; we've already seen that it terminates declarations, too.)

Expression statements do all of the real work in a C programme. Whenever you need to compute new values for variables, you'll typically use expression statements (and they'll typically contain assignment operators). Whenever you want your programme to do something visible, in the real world, you'll typically call a function (as part of an expression statement). We've already seen the most basic example: calling the function printf to print text to the screen.

But anything else you might do—read or write a disk file, talk to a modem or printer, draw pictures on the screen—will also involve function calls. (Furthermore, the functions you call to do these things are usually different depending on which operating system you're using. The C language does not define them, so we won't be talking about or using them much.) Expressions and expression statements can be arbitrarily complicated. They don't have to consist of exactly one simple function call, or of one simple assignment to a variable. For one thing, many functions return values, and the values they return can then be used by other parts of the expression. For example, C provides a sqrt (square root) function, which we might use to compute the hypotenuse of a right triangle like this:

```
c = sqrt(a*a + b*b);
```

To be useful, an expression statement must do something; it must have some lasting effect on the state of the programme. (Formally, a useful statement must have at least one *side effect*.) The first two sample expression statements in this section (above) assign new values to the variable i, and the third one calls printf to print something out, and these are good examples of statements that do something useful.

```
0;
i;
or
i + 1;
```

(To make the distinction clear, we may note that degenerate constructions such as are syntactically valid statements—they consist of an expression followed by a semicolon—but in each case, they compute a value without doing anything with it, so the computed value is discarded, and the statement is useless. But if the "degenerate" statements in this paragraph don't make much sense to you, don't worry; it's because they, frankly, don't make much sense.)

It's also possible for a single expression to have multiple side effects, but it's easy for such an expression to be (a) confusing or (b) undefined. For now, we'll only be looking at expressions (and, therefore, statements) which do one well-defined thing at a time.

IF STATEMENTS

The simplest way to modify the control flow of a

programme is with an if statement, which in its simplest form looks like this:

```
if(x > max)
max = x;
```

Even if you didn't know any C, it would probably be pretty obvious that what happens here is that if x is greater than max,x gets assigned to max. (We'd use code like this to keep track of the maximum value of x we'd seen—for each new x, we'd compare it to the old maximum value max, and if the new value was greater, we'd update max.)

More generally, we can say that the syntax of an if statement is:

```
if( expression )
statement
```

where *expression* is any expression and *statement* is any statement. What if you have a series of statements, all of which should be executed together or not at all depending on whether some condition is true?

The answer is that you enclose them in braces:

```
if( expression )
{
statement<sub>1</sub>
statement<sub>2</sub>
statement<sub>3</sub>
}
```

As a general rule, anywhere the syntax of C calls for a statement, you may write a series of statements enclosed by braces. (You do not need to, and should not, put a semicolon after the closing brace, because the series of statements enclosed by braces is not itself a simple expression statement.) An if statement may also optionally contain a second statement, the "else clause," which is to be executed if the condition is not met. Here is an example.

```
if(n > 0)
average = sum / n;
else{
printf("can't compute average\n");
average = 0;
}
```

The first statement or block of statements is executed if the condition *is* true, and the second statement or block of statements (following the keyword else) is executed if the condition is *not* true. In this example, we can compute a meaningful average only if n is greater than 0; otherwise, we print a message saying that we cannot compute the average. The general syntax of an if statement is therefore

```
if( expression )
statement<sub>1</sub>
else
statement<sub>2</sub>
```

(where both *statement₁* and *statement₂* may be lists of statements enclosed in braces).

It's also possible to nest one if statement inside another. (For that matter, it's in general possible to nest any kind of statement or control flow construct within another.) For example, here is a little piece of code which decides roughly which quadrant of the compass you're walking into, based on an x value which is positive if you're walking east, and a y value which is positive if you're walking north:

```
if(x > 0)
{
   if(y > 0)
   printf("Northeast.\n");
   else printf("Southeast.\n");
}
   else {
   if(y > 0)
   printf("Northwest.\n");
   else printf("Southwest.\n");
}
```

When you have one if statement (or loop) nested inside another, it's a very good idea to use explicit braces {}, as shown, to make it clear (both to you and to the compiler) how they're nested and which else goes with which if. It's also a good idea to indent the various levels, also as shown, to make the code more readable to humans. Why do both? You use indentation to make the code visually more readable to yourself and other humans, but the compiler doesn't pay attention to the indentation (since all whitespace is essentially equivalent and is essentially ignored). Therefore, you also have to make sure that the punctuation is right.

Here is an example of another common arrangement of if and else. Suppose we have a variable grade containing a student's numeric grade, and we want to print out the corresponding letter grade.

Here is code that would do the job:

```
if(grade >= 90)
printf("A");
else if(grade >= 80)
printf("B");
else if(grade >= 70)
printf("C");
else if(grade >= 60)
printf("D");
elseprintf("F");
```

What happens here is that exactly one of the five printf calls is executed, depending on which of the conditions is true. Each condition is tested in turn, and if one is true, the corresponding statement is executed, and the rest are skipped. If none of the conditions is true, we fall through to the last one, printing "F". In the cascaded if/else/if/else/... chain, each else clause is another if statement. This may be more obvious at first if we reformat the example, including every set of braces and indenting each if statement relative to the previous one:

```
if(grade >= 90)
{
  printf("A");
}
  else  {
  if(grade >= 80)
{
  printf("B");
}
  else  {
```

```
    if(grade >= 70)
  {
    printf("C");
  }
    else  {
    if(grade >= 60)
  {
    printf("D");
  }
    else   {
    printf("F");
  }
  }
  }
  }
```

By examining the code this way, it should be obvious that exactly one of the printf calls is executed, and that whenever one of the conditions is found true, the remaining conditions do not need to be checked and none of the later statements within the chain will be executed.

But once you've convinced yourself of this and learned to recognize the idiom, it's generally preferable to arrange the statements as in the first example, without trying to indent each successive if statement one tabstop further out. (Obviously, you'd run into the right margin very quickly if the chain had just a few more cases!)

BOOLEAN EXPRESSIONS

An if statement like

```
if(x > max)
max = x;
```

is perhaps deceptively simple. Conceptually, we say that it checks whether the condition x > max is "true" or "false". The mechanics underlying C's conception of "true" and "false," however, deserve some explanation.

We need to understand how true and false values are represented, and how they are interpreted by statements like if. As far as C is concerned, a true/false condition can be represented as an integer. (An integer can represent many values; here we care about only two values: "true" and "false." The study of mathematics involving only two values is called Boolean algebra, after George Boole, a mathematician who refined this study.)

In C, "false" is represented by a value of 0 (zero), and "true" is represented by any value that is nonzero. Since there are many nonzero values (at least 65,534, for values of type int), when we have to pick a specific value for "true," we'll pick 1. The *relational operators* such as <, <=, >, and >= are in fact operators, just like +, -, *, and /. The relational operators take two values, look at them, and "return" a value of 1 or 0 depending on whether the tested relation was true or false.

The complete set of relational operators in C is:

```
< less than
<=   less than or equal
> greater than
>=   greater than or equal
==   equal
!=   not equal
```

For example, 1 < 2 is 1, 3 > 4 is 0, 5 == 5 is 1, and 6 != 6 is 0. We've now encountered perhaps the most easy-to-stumble-on "gotcha!" in C: the equality-testing operator is ==, not a single =, which is assignment. If you accidentally write

```
if(a = 0)
```

(and you probably will at some point; everybody makes this mistake), it will *not* test whether a is zero, as you probably intended. Instead, it will *assign* 0 to a, and then perform the "true" branch of the if statement if a is *non*zero.

But a will have just been assigned the value 0, so the "true" branch will never be taken! (This could drive you crazy while debugging—you wanted to do something if a was 0, and after the test, a *is* 0, whether it was supposed to be or not, but the "true" branch is nevertheless not taken.)

The relational operators work with arbitrary numbers and generate true/false values. You can also combine true/false values by using the *Boolean operators*, which take true/false values as operands and compute new true/false values.

The three Boolean operators are:

```
&&   and
||   or
! not (takes one operand; "unary")
```

The && ("and") operator takes two true/false values and produces a true (1) result if both operands are true (that is, if the left-hand side is true and the right-hand side is true). The || ("or") operator takes two true/false values and produces a true (1) result if either operand is true. The ! ("not") operator takes a single true/false value and negates it, turning false to true and true to false (0 to 1 and nonzero to 0).

For example, to test whether the variable i lies between 1 and 10, you might use

```
if(1 < i && i < 10)
...
```

Here we're expressing the relation "i is between 1 and 10" as "1 is less than i and i is less than 10." It's important to understand why the more obvious expression

```
if(1 < i < 10)    /* WRONG */
```

would not work. The expression 1 < i < 10 is parsed by the compiler analogously to 1 + i + 10. The expression 1 + i + 10 is parsed as (1 + i) + 10 and means "add 1 to i, and then add the result to 10." Similarly, the expression 1 < i < 10 is parsed as (1 < i) < 10 and means "see if 1 is less than i, and then see if the result is less than 10." But in this case, "the result" is 1 or 0, depending on whether i is greater than 1. Since both 0 and 1 are less than 10, the expression 1 < i < 10 would *always* be true in C, regardless of the value of i! Relational and Boolean expressions are usually used in contexts such as an if statement, where something is to be done or not done depending on some condition. In these cases what's actually checked is whether the expression representing the condition has a zero or nonzero value. As long as the expression is a relational or Boolean expression, the interpretation is just what we want. For example, when we wrote

```
if(x > max)
```

the > operator produced a 1 if x was greater than max, and a 0 otherwise. The if statement interprets 0 as false and 1 (or any nonzero value) as true. But what if the expression is not a relational or Boolean expression? As far as C is concerned, the controlling expression (of conditional statements like if) can in fact be *any* expression: it doesn't have to "look like" a Boolean expression; it doesn't have to contain relational or logical operators. All C looks at (when it's evaluating an if statement, or anywhere else where it needs a true/false value) is whether the expression evaluates to 0 or nonzero. For example, if you have a variable x, and you want to do something if x is nonzero, it's possible to write

```
if(x)
statement
```

and the statement will be executed if x is nonzero (since nonzero means "true").

This possibility (that the controlling expression of an if statement doesn't have to "look like" a Boolean expression) is both useful and potentially confusing. It's useful when you have a variable or a function that is "conceptually Boolean," that is, one that you consider to hold a true or false (actually nonzero or zero) value. For example, if you have a variableverbose which contains a nonzero value when your programme should run in verbose mode and zero when it should be quiet, you can write things like

```
if(verbose)
printf("Starting first pass\n");
```

and this code is both legal and readable, besides which it does what you want. The standard library contains a functionisupper() which tests whether a character is an upper-case letter, so if c is a character, you might write

```
if(isupper(c))
...
```

Both of these examples (verbose and isupper()) are useful and readable. However, you will eventually come across code like

```
if(n)
average = sum / n;
```

where n is just a number. Here, the programmer wants to compute the average only if n is nonzero (otherwise, of course, the code would divide by 0), and the code works, because, in the context of the if statement, the trivial expression n is (as always) interpreted as "true" if it is nonzero, and "false" if it is zero.

"Coding shortcuts" like these can seem cryptic, but they're also quite common, so you'll need to be able to recognize them even if you don't choose to write them in your own code. Whenever you see code like

```
if(x)
or
if(f())
```

where x or f() do not have obvious "Boolean" names, you can read them as "if x is nonzero" or "if f() returns nonzero."

WHILE LOOPS

Loops generally consist of two parts: one or more *control expressions* which (not surprisingly) control the execution of the loop, and the *body*, which is the statement or set of statements which is executed over and over. The most basic *loop* in C is the while loop. A while loop has one control expression, and executes as long as that expression is true. This example repeatedly doubles the number 2 (2, 4, 8, 16,...) and prints the resulting numbers as long as they are less than 1000:

```
int x = 2;
while(x < 1000)
{
printf("%d\n", x);
x = x * 2;
}
```

(Once again, we've used braces {} to enclose the group of statements which are to be executed together as the body of the loop.)

The general syntax of a while loop is:

```
while( expression )
statement
```

A while loop starts out like an if statement: if the condition expressed by the *expression* is true, the *statement* is executed. However, after executing the statement, the condition is tested again, and if it's still true, the statement is executed again. (Presumably, the condition depends on some value which is changed in the body of the loop.)

As long as the condition remains true, the body of the loop is executed over and over again. (If the condition is false right at the start, the body of the loop is not executed at all.) As another example, if you wanted to print a number of blank lines, with the variable n holding the number of blank lines to be printed, you might use code like this:

```
while(n > 0)
{
printf("\n");
n = n - 1;
}
```

After the loop finishes (when control "falls out" of it, due to the condition being false), n will have the value 0. You use a while loop when you have a statement or group of statements which may have to be executed a number of times to complete their task. The controlling expression represents the condition "the loop is not done" or "there's more work to do." As long as the expression is true, the body of the loop is executed; presumably, it makes at least some progress at its task. When the expression becomes false, the task is done, and the rest of the programme (beyond the loop) can proceed. When we think about a loop in this way, we can seen an additional important property: if the expression evaluates to "false" before the very first trip through the loop, we make *zero* trips through the loop. In other words, if the task is already done (if there's no work to do) the body of the loop is not executed at all. (It's always a good idea to think about the "boundary conditions" in a piece of code, and to make sure that the code will work correctly when there is no work to do, or when there is a trivial task to do, such as sorting an array of one number. Experience has shown that bugs at boundary conditions are quite common.)

FOR LOOPS

Our second loop, which we've seen at least one example of already, is the for loop. The first one we saw was.

```
for (i = 0; i < 10; i = i + 1)
printf("i is %d\n", i);
```

More generally, the syntax of a for loop is

```
for( expr<sub>1</sub> ; expr<sub>2</sub>
expr<sub>3</sub>)
statement
```

(Here we see that the for loop has three control expressions. As always, the *statement* can be a brace-enclosed block.) Many loops are set up to cause some variable to step through a range of values, or, more generally, to set up an initial condition and then modify some value to perform each succeeding loop as long as some condition is true.

The three expressions in a for loop encapsulate these conditions: *expr₁* sets up the initial condition, *expr₂* tests whether another trip through the loop should be taken, and *expr₃* increments or updates things after each trip through the loop and prior to the next one. In our first example, we had i = 0 as*expr₁*, i < 10 as *expr₂*, i = i + 1 as *expr₃*, and the call to printf as*statement*, the body of the loop. So the loop began by setting i to 0, proceeded as long as i was less than 10, printed outi's value during each trip through the loop, and added 1 to i between each trip through the loop.

When the compiler sees a for loop, first, *expr₁* is evaluated. Then, *expr₂* is evaluated, and if it is true, the body of the loop (*statement*) is executed. Then, *expr₃* is evaluated to go to the next step, and*expr₂* is evaluated again, to see if there *is* a next step. During the execution of a for loop, the sequence is:

```
expr<sub>1</sub>
expr<sub>2</sub>
statement
expr<sub>3</sub>
expr<sub>2</sub>
statement
expr<sub>3</sub>
...
expr<sub>2</sub>
```

```
statement
expr<sub>3</sub>
expr<sub>2</sub>
```

The first thing executed is *expr₁*. *expr₃* is evaluated after *every* trip through the loop. The last thing executed is always *expr₂*, because when *expr₂* evaluates false, the loop exits.

All three expressions of a for loop are optional. If you leave out *expr₁*, there simply is no initialization step, and the variable(s) used with the loop had better have been initialized already. If you leave out *expr₂*, there is no test, and the default for the for loop is that another trip through the loop should be taken (such that unless you break out of it some other way, the loop runs forever). If you leave out *expr₃*, there is no increment step.

The semicolons separate the three controlling expressions of a for loop. (These semicolons, by the way, have nothing to do with statement terminators.) If you leave out one or more of the expressions, the semicolons remain. Therefore, one way of writing a deliberately infinite loop in C is

```
for(;;)
...
```

It's useful to compare C's for loop to the equivalent loops in other computer languages you might know. The C loop

```
for(i = x; i <= y; i = i + z)
```

is roughly equivalent to:

```
for I = X to Y step Z    (BASIC)
do 10 i=x,y,z   (FORTRAN)
for i := x to y (Pascal)
```

In C (unlike FORTRAN), if the test condition is false before the first trip through the loop, the loop won't be traversed at all. In C (unlike Pascal), a loop control variable (in this case, i) is guaranteed to retain its final value after the loop completes, and it is also legal to modify the control variable within the loop, if you really want to. (When the loop terminates due to the test condition turning false, the value of the control variable after the loop will be the first value for which the condition failed, not the last value for which it succeeded.)

It's also worth noting that a for loop can be used in more general ways than the simple, iterative examples we've seen so far. The "control variable" of a for loop does not have to be an integer, and it does not have to be incremented by an additive increment.

It could be "incremented" by a multiplicative factor (1, 2, 4, 8,...) if that was what you needed, or it could be a floating-point variable, or it could be another type of variable which we haven't met yet which would step, not over numeric values, but over the elements of an array or other data structure.

Strictly speaking, a for loop doesn't have to have a "control variable" at all; the three expressions can be anything, although the loop will make the most sense if they are related and together form the expected initialize, test, increment sequence.

The powers-of-two example of the previous section does fit this pattern, so we could rewrite it like this:

```
int x;
for(x = 2; x < 1000; x = x * 2)
printf("%d\n", x);
```

There is no earth-shaking or fundamental difference between the while and for loops. In fact, given the general for loop

```
for(expr<sub>1</sub>; expr<sub>2</sub>;
expr<sub>3</sub>)
statement
```

you could usually rewrite it as a while loop, moving the initialize and increment expressions to statements before and within the loop:

```
expr<sub>1</sub> ;
while(expr<sub>2</sub>)
{
  statement
  expr<sub>3</sub> ;
}
  Similarly, given the general while loop
  while(expr)
  statement
```

you could rewrite it as a for loop:

```
for(; expr;)
statement
```

Another contrast between the for and while loops is that although the test expression (*expr₂*) is optional in a for loop, it is required in a while loop. If you leave out the controlling expression of a while loop, the compiler will complain about a syntax error. (To write a deliberately infinite while loop, you have to supply an expression which is always nonzero. The most obvious one would simply be while(1) .)

If it's possible to rewrite a for loop as a while loop and vice versa, why do they both exist? Which one should you choose? In general, when you choose a for loop, its three expressions should all manipulate the same variable or data structure, using the initialize, test, increment pattern. If they don't manipulate the same variable or don't follow that pattern, wedging them into a for loop buys nothing and a while loop would probably be clearer. (The reason that one loop or the other can be clearer is simply that, when you see a for loop, you *expect* to see an idiomatic initialize/test/increment of a single variable, and if the for loop you're looking at doesn't end up matching that pattern, you've been momentarily misled.)

BREAK AND CONTINUE

Sometimes, due to an exceptional condition, you need to jump out of a loop early, that is, before the main controlling expression of the loop causes it to terminate normally. Other times, in an elaborate loop, you may want to jump back to the top of the loop (to test the controlling expression again, and perhaps begin a new trip through the loop) without playing out all the steps of the current loop.

The break and continue statements allow you to do these two things. (They are, in fact, essentially restricted forms of goto.). To put everything we've seen in this chapter together, as well as demonstrate the use of the break statement, here is a programme for printing prime numbers between 1 and 100:

```
#include <stdio.h>
#include <math.h>
main()
{
  int i, j;
  printf("%d\n", 2);
  for(i = 3; i <= 100; i = i + 1)
{
  for(j = 2; j < i; j = j + 1)
{
  if(i % j == 0)
  break;
  if(j > sqrt(i))
{
  printf("%d\n", i);
  break;
}
}
}
  return 0;
}
```

The outer loop steps the variable i through the numbers from 3 to 100; the code tests to see if each number has any divisors other than 1 and itself. The trial divisor j loops from 2 up to i. j is a divisor of i if the remainder of i divided by jis 0, so the code uses C's "remainder" or "modulus" operator % to make this test. (Remember that i % j gives the remainder when i is divided by j.)

If the programme finds a divisor, it uses break to break out of the inner loop, without printing anything. But if it notices that jhas risen higher than the square root of i, without its having found any divisors, then i must not have any divisors, so i is prime, and its value is printed.

(Once we've determined that i is prime by noticing that j > sqrt(i), there's no need to try the other trial divisors, so we use a second break statement to break out of the loop in that case, too.) The simple algorithm and implementation we used here (like many simple prime number algorithms) does not work for 2, the only even prime number, so the programme "cheats" and prints out 2 no matter what, before going on to test the numbers from 3 to 100. Many improvements to this simple programme are of course possible; you might experiment with it. (Did you notice that the "test" expression of the inner loop for(j = 2; j < i; j = j + 1) is in a sense unnecessary, because the loop always terminates early due to one of the two break statements?)

Chapter 5

Declarations and Initialization

ARRAYS

So far, we've been declaring simple variables: the declaration

```
int i;
```

declares a single variable, named i, of type int. It is also possible to declare an *array* of several elements. The declaration

```
int a[10];
```

declares an array, named a, consisting of ten elements, each of type int. Simply speaking, an array is a variable that can hold more than one value. You specify which of the several values you're referring to at any given time by using a numeric*subscript*. (Arrays in programming are similar to vectors or matrices in mathematics.)

We can represent the array a above with a picture like this:

a:
[0] [1] [2] [3] [4] [5] [6] [7] [8] [9]

In C, arrays are *zero-based*: tne ten elements of a 10-element array are numbered from 0 to 9. The subscript which specifies a single element of an array is simply an integer expression in square brackets. The first element of the array isa[0], the second element is a[1], etc. You can use these "array subscript expressions" anywhere you can use the name of a simple variable.

For example:

```
a[0] = 10;
```

```
a[1] = 20;
a[2] = a[0] + a[1];
```

Notice that the subscripted array references (i.e. expressions such as a[0] and a[1]) can appear on either side of the assignment operator.

The subscript does not have to be a constant like 0 or 1; it can be any integral expression. For example, it's common to loop over all elements of an array:

```
int i;
for(i = 0; i < 10; i = i + 1)
a[i] = 0;
```

This loop sets all ten elements of the array a to 0. Arrays are a real convenience for many problems, but there is not a lot that C will do with them for you automatically. In particular, you can neither set all elements of an array at once nor assign one array to another; both of the assignments

```
a = 0;    /* WRONG */
```

and

```
int b[10];
b = a;    /* WRONG */
```

are illegal.

To set all of the elements of an array to some value, you must do so one by one, as in the loop example above. To copy the contents of one array to another, you must again do so one by one:

```
int b[10];
for(i = 0; i < 10; i = i + 1)
b[i] = a[i];
```

Remember that for an array declared

```
int a[10];
```

there is no element a[10]; the topmost element is a[9]. This is one reason that zero-based loops are also common in C. Note that the for loop

```
for(i = 0; i < 10; i = i + 1)
...
```

does just what you want in this case: it starts at 0, the number 10 suggests (correctly) that it goes through 10 iterations, but the less-than comparison means that the last trip through the loop has i set to 9. (The comparison i <= 9 would also work, but it would be less clear and therefore poorer style.) In the little examples so far, we've always looped over all 10 elements of the sample array a. It's common, however, to use an array that's bigger than necessarily needed, and to use a second variable to keep track of how many elements of the array are currently in use. For example, we might have an integer variable

```
nt na; /* number of elements of a[] in use
*/
```

Then, when we wanted to do something with a (such as print it out), the loop would run from 0 to na, not 10 (or whatevera's size was):

```
for(i = 0; i < na; i = i + 1)
printf("%d\n", a[i]);
```

Naturally, we would have to ensure ensure that na's value was always less than or equal to the number of elements actually declared in a. Arrays are not limited to type int; you can have arrays of char or double or any other type.

Here is a slightly larger example of the use of arrays. Suppose we want to investigate the behaviour of rolling a pair of dice. The total roll can be anywhere from 2 to 12, and we want to count how often each roll comes up. We will use an array to keep track of the counts: a[2] will count how many times we've rolled 2, etc.

We'll simulate the roll of a die by calling C's random number generation function, rand(). Each time you call rand(), it returns a different, pseudo-random integer. The values that rand() returns typically span a large range, so we'll use C'*smodulus* (or "remainder") operator % to produce random numbers in the range we want. The expression rand()% 6produces random numbers in the range 0 to 5, and rand()% 6 + 1 produces random numbers in the range 1 to 6.

```
Here is the programme:
#include <stdio.h>
#include <stdlib.h>
main()
{
```

```
int i;
int d1, d2;
int a[13];    /* uses [2..12] */
for(i = 2; i <= 12; i = i + 1)
a[i] = 0;
for(i = 0; i < 100; i = i + 1)
{
  d1 = rand()% 6 + 1;
  d2 = rand()% 6 + 1;
  a[d1 + d2] = a[d1 + d2] + 1;
}
  for(i = 2; i <= 12; i = i + 1)
  printf("%d: %d\n", i, a[i]);
  return 0;
}
```

We include the header <stdlib.h> because it contains the necessary declarations for the rand() function. We declare the array of size 13 so that its highest element will be a[12]. (We're wasting a[0] and a[1]; this is no great loss.) The variables d1 and d2 contain the rolls of the two individual dice; we add them together to decide which cell of the array to increment, in the line

```
a[d1 + d2] = a[d1 + d2] + 1;
```

After 100 rolls, we print the array out. Typically (as craps players well know), we'll see mostly 7's, and relatively few 2's and 12's. (By the way, it turns out that using the % operator to reduce the range of the rand function is *not* always a good idea. We'll say more about this problem in an exercise.)

ARRAY INITIALIZATION

Although it is not possible to assign to all elements of an array at once using an assignment expression, it is possible to initialize some or all elements of an array when the array is defined.

The syntax looks like this:

```
int a[10] = {0, 1, 2, 3, 4, 5, 6, 7, 8, 9};
```

The list of values, enclosed in braces {}, separated by commas, provides the initial values for successive elements of the array. (Under older, pre-ANSI C compilers, you could not always supply initializers for "local" arrays inside functions; you could only initialize "global" arrays, those outside of any function. Those compilers are now rare, so you shouldn't have to worry about this distinction any more. We'll talk more about local and global variables later in this chapter.)

If there are fewer initializers than elements in the array, the remaining elements are automatically initialized to 0.

For example:

```
int a[10] = {0, 1, 2, 3, 4, 5, 6};
```

would initialize a[7], a[8], and a[9] to 0. When an array definition includes an initializer, the array dimension may be omitted, and the compiler will infer the dimension from the number of initializers.

For example:

```
int b[] = {10, 11, 12, 13, 14};
```

would declare, define, and initialize an array b of 5 elements (i.e. just as if you'd typed int b[5]). Only the dimension is omitted; the brackets [] remain to indicate that b is in fact an array.

In the case of arrays of char, the initializer may be a string constant:

```
char s1[7] = "Hello,";
char s2[10] = "there,";
char s3[] = "world!";
```

As before, if the dimension is omitted, it is inferred from the size of the string initializer. (We haven't covered strings in detail yet—we'll do so in chapter 8—but it turns out that all strings in C are terminated by a special character with the value 0. Therefore, the array s3 will be of size 7, and the explicitly-sized s1 does need to be of size at least 7. For s2, the last 4 characters in the array will all end up being this zero-value character.)

MULTIDIMENSIONAL ARRAYS

When we said that "Arrays are not limited to type int; you can have arrays of... any other type," we meant that more literally than you might have guessed. If you have an "array of int," it means that you have an array each of whose elements is of type int. But you can have an array each of whose elements is of type *x*, where *x* is any type you choose. In particular, you can have an array each of whose elements is another array! We can use these arrays of arrays for the same sorts of tasks as we'd use multidimensional arrays in other computer languages (or matrices in mathematics). Naturally, we are not limited to arrays of arrays, either; we could have an array of arrays of arrays, which would act like a 3-dimensional array, etc.

The declaration of an array of arrays looks like this:

```
int a2[5][7];
```

You have to read complicated declarations like these "inside out." What this one says is that a2 is an array of 5 somethings, and that each of the somethings is an array of 7 ints. More briefly, "a2 is an array of 5 arrays of 7 ints," or, "a2 is an array of array of int." In the declaration of a2, the brackets closest to the identifier a2 tell you what a2 first and foremost is. That's how you know it's an array of 5 arrays of size 7, not the other way around. You can think of a2 as having 5 "rows" and 7 "columns," although this interpretation is not mandatory. (You could also treat the "first" or inner subscript as "x" and the second as "y." Unless you're doing something fancy, all you have to worry about is that the subscripts when you access the array match those that you used when you declared it, as in the examples below.)

To illustrate the use of multidimensional arrays, we might fill in the elements of the above array a2 using this piece of code:

```
int i, j;
for(i = 0; i < 5; i = i + 1)
{
   for(j = 0; j < 7; j = j + 1)
   a2[i][j] = 10 * i + j;
}
```

This pair of nested loops sets a[1][2] to 12, a[4][1] to 41, etc. Since the first dimension of a2 is 5, the first subscripting index variable, i, runs from 0 to 4. Similarly, the second subscript varies from 0 to 6.

We could print a2 out (in a two-dimensional way, suggesting its structure) with a similar pair of nested loops:

```
for(i = 0; i < 5; i = i + 1)
{
  for(j = 0; j < 7; j = j + 1)
  printf("%d\t", a2[i][j]);
  printf("\n");
}
```

(The character \t in the printf string is the tab character.) Just to see more clearly what's going on, we could make the "row" and "column" subscripts explicit by printing them, too:

```
for(j = 0; j < 7; j = j + 1)
printf("\t%d:", j);
printf("\n");
for(i = 0; i < 5; i = i + 1)
{
  printf("%d:", i);
  for(j = 0; j < 7; j = j + 1)
  printf("\t%d", a2[i][j]);
  printf("\n");
}
```

This last fragment would print:

```
0: 1: 2: 3: 4: 5: 6:
0: 0 1 2 3 4 5 6
1: 10 11 12 13 14 15 16
2: 20 21 22 23 24 25 26
3: 30 31 32 33 34 35 36
4: 40 41 42 43 44 45 46
```

Finally, there's no reason we have to loop over the "rows" first and the "columns" second; depending on what we wanted to do.

we could interchange the two loops, like this:

```
for(j = 0; j < 7; j = j + 1)
{
  for(i = 0; i < 5; i = i + 1)
  printf("%d\t", a2[i][j]);
  printf("\n");
}
```

Notice that i is still the first subscript and it still runs from 0 to 4, and j is still the second subscript and it still runs from 0 to 6.

VISIBILITY

We haven't said so explicitly, but variables are channels of communication within a programme. You set a variable to a value at one point in a programme, and at another point (or points) you read the value out again. The two points may be in adjoining statements, or they may be in widely separated parts of the programme.

How long does a variable last? How widely separated can the setting and fetching parts of the programme be, and how long after a variable is set does it persist? Depending on the variable and how you're using it, you might want different answers to these questions. The *visibility* of a variable determines how much of the rest of the programme can access that variable.

You can arrange that a variable is visible only within one part of one function, or in one function, or in one source file, or anywhere in the programme. (We haven't really talked about source files yet; we'll be exploring them soon.) Why would you want to limit the visibility of a variable? For maximum flexibility, wouldn't it be handy if all variables were potentially visible everywhere?

As it happens, that arrangement would be *too* flexible: everywhere in the programme, you would have to keep track of the names of all the variables declared anywhere else in the programme, so that you didn't accidentally re-use one. Whenever a variable had the wrong value by mistake, you'd have to search the entire programme for the bug, because any statement in the entire programme could potentially have modified that variable.

You would constantly be stepping all over yourself by using a common variable name like i in two parts of your programme, and having one snippet of code accidentally overwrite the values being used by another part of the code. The communication would be sort of like an old party line—

you'd always be accidentally interrupting other conversations, or having your conversations interrupted. To avoid this confusion, we generally give variables the narrowest or smallest visibility they need.

A variable declared within the braces {} of a function is visible only within that function; variables declared within functions are called *local variables*. If another function somewhere else declares a local variable with the same name, it's a different variable entirely, and the two don't clash with each other.

On the other hand, a variable declared outside of any function is a *global variable*, and it is potentially visible anywhere within the programme. You use global variables when you *do* want the communications path to be able to travel to any part of the programme.

When you declare a global variable, you will usually give it a longer, more descriptive name (not something generic like i) so that whenever you use it you will remember that it's the same variable everywhere. Another word for the visibility of variables is *scope*.

How long do variables last? By default, local variables (those declared within a function) have *automatic duration*: they spring into existence when the function is called, and they (and their values) disappear when the function returns. Global variables, on the other hand, have *static duration*: they last, and the values stored in them persist, for as long as the programme does. (Of course, the values can in general still be overwritten, so they don't necessarily persist forever.)

Finally, it is possible to split a function up into several source files, for easier maintenance. When several source files are combined into one programme (we'll be seeing how in the next chapter) the compiler must have a way of correlating the global variables which might be used to communicate between the several source files.

Furthermore, if a global variable is going to be useful for communication, there must be exactly one of it: you wouldn't want one function in one source file to store a value in one global variable named globalvar, and then have another function in another source file read from a*different* global variable named globalvar. Therefore, a global variable should have exactly one *defining instance,* in one place in one source file. If the same variable is to be used anywhere else (i.e. in some other source file or files), the variable is declared in those other files with an *external declaration,* which is not a defining instance.

The external declaration says, "hey, compiler, here's the name and type of a global variable I'm going to use, but don't define it here, don't allocate space for it; it's one that's defined somewhere else, and I'm just referring to it here." If you accidentally have two distinct defining instances for a variable of the same name, the compiler (or the linker) will complain that it is "multiply defined."

It is also possible to have a variable which is global in the sense that it is declared outside of any function but private to the one source file it's defined in. Such a variable is visible to the functions in that source file but not to any functions in any other source files, even if they try to issue a matching declaration.

You get any extra control you might need over visibility and lifetime, and you distinguish between defining instances and external declarations, by using *storage classes.* A storage class is an extra keyword at the beginning of a declaration which modifies the declaration in some way. Generally, the storage class (if any) is the first word in the declaration, preceding the type name. (Strictly speaking, this ordering has not traditionally been necessary, and you may see some code with the storage class, type name, and other parts of a declaration in an unusual order.)

We said that, by default, local variables had automatic duration. To give them static duration (so that, instead of coming and going as the function is called, they persist for as long as the function does), you precede their declaration with thestatic keyword:

```
static int i;
```

By default, a declaration of a global variable (especially if it specifies an initial value) is the defining instance. To make it an external declaration, of a variable which is defined somewhere else, you precede it with the keyword extern.

```
extern int j;
```

Finally, to arrange that a global variable is visible only within its containing source file, you precede it with the statickeyword:

```
static int k;
```

Notice that the static keyword can do two different things: it adjusts the duration of a local variable from automatic to static, or it adjusts the visibility of a global variable from truly global to private-to-the-file.

To summarize, we've talked about two different attributes of a variable: visibility and duration. These are orthogonal, as shown in this table.

	duration:	
visibility:	automatic	static
local	normal local variables	static local variables
global	N/A	normal global variables

We can also distinguish between file-scope global variables and truly global variables, based on the presence or absence of the static keyword. We can also distinguish between external declarations and defining instances of global variables, based on the presence or absence of the extern keyword.

DEFAULT INITIALIZATION

The duration of a variable (whether static or automatic) also affects its default initialization. If you do not explicitly initialize them, automatic-duration variables (that is, local, non-static ones) are not guaranteed to have any particular initial value; they will typically contain garbage. It is therefore a fairly serious error to attempt to use the value of an automatic variable which has never been initialized or assigned to: the programme will either work incorrectly, or the garbage value may just happen to be "correct" such that the programme appears to work correctly! However, the particular value that the garbage takes on can vary depending literally on *anything*: other parts of the programme, which compiler was used, which hardware or operating system the programme is running on, the time of day, the phase of the moon.So you hardly want to say that a programme which uses an uninitialized variable "works"; it may seem to work, but it works for the wrong reason, and it may stop working tomorrow.

Static-duration variables (global and static local), on the other hand, are guaranteed to be initialized to 0 if you do not use an explicit initializer in the definition. (Once upon a time, there was another distinction between the initialization of automatic vs. static variables: you could initialize *aggregate* objects, such as arrays, only if they had static duration. If your compiler complains when you try to initialize a local array, it's probably an old, pre-ANSI compiler. Modern, ANSI-compatible compilers remove this limitation, so it's no longer much of a concern.)

EXAMPLES

Here is an example demonstrating almost everything we've seen so far:

```
int globalvar = 1;
extern int anotherglobalvar;
static int privatevar;
f()
{
  int localvar;
  int localvar2 = 2;
  static int persistentvar;
}
```

Here we have six variables, three declared outside and three declared inside of the function f(). Globalvar is a global variable. The declaration we see is its defining instance (it happens also to include an initial value).globalvar can be used anywhere in this source file, and it could be used in other source files, too (as long as corresponding external declarations are issued in those other source files).

Anotherglobalvar is a second global variable. It is *not* defined here; the defining instance for it (and its initialization) is somewhere else. Privatevar is a "private" global variable. It can be used anywhere within this source file, but functions in other source files cannot access it, even if they try to issue external declarations for it. (If other source files try to declare a global variable called "privatevar", they'll get their own; they won't be sharing this one.) Since it has static duration and receives no explicit initialization, privatevar will be initialized to 0.

Localvar is a local variable within the function f(). It can be accessed only within the function f(). (If any other part of the programme declares a variable named "localvar", that variable will be distinct from the one we're looking at here.)localvar is conceptually "created" each time f() is called, and disappears when f() returns. Any value which was stored in localvar last time f() was running will be lost and will not be available next time f() is called. Furthermore, since it has no explicit initializer, the value of localvar will in general be garbage each time f() is called.

Localvar2 is also local, and everything that we said about localvar applies to it, except that since its declaration includes an explicit initializer, it will be initialized to 2 each time f() is called. Finally, persistentvar is again local to f(), but it *does* maintain its value between calls to f(). It has static duration but no explicit initializer, so its initial value will be 0. The defining instances and external declarations we've been looking at so far have all been of simple variables. There are also defining instances and external declarations of functions, which we'll be looking at in the next chapter. (Also, don't worry about static variables for now if they don't make sense to you; they're a relatively sophisticated concept, which you won't need to use at first.)

The term *declaration* is a general one which encompasses defining instances and external declarations; defining instances and external declarations are two different kinds of declarations. Furthermore, either kind of declaration suffices to inform the compiler of the name and type of a particular variable (or function). If you have the defining instance of a global variable in a source file, the rest of that source file can use that variable without having to issue any external declarations. It's only in source files where the defining instance hasn't been seen that you need external declarations. You will sometimes hear a defining instance referred to simply as a "definition," and you will sometimes hear an external declaration referred to simply as a "declaration."

These usages are mildly ambiguous, in that you can't tell out of context whether a "declaration" is a generic declaration (that might be a defining instance or an external declaration) or whether it's an external declaration that specifically is not a defining instance. (Similarly, there are other constructions that can be called "definitions" in C, namely the definitions of preprocessor macros, structures, and typedefs, none of which we've met.) In these notes, we'll try to make things clear by using the unambiguous terms *defining instance* and *external declaration*. Elsewhere, you may have to look at the context to determine how the terms "definition" and "declaration" are being used.

Chapter 6

Functions and Programme Structure

FUNCTIONS

So what defines a function? It has a *name* that you call it by, and a list of zero or more *arguments* or *parameters* that you hand to it for it to act on or to direct its work; it has a *body* containing the actual instructions (statements) for carrying out the task the function is supposed to perform; and it may give you back a *return value*, of a particular type. Here is a very simple function, which accepts one argument, multiplies it by 2, and hands that value back:

```
int multbytwo(int x)
{
  int retval;
  retval = x * 2;
  return retval;
}
```

On the first line we see the return type of the function (int), the name of the function (multbytwo), and a list of the function's arguments, enclosed in parentheses. Each argument has both a name and a type; multbytwo accepts one argument, of type int, named x. The name x is arbitrary, and is used only within the definition of multbytwo. The caller of this function only needs to know that a single argument of type int is expected; the caller does not need to know what name the function will use internally to refer to that argument. (In particular, the caller does not have to pass the value of a variable named x.) Next we see, surrounded by the familiar braces, the body of the function itself. This function consists of one declaration (of a local variable retval) and two statements. The first statement is a conventional expression statement, which computes and assigns a value to retval, and the second statement is a return statement, which causes the function to return to its caller, and also specifies the value which the function returns to its caller.

The return statement can return the value of any expression, so we don't really need the local retval variable; the function could be collapsed to

```
int multbytwo(int x)
{
  return x * 2;
}
```

How do we call a function? We've been doing so informally since day one, but now we have a chance to call one that we've written, in full detail. Here is a tiny skeletal programme to call multby2:

```
#include <stdio.h>
extern int multbytwo(int);
int main()
{
  int i, j;
  i = 3;
  j = multbytwo(i);
  printf("%d\n", j);
  return 0;
}
```

This looks much like our other test programmes, with the exception of the new line

```
extern int multbytwo(int);
```

This is an *external function prototype declaration*. It is an external declaration, in that it declares something which is defined somewhere else. (We've already seen the defining instance of the function multbytwo, but maybe the compiler hasn't seen it yet.) The function prototype declaration contains the three pieces of information about the function that a caller needs to know: the function's name, return type, and argument type(s). Since we don't care what name the multbytwo function will use to refer to its first argument, we don't need to mention it. (On the other hand, if a function takes several arguments, giving them names in the prototype may make it easier to remember which is which, so names may optionally be used in function prototype declarations.) Finally, to remind us that this is an external declaration and not a defining instance, the prototype is preceded by the keyword extern.

The presence of the function prototype declaration lets the compiler know that we intend to call this function, multbytwo. The information in the prototype lets the compiler generate the correct code for calling the function, and also enables the compiler to check up on our code (by making sure, for example, that we pass the correct number of arguments to each function we call).

Down in the body of main, the action of the function call should be obvious:

```
j = multbytwo(i);
```

The line calls multbytwo, passing it the value of i as its argument. When multbytwo returns, the return value is assigned to the variable j. (Notice that the value of main's local variable i will become the value of multbytwo's parameter x; this is absolutely not a problem, and is a normal sort of affair.)

This example is written out in "longhand," to make each step equivalent. The variable i isn't really needed, since we could just as well call

```
j = multbytwo(3);
```

And the variable j isn't really needed, either, since we could just as well call

```
printf("%d\n", multbytwo(3));
```

Here, the call to multbytwo is a subexpression which serves as the second argument to printf. The value returned bymultbytwo is passed immediately to printf. (Here, as in general, we see the flexibility and generality of expressions in C. An argument passed to a function may be an arbitrarily complex subexpression, and a function call is itself an expression which may be embedded as a subexpression within arbitrarily complicated surrounding expressions.) We should say a little more about the mechanism by which an argument is passed down from a caller into a function. Formally, C is *call by value,* which means that a function receives *copies* of the values of its arguments. We can illustrate this with an example. Suppose, in our implementation of multbytwo, we had gotten rid of the unnecessary retvalvariable like this:

```
int multbytwo(int x)
{
    x = x * 2;
    return x;
}
```

We might wonder, if we wrote it this way, what would happen to the value of the variable i when we called

```
j = multbytwo(i);
```

When our implementation of multbytwo changes the value of x, does that change the value of i up in the caller? The answer is no. x receives a copy of i's value, so when we change x we don't change i.

However, there is an exception to this rule. When the argument you pass to a function is not a single variable, but is rather an array, the function does *not* receive a copy of the array, and it therefore *can* modify the array in the caller. The reason is that it might be too expensive to copy the entire array, and furthermore, it can be useful for the function to write into the caller's array, as a way of handing back more data than would fit in the function's single return value.

FUNCTION PROTOTYPES

In modern C programming, it is considered good practice to use prototype declarations for all functions that you call. As we mentioned, these prototypes help to ensure that the compiler can generate correct code for calling the functions, as well as allowing the compiler to catch certain mistakes you might make.

Strictly speaking, however, prototypes are optional. If you call a function for which the compiler has not seen a prototype, the compiler will do the best it can, assuming that you're calling the function correctly. If prototypes are a good idea, and if we're going to get in the habit of writing function prototype declarations for functions we call that we've written (such as multbytwo), what happens for library functions such as printf? Where are their prototypes? The answer is in that boilerplate line

```
#include <stdio.h>
```

we've been including at the top of all of our programmes. stdio.h is conceptually a file full of external declarations and other information pertaining to the "Star.dard I/O" library functions, including printf. The #include directive (which we'll meet formally in a later chapter) arranges that all of the declarations within stdio.h are considered by the compiler, rather as if we'd typed them all in ourselves. Somewhere within these declarations is an external function prototype declaration forprintf, which satisfies the rule that there should be a prototype for each function we call.

(For other standard library functions we call, there will be other "header files" to include.) Finally, one more thing about external function prototype declarations. We've said that the distinction between external declarations and defining instances of normal variables hinges on the presence or absence of the keyword extern.

The situation is a little bit different for functions. The "defining instance" of a function is the function, including its body (that is, the brace-enclosed list of declarations and statements implementing the function). An external declaration of a function, even without the keyword extern, looks nothing like a function declaration. Therefore, the keyword extern is optional in function prototype declarations. If you wish, you can write

```
int multbytwo(int);
```

and this is just as good an external function prototype declaration as

```
extern int multbytwo(int);
```

(In the first form, without the extern, as soon as the compiler sees the semicolon, it knows it's not going to see a function body, so the declaration can't be a definition.) You may want to stay in the habit of using extern in all external declarations, including function declarations, since "extern = external declaration" is an easier rule to remember.

FUNCTION PHILOSOPHY

What makes a good function? The most important aspect of a good "building block" is that have a single, well-defined task to perform. When you find that a programme is hard to manage, it's often because it has not been designed and broken up into functions cleanly. Two obvious reasons for moving code down into a function are because:

- It appeared in the main programme several times, such that by making it a function, it can be written just once, and the several places where it used to appear can be replaced with calls to the new function.
- The main programme was getting too big, so it could be made (presumably) smaller and more manageable by lopping part of it off and making it a function.

These two reasons are important, and they represent significant benefits of well-chosen functions, but they are not sufficient to automatically identify a good function. As we've been suggesting, a good function has at least these two additional attributes:

- It does just one well-defined task, and does it well.
- Its interface to the rest of the programme is clean and narrow.

Attribute 3 is just a restatement of two things we said above. Attribute 4 says that you shouldn't have to keep track of too many things when calling a function. If you know what a function is supposed to do, and if its task is simple and well-defined, there should be just a few pieces of information you have to give it to act upon, and one or just a few pieces of information which it returns to you when it's done.

If you find yourself having to pass lots and lots of information to a function, or remember details of its internal implementation to make sure that it will work properly this time, it's often a sign that the function is not sufficiently well-defined. (A poorly-defined function may be an arbitrary chunk of code that was ripped out of a main programme that was getting too big, such that it essentially has to have access to all of that main function's local variables.)

The whole point of breaking a programme up into functions is so that you don't have to think about the entire programme at once; ideally, you can think about just one function at a time. We say that a good function is a "black box," which is supposed to suggest that the "container" it's in is opaque—callers can't see inside it (and the function inside can't see out). When you call a function, you only have to know what it does, not how it does it. When you're *writing* a function, you only have to know what it's supposed to do, and you don't have to know why or under what circumstances its caller will be calling it. (When designing a function, we should perhaps think about the callers just enough to ensure that the function we're designing will be easy to call, and that we aren't accidentally setting things up so that callers will have to think about any internal details.)

Some functions may be hard to write (if they have a hard job to do, or if it's hard to make them do it truly well), but that difficulty should be compartmentalized along with the function itself. Once you've written a "hard" function, you should be able to sit back and relax and watch it do that hard work on call from the rest of your programme.

It should be pleasant to notice (in the ideal case) how much easier the rest of the programme is to write, now that the hard work can be deferred to this workhorse function. (In fact, if a difficult-to-write function's interface is well-defined, you may be able to get away with writing a quick-and-dirty version of the function first, so that you can begin testing the rest of the programme, and then go back later and rewrite the function to do the hard parts. As long as the function's original interface anticipated the hard parts, you won't have to rewrite the rest of the programme when you fix the function.)

What I've been trying to say in the preceding few paragraphs is that functions are important for far more important reasons than just saving typing. Sometimes, we'll write a function which we only call once, just because breaking it out into a function makes things clearer and easier. If you find that difficulties pervade a programme, that the hard parts can't be buried inside black-box functions and then forgotten about; if you find that there are hard parts which involve complicated interactions among multiple functions, then the programme probably needs redesigning.

For the purposes of explanation, we've been seeming to talk so far only about "main programmes" and the functions they call and the rationale behind moving some piece of code down out of a "main programme" into a function. But in reality, there's obviously no need to restrict ourselves to a two-tier scheme. Any function we find ourself writing will often be appropriately written in terms of sub-functions, sub-sub-functions, etc.

SEPARATE COMPILATION LOGISTICS

When a programme consists of many functions, it can be convenient to split them up into several source files. Among other things, this means that when a change is made, only the source file containing the change has to be recompiled, not the whole programme.

The job of putting the pieces of a programme together and producing the final executable falls to a tool called the *linker*. (We may or may not need to invoke the linker explicitly; a compiler often invokes it automatically, as needed.) The linker looks through all of the pieces making up the programme, sorting out the external declarations and defining instances. The compiler has noted the definitions made by each source file, as well as the declarations of things used by each source file but (presumably) defined elsewhere. For each thing (global variable or function) used but not defined by one piece of the programme, the linker looks for another piece which does define that thing.

The logistics of writing a programme in several source files, and then compiling and linking all of the source files together, depend on the programming environment you're using. We'll cover two possibilities, depending on whether you're using a traditional command-line compiler or a newer integrated development environment (IDE) or other graphical user interface (GUI) compiler. When using a command-line compiler, there are usually two main steps involved in building an executable programme from one or more source files. First, each source file is compiled, resulting in an *object file* containing the machine instructions (generated by the compiler) corresponding to just the code in that source file. Second, the various object files are *linked*together, with each other and with *libraries* containing code for functions which you did not write (such as printf), to produce a final, executable programme.

Under Unix, the cc command can perform one or both steps. So far, we've been using extremely simple invocations of ccsuch as

```
cc -o hello hello.c
```

This invocation compiles a single source file, hello.c, links it, and places the executable in a file named hello.

Suppose we have a programme which we're trying to build from three separate source files, x.c, y.c, and z.c. We could compile all three of them, and link them together, all at once, with the command

```
cc -o myprog x.c y.c z.c
```

Alternatively, we could compile them separately: the -c option to cc tells it to compile only, but not to link. Instead of building an executable, it merely creates an object file, with a name ending in .o, for each source file compiled.

So the three commands:

```
cc -c x.c
cc -c y.c
cc -c y.c
```

would compile x.c, y.c, and z.c and create object files x.o, y.o, and z.o. Then, the three object files could be linked together using

```
cc -o myprog x.o y.o z.o
```

When the cc command is given an .o file, it knows that it does not have to compile it (it's an object file, already compiled); it just sends it through to the link process. Above we mentioned that the second, linking step also involves pulling in library functions. Normally, the functions from the Standard C library are linked in automatically. Occasionally, you must request a library manually; one common situation under Unix is that the math functions tend to be in a separate math library, which is requested by using -lm on the command line. Since the libraries must typically be searched *after* your program's own object files are linked (so that the linker knows which library functions your programme uses), any -l option must appear *after* the names of your files on the command line. For example, to link the object file mymath.o (previously compiled with cc -c mymath.c) together with the math library, you might use

```
cc -o mymathprog mymath.o -lm
```

Everything we've said about cc also applies to most other Unix C compilers. (Many of you will be using gcc, the FSF's GNU C Compiler.) There are command-line compilers for MS-DOS systems which work similarly. For example, the Microsoft C compiler comes with a CL ("compile and link") command, which works almost the same as Unix cc.

You can compile and link in one step:

```
cl hello.c
```

or you can compile only:

```
cl /c hello.c
```

creating an object file named hello.obj which you can link later. The preceding has all been about command-line compilers. If you're using some kind of integrated development environment, such as Borland's Turbo C or the Microsoft Programmer's Workbench or Visual C or Think C or Codewarrior, most of the mechanical details are taken care of for you. Typically you define a "project," and there's a way to specify the list of files which make up your project.

Chapter 7

Input/Output Model

MODEL

The I/O model does not distinguish between the types of physical devices supporting the I/O. Each source or sink of data is treated in the same way, and is viewed as a *stream* of bytes. Since the smallest object that can be represented in C is the character, access to a file is permitted at any character boundary.

Any number of characters can be read or written from a movable point, known as the *file position indicator*. The characters will be read, or written, in sequence from this point, and the position indicator moved accordingly. The position indicator is initially set to the beginning of a file when it is opened, but can also be moved by means of positioning requests.

Opening a file in append mode has an implementation defined effect on the stream's file position indicator. The overall effect is to provide sequential reads or writes unless the stream was opened in append mode, or the file position indicator is explicitly moved. There are two types of file, *text files* and *binary files*, which, within a programme, are manipulated as *text streams* and *binary* streams once they have been opened for I/O. The stdio package does not permit operations on the contents of files 'directly', but only by viewing them as streams.

TEXT STREAMS

The Standard specifies what is meant by the term *text*

stream, which essentially considers a file to contain lines of text. A line is a sequence of zero or more characters terminated by a newline character.

It is quite possible that the actual representation of lines in the external environment is different from this and there may be transformations of the data stream on the way in and out of the programme; a common requirement is to translate the '\n' line-terminator into the sequence '\r\n' on output, and do the reverse on input. Other translations may also be necessary.

Data read in from a text stream is guaranteed to compare equal to the data that was earlier written out to the file if the data consists only of complete lines of printable characters and the control characters horizontal-tab and newline, no newline character is immediately preceded by space characters and the last character is a newline.

It is guaranteed that, if the last character written to a text file is a newline, it will read back as the same. It is implementation defined whether the last line written to a text file must terminate with a newline character; this is because on some implementations text files and binary files are the same. Some implementations may strip the leading space from lines consisting only of a space followed by a newline, or strip trailing spaces at the end of a line!

An implementation must support text files with lines containing at least 254 characters, including the terminating newline.Opening a text stream in update mode may result in a binary stream in some implementations. Writing on a text stream may cause some implementations to truncate the file at that point—any data beyond the last byte of the current write being discarded.

BINARY STREAMS

A binary stream is a sequence of characters that can be used to record a program's internal data, such as the contents of structures or arrays in binary form. Data read in from a binary stream will always compare equal to data written out earlier to the same stream, under the same implementation.

In some circumstances, an implementation-defined number of NUL characters may be appended to a binary stream.

STDIO.H HEADER FILE

To provide support for streams of the various kinds, a number of functions and macros exist. The <stdio.h> header file contains the various declarations necessary for the functions, together with the following macro and type declarations.

FILE

The type of an object used to contain stream control information. Users of stdio never need to know the contents of these objects, but simply manipulate pointers to them. It is not safe to copy these objects within the programme; sometimes their addresses may be 'magic'.

fpos_t

A type of object that can be used to record unique values of a stream's file position indicator.

_IOFBF _IOLBF _IONBF

Values used to control the buffering of a stream in conjunction with thesetvbuf function.

BUFSIZ

The size of the buffer used by the setbuf function. An integral constant expression whose value is at least 256.

EOF

A negative integral constant expression, indicating the end-of-file condition on a stream i.e. that there is no more input.

FILENAME_MAX

The maximum length which a filename can have, if there is a limit, or otherwise the recommended size of an array intended to hold a file name.

FOPEN_MAX

The minimum number of files that the implementation guarantees may be held open concurrently; at least eight are guaranteed. Note that three predefined streams exist and may need to be closed if a programme needs to open more than five files explicitly.

L_tmpnam

The maximum length of the string generated by tmpnam; an integral constant expression.

SEEK_CUR SEEK_END SEEK_SET

Integral constant expressions used to control the actions of fseek.

TMP_MAX

The minimum number of unique filenames generated by tmpnam; an integral constant expression with a value of at least 25.

stdin stdout stderr

Predefined objects of type (FILE *) referring to the standard input, output and error streams respectively. These streams are automatically open when a programme starts execution.

OPENING, CLOSING AND BUFFERING OF STREAMS

OPENING

A stream is connected to a file by means of the fopen, freopen or tmpfilefunctions. These functions will, if successful, return a pointer to a FILE object. Three streams are available without any special action; they are normally all connected to the physical device associated with the executing programme: usually your terminal. They are referred to by the names stdin, the *standard input*, stdout, the *standard output*, and stderr, the *standard error* streams.

Normal keyboard input is from stdin, normal terminal output is to stdout, and error messages are directed to stderr. The separation of error messages from normal output messages allows the stdout stream to be connected to something other than the terminal device, and still to have error messages appear on the screen in front of you, rather than to be redirected to this file. These files are only fully buffered if they do not refer to interactive devices.

As mentioned earlier, the file position indicator may or may not be movable, depending on the underlying device. It is not possible, for example, to move the file position indicator on stdin if that is connected to a terminal, as it usually is. All non-temporary files must have a *filename*, which is a string. The rules for what constitutes valid filenames are implementation defined. Whether a file can be simultaneously open multiple times is also implementation defined. Opening a new file may involve creating the file. Creating an existing file causes its previous contents to be discarded.

CLOSING

Files are closed by explicitly calling fclose, exit or by returning from main. Any buffered data is flushed. If a programme stops for some other reason, the status of files which it had open is undefined.

BUFFERING

There are three types of buffering:

`Unbuffered`

Minimum internal storage is used by stdio in an attempt to send or receive data as soon as possible.

`Line buffered`

Characters are processed on a line-by-line basis. This is commonly used in interactive environments, and internal buffers are flushed only when full or when a newline is processed.

`Fully buffered`

Internal buffers are only flushed when full. The buffering associated with a stream can always be flushed by using fflushexplicitly. Support for the various types of buffering is implementation defined, and can be controlled within these limits using setbuf and setvbuf.

DIRECT FILE MANIPULATION

A number of functions exist to operate on files directly.

```
#include <stdio.h>
int remove(const char *filename);
int rename(const char *old, const char *new);
char *tmpnam(char *s);
FILE *tmpfile(void);
remove
```

Causes a file to be removed. Subsequent attempts to open the file will fail, unless it is first created again. If the file is already open, the operation ofremove is implementation defined. The return value is zero for success, any other value for failure.

`rename`

Changes the name of the file identified by old to new. Subsequent attempts to open the original name will fail, unless another file is created with the old name. As with remove, rename returns zero for a successful operation, any other value indicating a failure. If a file with the new name exists prior to calling rename, the behaviour is implementation defined. If rename fails for any reason, the original file is unaffected.

`tmpnam`

Generates a string that may be used as a filename and is guaranteed to be different from any existing filename. It may be called repeatedly, each time generating a new name. The constant TMP_MAX is used to specify how many times tmpnam may be called before it can no longer find a unique name.TMP_MAX will be at least 25.

If tmpnam is called more than this number of times, its behaviour is undefined by the Standard, but many implementations offer no practical limit. If the argument s is set to NULL, then tmpnam uses an internal buffer to build the name, and returns a pointer to that. Subsequent calls may alter the same internal buffer.

The argument may instead point to an array of at leastL_tmpnam characters, in which case the name will be filled into the supplied buffer. Such a filename may then be created, and used as a temporary file. Since the name is generated by the function, it is unlikely to be very useful in any other context. Temporary files of this nature are not removed, except by direct calls to the remove function. They are most often used to pass temporary data between two separate programmes.

`tmpfile`

Creates a temporary binary file, opened for update, and returns a pointer to the stream of that file. The file will be removed when the stream is closed. If no file could be opened, tmpfile returns a null pointer.

OPENING NAMED FILES

Named files are opened by a call to the fopen function, whose declaration is this:

```
#include <stdio.h>
FILE *fopen(const char *pathname, const char
*mode);
```

The pathname argument is the name of the file to open, such as that returned fromtmpnam, or some programme-specific filename. Files can be opened in a variety of *modes,* such as *read* mode for reading data,*write* mode for writing data, and so on.

Note that if you only want to write data to a file, open will *create* the file if it does not already exist, or truncate it to zero length if it did exist. The Standard list of modes is shown in Table, although implementations may permit extra modes by appending extra characters at the end of the modes.

Table. File Opening Modes.

Mode	Type of file	Read	Write	Create	Truncate
"r"	text	yes	n–	n–	no
"rb"	binary	yes	n–	n–	no
"r+"	text	yes	yes	n–	no
"r+b"	binary	yes	yes	n–	no
"rb+"	binary	yes	yes	n–	no
"w"	text	n–	yes	yes	yes
"wb"	binary	n–	yes	yes	yes
"w+"	text	yes	yes	yes	yes
"w+b"	binary	yes	yes	yes	yes
"wb+"	binary	yes	yes	yes	yes
"a"	text	n–	yes	yes	no
"ab"	binary	n–	yes	yes	no
"a+"	text	yes	yes	yes	no
"a+b"	binary	n–	yes	yes	no
"ab+"	binary	n–	yes	yes	no

Beware that some implementations of binary files may pad the last record withNULL characters, so opening them with modes ab, ab+ or a+b could position the file pointer beyond the last data written. If a file is opened in append mode, *all* writes will occur at the end of the file, regardless of attempts to move the file position indicator with fseek. The initial position fo the file position indicator will be implementation defined.

Attempts to open a file in read mode, indicated by an 'r' as the first character in the mode string, will fail if the file does not already exist or can't be read. Files opened for update ('+' as the second or third character of mode) may be both read and written, but a read may not immediately follow a write, or a write follow a read, without an intervening call to one (or more) of fflush, fseek, fsetpos or rewind. The only exception is that a write may immediately follow a read if EOF was read.

It may also be possible in some implementations to omit the b in the binary modes, using the same modes for text and binary files. Streams opened by fopen are fully buffered only if they are not connected to an interactive device; this ensures that prompts and responses are handled properly.

If fopen fails to open a file, it returns a null pointer; otherwise, it returns a pointer to the object controlling the stream. The stdin, stdout and stderr objects are not necessarily modifiable and it may not be possible to use the value returned fromfopen for assignment to one of them. For this reason, freopen is provided.

FREOPEN

The freopen function is used to take an existing stream pointer and associate it with another named file:

```
#include <stdio.h>
FILE *freopen(const char *pathname,
const char *mode, FILE *stream);
```

The mode argument is the same as for fopen. The stream is closed first, and any errors from the close are ignored. On error, NULL is returned, otherwise the new value for stream is returned.

CLOSING FILES

An open file is closed using fclose.

```
#include <stdio.h>
int fclose(FILE *stream);
```

Any unwritten data buffered for stream is flushed out and any unread data is thrown away. If a buffer had been automatically allocated for the stream, it is freed. The file is then closed. Zero is returned on success, EOF if any error occurs.

SETBUF, SETVBUF

These two functions are used to change the buffering strategy for an open stream:

```
#include <stdio.h>
int setvbuf(FILE *stream, char *buf,
int type, size_t size);
void setbuf(FILE *stream, char *buf);
```

They must be used *before* the file is either read from or written to. The typeargument defines how the stream will be buffered.

Table. Type of Buffering

Value	Effect
_IONBF	Do not buffer I/O
_IOFBF	Fully buffer I/O
_IOLBF	Line buffer: flush buffer when full, when newline is written or when a read is requested.

The buf argument can be a null pointer, in which case an array is automatically allocated to hold the buffered data. Otherwise, the user can provide a buffer, but should ensure that its lifetime is at least as long as that of the stream: a common mistake is to use automatic storage allocated inside a compound statement; in correct usage it is usual to obtain the storage from malloc instead. The size of the buffer is specified by the size argument. A call of setbuf is exactly the same as a call of setvbuf with IOFBF for the typeargument, and BUFSIZ for the size argument. If buf is a null pointer, the value_IONBF is used for type instead. No value is returned by setbuf, setvbuf returns zero on success, non-zero if invalid values are provided for type or size, or the request cannot be complied with.

FFLUSH

```
#include <stdio.h>
int fflush(FILE *stream);
```

If stream refers to a file opened for output or update, any unwritten data is 'written' out. Exactly what that means is a function of the host environment, and C cannot guarantee, for example, that data immediately reaches the surface of a disk which might be supporting the file. If the stream is associated with a file opened for input or update, any preceding ungetc operation is forgotten.

The most recent operation on the stream must have been an output operation; if not, the behaviour is undefined. A call of fflush with an argument of zero flushes every output or update stream. Care is taken to avoid those streams that have not had an output as their last operation, thus avoiding the undefined behaviour mentioned above. EOF is returned if an error occurs, otherwise zero.

PRINTF

Printf's name comes from print formatted. It generates output under the control of a *format string* (its first argument) which consists of literal characters to be printed and also special character sequences—*format specifiers*—which request that other arguments be fetched, formatted, and inserted into the string.

Our very first programme was nothing more than a call to printf, printing a constant string:

```
printf("Hello, world!\n");
Our second programme also featured a call
to printf:
printf("i is %d\n", i);
```

In that case, whenever printf "printed" the string "i is %d", it did not print it verbatim; it replaced the two characters%d with the value of the variable i.

There are quite a number of format specifiers for printf. Here are the basic ones:

```
%d  print an int argument in decimal
%ld print a long int argument in decimal
%c  print a character
%s  print a string
%f  print a float or double argument
%e  same as %f, but use exponential notation
%g  use %e or %f, whichever is better
%-  print an int argument in octal (base 8)
%x  print an int argument in hexadecimal
(base 16)
%%  print a single %
```

It is also possible to specify the width and precision of numbers and strings as they are inserted (somewhat like FORTRAN format statements); we'll present those details in a later chapter.

(Very briefly, for those who are curious: a notation like %3d means to print an int in a field at least 3 spaces wide; a notation like %5.2f means to print a float ordouble in a field at least 5 spaces wide, with two places to the right of the decimal.)

To illustrate with a few more examples: the call

```
printf("%c %d %f %e %s %d%%\n", '1', 2,
3.14, 56000000., "eight", 9);
would print
1 2 3.140000 5.600000e+07 eight 9%
The call
printf("%d %o %x\n", 100, 100, 100);
would print
100 144 64
```

Successive calls to printf just build up the output a piece at a time, so the calls

```
printf("Hello, ");
printf("world!\n");
```

would also print Hello, world! (on one line of output).

Earlier we learned that C represents characters internally as small integers corresponding to the characters' values in the machine's character set (typically ASCII). This means that there isn't really much difference between a character and an integer in C; most of the difference is in whether we choose to interpret an integer as an integer or a character. printf is one place where we get to make that choice: %d prints an integer value as a string of digits representing its decimal value, while %c prints the character corresponding to a character set value.

So the lines:

```
char c = 'A';
int i = 97;
printf("c = %c, i = %d\n", c, i);
```

would print c as the character A and i as the number 97. But if, on the other hand, we called

```
printf("c = %d, i = %c\n", c, i);
```

we'd see the decimal value (printed by %d) of the character 'A', followed by the character (whatever it is) which happens to have the decimal value 97. You have to be careful when calling printf. It has no way of knowing how many arguments you've passed it or what their types are other than by looking for the format specifiers in the format string.

If there are more format specifiers (that is, more % signs) than there are arguments, or if the arguments have the wrong types for the format specifiers, printf can misbehave badly, often printing nonsense numbers or (even worse) numbers which mislead you into thinking that some other part of your programme is broken. Because of some automatic conversion rules which we haven't covered yet, you have a small amount of latitude in the types of the expressions you pass as arguments to printf.

The argument for %c may be of type char or int, and the argument for %d may be of type char or int. The string argument for %s may be a string constant, an array of characters, or a pointer to some characters (though we haven't really covered strings or pointers yet).

Finally, the arguments corresponding to %e, %f, and %g may be of types float or double. But other combinations do *not* work reliably: %d will not print a long int or a float or a double; %ld will not print an int; %e, %f, and %g will not print an int.

CHARACTER INPUT AND OUTPUT

Unless a programme can read some input, it's hard to keep it from doing exactly the same thing every time it's run, and thus being rather boring after a while.

The most basic way of reading input is by calling the function getchar. getchar reads one character from the "standard input," which is usually the user's keyboard, but which can sometimes be redirected by the operating system. getcharreturns the character it reads, or, if there are no more characters available, the special value EOF.A companion function is putchar, which writes one character to the "standard output."

(The standard output is, again not surprisingly, usually the user's screen, although it, too, can be redirected. printf, like putchar, prints to the standard output; in fact, you can imagine that printf calls putchar to actually print each of the characters it formats.) Using these two functions, we can write a very basic programme to copy the input, a character at a time, to the output:

```
#include <stdio.h>
/* copy input to output */
main()
{
  int c;
  c = getchar();
  while(c != EOF)
{
  putchar(c);
  c = getchar();
}
  return 0;
}
```

This code is straightforward, and I encourage you to type it in and try it out. It reads one character, and if it is not the EOFcode, enters a while loop, printing one character and reading another, as long as the character read is not EOF. This is a straightforward loop, although there's one mystery surrounding the declaration of the variable c: if it holds characters, why is it an int?

We said that a char variable could hold integers corresponding to character set values, and that an int could hold integers of more arbitrary values. Since most character sets contain a few hundred characters, an int variable can in general comfortably hold all char values, and then some. Therefore, there's nothing wrong with declaring c as an int. But in fact, it's important to do so, because getchar can return every character value,*plus* that special, non-character value EOF, indicating that there are no more characters.

Type char is only guaranteed to be able to hold all the character values; it is *not* guaranteed to be able to hold this "no more characters" value without possibly mixing it up with some actual character value. Therefore, you should always remember to use an int for anything you assigngetchar's return value to.

When you run the character copying programme, and it begins copying its input (your typing) to its output (your screen), you may find yourself wondering how to stop it. It stops when it receives end-of-file (EOF), but how do you send EOF? The answer depends on what kind of computer you're using. On Unix and Unix-related systems, it's almost always control-D. On MS-DOS machines, it's control-Z followed by the RETURN key. Under Think C on the Macintosh, it's control-D, just like Unix. On other systems, you may have to do some research to learn how to send EOF.

(Note, too, that the character you type to generate an end-of-file condition from the keyboard is *not* the same as the special EOF value returned by getchar. The EOF value returned by getchar is a code indicating that the input system has detected an end-of-file condition, whether it's reading the keyboard or a file or a magnetic tape or a network connection or anything else. In a disk file, at least, there is not likely to be any character *in* the file corresponding to EOF; as far as your programme is concerned, EOF indicates the absence of any more characters to read.) Another excellent thing to know when doing any kind of programming is how to terminate a runaway programme. If a programme is running forever waiting for input, you can usually stop it by sending it an end-of-file, as above, but if it's running forever *not* waiting for something, you'll have to take more drastic measures.

Under Unix, control-C (or, occasionally, the DELETE key) will terminate the current programme, almost no matter what. Under MS-DOS, control-C or control-BREAK will sometimes terminate the current programme, but by default MS-DOS only checks for control-C when it's looking for input, so an infinite loop can be unkillable. There's a DOS command,

```
break on
```

which tells DOS to look for control-C more often, and I recommend using this command if you're doing any programming. (If a programme is in a really tight infinite loop under MS-DOS, there can be no way of killing it short of rebooting.) On the Mac, try command-period or command-option-ESCAPE.

You'll type a character, and see it on the screen right away, and assume it's your programme working, but it's only your computer echoing every key you type, as it always does. When you hit RETURN, a full line of characters is made available to your programme. It then zips several times through its loop, reading and printing all the characters in the line in quick succession. In other words, when you run this programme, it will probably seem to copy the input a line at a time, rather than a character at a time. You may wonder how a programme could instead read a character right away, without waiting for the user to hit RETURN. That's an excellent question, but unfortunately the answer is rather complicated, and beyond the scope of our discussion here. (Among other things, how to read a character right away is one of the things that's not defined by the C language, and it's not defined by any of the standard library functions, either.

Stylistically, the character-copying programme above can be said to have one minor flaw: it contains two calls to getchar, one which reads the first character and one which reads (by virtue of the fact that it's in the body of the loop) all the other characters. This seems inelegant and perhaps unnecessary, and it can also be risky: if there were more things going on within the loop, and if we ever changed the way we read characters, it would be easy to change one of the getchar calls but forget to change the other one. Is there a way to rewrite the loop so that there is only one call to getchar, responsible for reading all the characters? Is there a way to read a character, test it for EOF, and assign it to the variable c, all at the same time?

There is. It relies on the fact that the assignment operator, =, is just another operator in C. An assignment is not (necessarily) a standalone statement; it is an expression, and it has a value (the value that's assigned to the variable on the left-hand side), and it can therefore participate in a larger, surrounding expression. Therefore, most C programmers would write the character-copying loop like this:

```
while((c = getchar()) != EOF)
putchar(c);
```

The function getchar is called, as before, and its return value is assigned to the variable c. Then the value is immediately compared against the value EOF. Finally, the true/false value of the comparison controls the whileloop: as long as the value is not EOF, the loop continues executing, but as soon as an EOF is received, no more trips through the loop are taken, and it exits. The net result is that the call to getchar happens inside the test at the top of the whileloop, and doesn't have to be repeated before the loop and within the loop (more on this in a bit).

Stated another way, the syntax of a while loop is always

```
while( expression )...
```

A comparison (using the != operator) is of course an expression; the syntax is

```
expression != expression
```

And an assignment is an expression; the syntax is

```
expression = expression
```

What we're seeing is just another example of the fact that expressions can be combined with essentially limitless generality and therefore infinite variety. The left-hand side of the != operator (its first *expression*) is the (sub)expression c = getchar(), and the combined expression is the *expression* needed by the while loop.

The extra parentheses around

```
(c = getchar())
```

are important, and are there because because the *precedence* of the != operator is higher than that of the = operator.

If we (incorrectly) wrote

```
while(c = getchar() != EOF)     /* WRONG */
```

the compiler would interpret it as

```
while(c = (getchar() != EOF))
```

That is, it would assign the result of the != operator to the variable c, which is *not* what we want.

("Precedence" refers to the rules for which operators are applied to their operands in which order, that is, to the rules controlling the default grouping of expressions and subexpressions. For example, the multiplication operator * has higher precedence than the addition operator +, which means that the expression a + b * c is parsed as a + (b * c). We'll have more to say about precedence later.)

The line

```
while((c = getchar()) != EOF)
```

epitomizes the cryptic brevity which C is notorious for. You may find this terseness infuriating (and you're not alone!), and it can certainly be carried too far, but bear with me for a moment while I defend it.

The simple example we've been discussing illustrates the tradeoffs well. We have four things to do:

- Call getchar,
- Assign its return value to a variable,
- Test the return value against EOF, and
- Process the character (in this case, print it out again).

We can't eliminate any of these steps. We have to assign getchar's value to a variable because we have to do two different things with it (test, and print). Therefore, compressing the assignment and test into the same line is the only good way of avoiding two distinct calls to getchar. You may not agree that the compressed idiom is better for being more compact or easier to read, but the fact that there is now only one call to getchar *is* a real virtue.

Don't think that you'll have to write compressed lines like

```
while((c = getchar()) != EOF)
```

right away, or in order to be an "expert C programmer." But, for better or worse, most experienced C programmers do like to use these idioms (whether they're justified or not), so you'll need to be able to at least recognize and understand them when you're reading other peoples' code.

READING LINES

It's often convenient for a programme to process its input not a character at a time but rather a line at a time, that is, to read an entire line of input and then act on it all at once. The standard C library has a couple of functions for reading lines, but they have a few awkward features, so we're going to learn more about character input (and about writing functions in general) by writing our own function to read one line. Here it is:

```
#include <stdio.h>
/* Read one line from standard input, */
/* copying it to line array (but no more
 than max chars). */
/* Does not place terminating \n in line
array. */
/* Returns line length, or 0 for empty line,
 or EOF for end-of-file. */
int getline(char line[], int max)
{
  int nch = 0;
  int c;
  max = max - 1; /* leave room for '\0' */
  while((c = getchar()) != EOF)
{
  if(c == '\n')
  break;
  if(nch < max)
{
```

```
    line[nch] = c;
    nch = nch + 1;
    }
}
    if(c == EOF && nch == 0)
    return EOF;
    line[nch] = '\0';
    return nch;
}
```

As the comment indicates, this function will read one line of input from the standard input, placing it into the line array. The size of the line array is given by the max argument; the function will never write more than max characters into line.

The main body of the function is a getchar loop, much as we used in the character-copying programme. In the body of this loop, however, we're storing the characters in an array. Also, we're only reading one line of characters, then stopping and returning.

First of all, the getline function accepts an array as a parameter. As we've said, array parameters are an exception to the rule that functions receive copies of their arguments—in the case of arrays, the function *does* have access to the actual array passed by the caller, and *can* modify it. Since the function is accessing the caller's array, not creating a new one to hold a copy, the function does not have to declare the argument array's size; it's set by the caller. However, so that we won't overflow the caller's array by reading too long a line into it, we allow the caller to pass along the size of the array, which we promise not to exceed.

Second, we see an example of the break statement. The top of the loop looks like our earlier character-copying loop—it stops when it reaches EOF—but we only want this loop to read one line, so we also stop (that is, break out of the loop) when we see the \n character signifying end-of-line. An equivalent loop, without the break statement, would be

```
    while((c = getchar()) != EOF && c != '\n')
    {
    if(nch < max)
```

```
    {
      line[nch] = c;
      nch = nch + 1;
    }
}
```

We haven't learned about the internal representation of strings yet, but it turns out that strings in C are simply arrays of characters, which is why we are reading the line into an array of characters. The end of a string is marked by the special character, '\0'. To make sure that there's always room for that character, on our way in we subtract 1 from max, the argument that tells us how many characters we may place in the line array. When we're done reading the line, we store the end-of-string character '\0' at the end of the string we've just built in the line array.

Finally, there's one subtlety in the code which isn't too important for our purposes now but which you may wonder about: it's arranged to handle the possibility that a few characters (i.e. the apparent beginning of a line) are read, followed immediately by an EOF, without the usual \n end-of-line character.

In any case, the function returns the length (number of characters) of the line it read, not including the \n. (Therefore, it returns 0 for an empty line.) Like getchar, it returns EOF when there are no more lines to read. (It happens that EOF is a negative number, so it will never match the length of a line that getline has read.) Here is an example of a test programme which calls getline, reading the input a line at a time and then printing each line back out:

```
#include <stdio.h>
extern int getline(char [], int);
main()
{
  char line[256];
  while(getline(line, 256) != EOF)
  printf("you typed \"%s\"\n", line);
  return 0;
}
```

The notation char [] in the function prototype for getline says that getline accepts as its first argument an array ofchar. When the programme calls getline, it is careful to pass along the actual size of the array. You might notice a potential problem: since the number 256 appears in two places, if we ever decide that 256 is too small, and that we want to be able to read longer lines, we could easily change one of the instances of 256, and forget to change the other one.

READING NUMBERS

The getline function of the previous section reads one line from the user, as a *string*. What if we want to read a number? One straightforward way is to read a string as before, and then immediately convert the string to a number. The standard C library contains a number of functions for doing this. The simplest to use are atoi(), which converts a string to an integer, and atof(), which converts a string to a floating-point number. (Both of these functions are declared in the header<stdlib.h>, so you should #include that header at the top of any file using these functions.) You could read an integer from the user like this:

```
#include <stdlib.h>
char line[256];
int n;
printf("Type an integer:\n");
getline(line, 256);
n = atoi(line);
```

Now the variable n contains the number typed by the user. (This assumes that the user *did* type a valid number, and thatgetline did not return EOF.)

Reading a floating-point number is similar:

```
#include <stdlib.h>
char line[256];
double x;
printf("Type a floating-point number:\n");
getline(line, 256);
x = atof(line);
```

(atof is actually declared as returning type double, but you could also use it with a variable of type float, because in general, C automatically converts between float and double as needed.) Another way of reading in numbers, which you're likely to see in other books on C, involves the scanf function, but it has several problems, so we won't discuss it for now. (Superficially, scanf seems simple enough, which is why it's often used, especially in textbooks. The trouble is that to perform input reliably using scanf is not nearly as easy as it looks, especially when you're not sure what the user is going to type.)

FORMATTED I/O

There are a number of related functions used for formatted I/O, each one determining the format of the I/O from a *format string*. For output, the format string consists of plain text, which is output unchanged, and embedded *format specifications* which call for some special processing of one of the remaining arguments to the function. On input, the plain text must match what is seen in the input stream; the format specifications again specify what the meaning of remaining arguments is. Each format specification is introduced by a % character, followed by the rest of the specification.

OUTPUT: THE PRINTF FAMILY

For those functions performing output, the format specification takes the following form, with optional parts enclosed in brackets:

```
%<flags><field
width><precision><length>conversion
```

The meaning of *flags, field width, precision, length,* and *conversion* are given below, although tersely. For more detail, it is worth looking at what the Standard says.

flags

Zero or more of the following:

-

Left justify the conversion within its field.

+

A signed conversion will always start with a plus or minus sign.

space

If the first character of a signed conversion is not a sign, insert a space. Overridden by + if present.

`#`

Forces an alternative form of output. The first digit of an octal conversion will always be a 0; inserts 0X in front of a non-zero hexadecimal conversion; forces a decimal point in all floating point conversions even if one is not necessary; does not remove trailing zeros from g and G conversions.

`0`

Pad d, i, o, u, x, X, e, E, f, F and G conversions on the left with zeros up to the field width. Overidden by the - flag. If a precision is specified for the d, i, o, u, x or X conversions, the flag is ignored. The behaviour is undefined for other conversions.

`field width`

A decimal integer specifying the minimum output field width. This will be exceeded if necessary. If an asterisk is used here, the next argument is converted to an integer and used for the value of the field width; if the value is negative it is treated as a - flag followed by a positive field width. Output that would be less than the field width is padded with spaces (zeros if the*field width* integer starts with a zero) to fit. The padding is on the left unless the left-adjustment flag is specified.

`precision`

This starts with a period '.'. It specifies the minimum number of digits for d,i, o, u, x, or X conversions; the number of digits after the decimal point for e,E, f conversions; the maximum number of digits for g and G conversions; the number of characters to be printed from a string for s conversion. The amount of padding overrides the field width. If an asterisk is used here, the next argument is converted to an integer and used for the value of the field width. If the value is negative, it is treated as if it were missing. If only the period is present, the precision is taken to be zero.

`length`

In preceding a specifier to print an integral type causes it to be treated as if it were a short. (Note that the various sorts of short are always promoted to one of the flavours of int when passed as an argument.) l works like h but applies to a long integral argument. L is used to indicate that a long doubleargument is to be printed, and only applies to the floating-point specifiers. These are cause undefined behaviour if they are used with the 'wrong' type of conversion.

Conversion

Table. Conversions

Specifier	Effect precision	Default
d	Signed decimal	1
i	Signed decimal	1
u	Unsigned decimal	1
–	Unsigned octal	1
x	Unsigned hexadecimal (0–f)	1
X	Unsigned hexadecimal (0–F)	1
	Precision specifies minimum number of digits, expanded with leading zeros if necessary. Printing a value of zero with zero precision outputs no characters.	
f	Print a double with *precision* digits (rounded) after the decimal point.	6
	To suppress the decimal point use a *precision* of explicitly zero. Otherwise, at least one digit appears in front of the point.	
e, E	Print a double in exponential format, rounded, with one digit before the decimal point, *precision* after it. A *precision* of zero suppresses the decimal point. There will be at least two digits in the exponent, which is printed as 1.23e15 in e format, or 1.23E15 inE format.	6
g,G	Use style f, or e (E with G) depending on the exponent. If the exponent is	unspecified

	less than "4 or e"*precision,* f is not used. Trailing zeros are suppressed, a decimal point is only printed if there is a following digit.	
c	The int argument is converted to an unsigned char and the resultant character printed.	
s	Print a string up to *precision* digits long. If *precision*is not specified, or is greater than the length of the string, the string must be NUL terminated.	infinite
p	Display the value of a (void *) pointer in a system-dependent way.	
n	The argument must be a pointer to an integer. The number of characters output so far by this call will be written into the integer.	
%	A %	—

The functions that use these formats are described in Table. All need the inclusion of <stdio.h>. Their declarations are as shown.

```
#include <stdio.h>
int fprintf(FILE *stream, const char
*format,...);
int printf(const char *format,...);
int sprintf(char *s, const char *format,...);
#include <stdarg.h> /* as well as stdio.h */
int vfprintf(FILE *stream, const char
*format, va list arg);
int vprintf(const char *format, va list arg);
int vsprintf(char *s, const char *format,
va list arg);
```

Table. Functions Performing Formatted Output.

Name	Purpose
fprintf	General formatted output as described. Output is written to the file indicated by stream.

printf	Identical to fprintf with a first argument equal to stdout.
sprintf	Identical to fprintf except that the output is not written to a file, but written into the character array pointed to by s.
vfprintf	Formatted output as for fprintf, but with the variable argument list replaced by arg which must have been initialized by va_start.va_end is not called by this function.
vprintf	Identical to vfprintf with a first argument equal to stdout.
vsprintf	Formatted output as for sprintf, but with the variable argument list replaced by arg which must have been initialized by va_start.va_end is not called by this function.

All of the above functions return the number of characters output, or a negative value on error. The trailing null is not counted by sprintf and vsprintf. Implementations must permit at least 509 characters to be produced by any single conversion.

INPUT SCANF

A number of functions exist analogous to the printf family, but for the purposes of input instead. The most immediate difference between the two families is that thescanf group needs to be passed *pointers* to their arguments, so that the values read can be assigned to the proper destinations.

Forgetting to pass a pointer is a very common error, and one which the compiler cannot detect—the variable argument list prevents it.

The format string is used to control interpretation of a stream of input data, which generally contains values to be assigned to the objects pointed to by the remaining arguments to scanf. The contents of the format string may contain:

`white space`

This causes the input stream to be read up to the next non-white-space character.

`ordinary character`

Anything except white-space or % characters. The next character in the input stream *must* match this character.

`conversion specification`

This is a % character, followed by an optional * character (which suppresses the conversion), followed by an optional nonzero decimal integer specifying the maximum field width, an optional h, l or L to control the length of the conversion and finally a non-optional conversion specifier. Note that use ofh, l, or L will affect the type of pointer which must be used.

Except for the specifiers c, n and [, a field of input is a sequence of non-space characters starting at the first non-space character in the input.

It terminates at the first conflicting character or when the input field width is reached. The result is put into wherever the corresponding argument points, unless the assignment is suppressed using the * mentioned already. The following conversion specifiers may be used.

`d i o u x`

Convert a signed integer, a signed integer in a form acceptable to strtol, an octal integer, an unsigned integer and a hexadecimal integer respectively.

`e f g`

Convert a float (*not* a double).

`s`

Read a string, and add a null at the end. The string is terminated by whitespace on input (which is not read as part of the string).

`[`

Read a string. A list of characters, called the *scan set* follows the [. A]delimits the list.

Characters are read until (but not including) the first character which is *not* in the scan set. If the first character in the list is a circumflex ^, then the scan set includes any character not in the list.

If the initial sequence is [^] or [], the] is not a delimiter, but part of the list and another] will be needed to end the list. If there is a minus sign (-) in the list, it must be either the first or the last character; otherwise the meaning is implementation defined.

`c`

Read a single character; white space is significant here. To read the first non-white space character, use %1s. A field width indicates that an array of characters is to be read.

`p`

Read a (void *) pointer previously written out using the %p of one of theprintfs.

`%`

A % is expected in the input, no assignment is made.

`n`

Return as an integer the number of characters read by this call so far. The size specifiers have the effect shown in Table.

Table. Size Specifiers.

Specifier	Modifies	Converts
l	d i o u x	Long int
h	d i o u x	Short int
l	e f	Double
L	e f	Long double

The functions are described below, with the following declarations:

```
#include <stdio.h>
int fscanf(FILE *stream, const char
*format,...);
int sscanf(const char *s, const char
*format,...);
int scanf(const char *format,...);
```

Fscanf takes its input from the designated stream, scanf is identical to fscanfwith a first argument of stdin, and sscanf takes its input from the designated character array. If an input failure occurs before any conversion, EOF is returned. Otherwise, the number of successful conversions is returned: this may be zero if no conversions are performed. An input failure is caused by reading EOF or reaching the end of the input string (as appropriate). A conversion failure is caused by a failure to match the proper pattern for a particular conversion.

OPERATORS

```
v = v op e
```

where *v* is any variable (or anything like a[i]), *op* is any of the binary arithmetic operators we've seen so far, and *e* is any expression, you can replace it with the simplified

```
v op= e
```

For example, you can replace the expressions

```
i = i + 1
j = j - 10
k = k * (n + 1)
a[i] = a[i] / b
```

with

```
i += 1
j -= 10
k *= n + 1
a[i] /= b
```

In an example in a previous chapter, we used the assignment

```
a[d1 + d2] = a[d1 + d2] + 1;
```

to count the rolls of a pair of dice. Using +=, we could simplify this expression to

```
a[d1 + d2] += 1;
```

As these examples show, you can use the "op=" form with any of the arithmetic operators (and with several other operators that we haven't seen yet). The expression, *e*, does not have to be the constant 1; it can be any expression. You don't always need as many explicit parentheses when using the *op*= operators: the expression

```
k *= n + 1
```

is interpreted as:

```
k = k * (n + 1)
```

INCREMENT AND DECREMENT OPERATORS

The assignment operators of the previous section let us replace *v* = *v op e* with *v op*= *e*, so that we didn't have to mention*v* twice. In the most common cases, namely when we're adding or subtracting the constant 1 (that is, when *op* is + or - and*e* is 1), C provides another set of shortcuts:

the *autoincrement* and *autodecrement* operators. In their simplest forms, they look like this:

```
++i add 1 to i
—j  subtract 1 from j
```

These correspond to the slightly longer i += 1 and j -= 1, respectively, and also to the fully "longhand" forms i = i + 1 and j = j - 1. The ++ and — operators apply to one operand (they're *unary* operators). The expression ++i adds 1 to i, and stores the incremented result back in i. This means that these operators don't just compute new values; they also modify the value of some variable. (They share this property—modifying some variable—with the assignment operators; we can say that these operators all have *side effects*. That is, they have some effect, on the side, other than just computing a new value.)

The incremented (or decremented) result is also made available to the rest of the expression, so an expression like

```
k = 2 * ++i
```

means "add one to i, store the result back in i, multiply it by 2, and store *that* result in k." (This is a pretty meaningless expression; our actual uses of ++ later will make more sense.) Both the ++ and — operators have an unusual property: they can be used in two ways, depending on whether they are written to the left or the right of the variable they're operating on. In either case, they increment or decrement the variable they're operating on; the difference concerns whether it's the old or the new value that's "returned" to the surrounding expression. The *prefix* form ++i increments i and returns the incremented value. The *postfix* form i++ increments i, but returns the *prior,* non-incremented value. Rewriting our previous example slightly, the expression

```
k = 2 * i++
```

means "take i's old value and multiply it by 2, increment i, store the result of the multiplication in k." The distinction between the prefix and postfix forms of ++ and — will probably seem strained at first, but it will make more sense once we begin using these operators in more realistic situations. For example, our getline function of the previous chapter used the statements

```
line[nch] = c;
nch = nch + 1;
```

as the body of its inner loop. Using the ++ operator, we could simplify this to

```
line[nch++] = c;
```

We wanted to increment nch *after* deciding which element of the line array to store into, so the postfix form nch++ is appropriate.

Notice that it only makes sense to apply the ++ and — operators to variables (or to other "containers," such as a[i]). It would be meaningless to say something like

```
1++
or
(2+3)++
```

The ++ operator doesn't just mean "add one"; it means "add one *to a variable*" or "make a variable's value one more than it was before." But (1+2) is not a variable, it's an expression; so there's no place for ++ to store the incremented result.

Another unfortunate example is:

```
i = i++;
```

which some confused programmers sometimes write, presumably because they want to be extra sure that i is incremented by 1. But i++ all by itself is sufficient to increment i by 1; the extra (explicit) assignment to i is unnecessary and in fact counterproductive, meaningless, and incorrect. If you want to increment i (that is, add one to it, and store the result back in i), either use

```
i = i + 1;
or
i += 1;
or
++i;
or
i++;
```

Don't try to use some bizarre combination.

Did it matter whether we used ++i or i++ in this last example? Remember, the difference between the two forms is what value (either the old or the new) is passed on to the surrounding expression. If there is no surrounding expression, if the++i or i++ appears all by itself, to increment i and do nothing else, you can use either form; it makes no difference. (Two ways that an expression can appear "all by itself," with "no surrounding expression," are when it is an expression statement terminated by a semicolon, as above, or when it is one of the controlling expressions of a for loop.) For example, both the loops

```
for(i = 0; i < 10; ++i)
printf("%d\n", i);
and
for(i = 0; i < 10; i++)
printf("%d\n", i);
```

will behave exactly the same way and produce exactly the same results. (In real code, postfix increment is probably more common, though prefix definitely has its uses, too.)

In the preceding section, we simplified the expression

```
a[d1 + d2] = a[d1 + d2] + 1;
from a previous chapter down to
a[d1 + d2] += 1;
Using ++, we could simplify it still further
to
a[d1 + d2]++;
or
++a[d1 + d2];
```

(Again, in this case, both are equivalent.)

ORDER OF EVALUATION

When you start using the ++ and — operators in larger expressions, you end up with expressions which do several things at once, i.e., they modify several different variables at more or less the same time. When you write such an expression, you must be careful not to have the expression "pull the rug out from under itself" by assigning two different values to the same variable, or by assigning a new value to a variable at the same time that another part of the expression is trying to use the value of that variable.

Actually, we had already started writing expressions which did several things at once even before we met the ++ and —operators. The expression

```
(c = getchar()) != EOF
```

assigns getchar's return value to c, *and* compares it to EOF. The ++ and — operators make it much easier to cram a lot into a small expression: the example

```
line[nch++] = c;
```

from the previous section assigned c to line[nch], *and* incremented nch. We'll eventually meet expressions which do*three* things at once, such as

```
a[i++] = b[j++];
```

which assigns b[j] to a[i], and increments i, *and* increments j. If you're not careful, though, it's easy for this sort of thing to get out of hand. Can you figure out exactly what the expression

```
a[i++] = b[i++]; /* WRONG */
```

should do? I can't, and here's the important part: *neither can the compiler*. We know that the definition of postfix ++ is that the former value, before the increment, is what goes on to participate in the rest of the expression, but the expressiona[i++] = b[i++] contains *two* ++ operators. Which of them happens first? Does this expression assign the old ith element of b to the new ith element of a, or vice versa? No one knows. When the order of evaluation matters but is not well-defined (that is, when we can't say for sure which order the compiler will evaluate the various dependent parts in) we say that the meaning of the expression is *undefined*, and if we're smart we won't write the expression in the first place. (Why would anyone ever write an "undefined" expression? Because sometimes, the compiler happens to evaluate it in the order a programmer wanted, and the programmer assumes that since it works, it must be okay.)

For example, suppose we carelessly wrote this loop:

```
int i, a[10];
i = 0;
while(i < 10)
a[i] = i++; /* WRONG */
```

It looks like we're trying to set a[0] to 0, a[1] to 1, etc. But what if the increment i++ happens before the compiler decides which cell of the array a to store the (unincremented) result in? We might end up setting a[1] to 0, a[2] to 1, etc., instead. Since, in this case, we can't be sure which order things would happen in, we simply shouldn't write code like this. In this case, what we're doing matches the pattern of a for loop, anyway, which would be a better choice:

```
for(i = 0; i < 10; i++)
a[i] = i;
```

Now that the increment i++ isn't crammed into the same expression that's setting a[i], the code is perfectly well-defined, and is guaranteed to do what we want. In general, you should be wary of ever trying to second-guess the order an expression will be evaluated in, with two exceptions:

- You can obviously assume that precedence will dictate the order in which binary operators are applied. This typically says more than just what order things happens in, but also what the expression actually *means*. (In other words, the precedence of * over + says more than that the multiplication "happens first" in 1 + 2 * 3; it says that the answer is 7, not 9.)
- Although we haven't mentioned it yet, it is guaranteed that the logical operators && and || are evaluated left-to-right, and that the right-hand side is not evaluated at all if the left-hand side determines the outcome.

To look at one more example, it might seem that the code

```
int i = 7;
printf("%d\n", i++ * i++);
```

would have to print 56, because no matter which order the increments happen in, 7*8 is 8*7 is 56. But ++ just says that the increment happens later, not that it happens immediately, so this code could print 49 (if the compiler chose to perform the multiplication first, and both increments later). And, it turns out that ambiguous expressions like this are such a bad idea that the ANSI C Standard does not require compilers to do anything reasonable with them at all. Theoretically, the above code could end up printing 42, or 8923409342, or 0, or crashing your computer.

Programmers sometimes mistakenly imagine that they can write an expression which tries to do too much at once and then predict exactly how it will behave based on "order of evaluation." For example, we know that multiplication has higher*precedence* than addition, which means that in the expression

```
i + j * k
```

j will be multiplied by k, and then i will be added to the result. Informally, we often say that the multiplication happens "before" the addition. That's true in this case, but it doesn't say as much as we might think about a more complicated expression, such as

```
i++ + j++ * k++
```

In this case, besides the addition and multiplication, i, j, and k are all being incremented. We can *not* say which of them will be incremented first; it's the compiler's choice. (In particular, it is *not* necessarily the case that j++ or k++ will happen first; the compiler might choose to save i's value somewhere and increment i first, even though it will have to keep the old value around until after it has done the multiplication.)

In the preceding example, it probably doesn't matter which variable is incremented first. It's not too hard, though, to write an expression where it does matter. In fact, we've seen one already: the ambiguous assignment a[i++] = b[i++]. We still don't know which i++ happens first. (We can *not* assume, based on the right-to-left behaviour of the = operator, that the right-hand i++ will happen first.) But if we had to know what a[i++] = b[i++] really did, we'd have to know whichi++ happened first.

Finally, note that parentheses don't dictate overall evaluation order any more than precedence does. Parentheses override precedence and say which operands go with which operators, and they therefore affect the overall meaning of an expression, but they don't say anything about the order of subexpressions or side effects. We could not "fix" the evaluation order of any of the expressions we've been discussing by adding parentheses. If we wrote

```
i++ + (j++ * k++)
```

we still wouldn't know which of the increments would happen first. (The parentheses would force the multiplication to happen before the addition, but precedence already would have forced that, anyway.) If we wrote

```
(i++) * (i++)
```

the parentheses wouldn't force the increments to happen before the multiplication or in any well-defined order; this parenthesized version would be just as undefined as i++ * i++ was. There's a line from Kernighan & Ritchie, which I am fond of quoting when discussing these issues [Sec. 2.12, p. 54]:

The moral is that writing code that depends on order of evaluation is a bad programming practice in any language. Naturally, it is necessary to know what things to avoid, but if you don't know *how* they are done on various machines, you won't be tempted to take advantage of a particular implementation. The first edition of K&R said ...if you don't know *how* they are done on various machines, that innocence may help to protect you. I actually prefer the first edition wording. Many textbooks encourage you to write small programmes to find out how your compiler implements some of these ambiguous expressions, but it's just one step from writing a small programme to find out, to writing a real programme which makes use of what you've just learned.

But you *don't* want to write programmes that work only under one particular compiler, that take advantage of the way that one compiler (but perhaps no other) happens to implement the undefined expressions. It's fine to be curious about what goes on "under the hood," and many of you will be curious enough about what's going on with these "forbidden" expressions that you'll want to investigate them, but please keep very firmly in mind that, for real programmes, the very easiest way of dealing with ambiguous, undefined expressions (which one compiler interprets one way and another interprets another way and a third crashes on) is not to write them in the first place.

Chapter 8

Strings and Preprocessor

C STRING

In fact, C's only truly built-in string-handling is that it allows us to use *string constants* (also called *string literals*) in our code. Whenever we write a string, enclosed in double quotes, C automatically creates an array of characters for us, containing that string, terminated by the \0 character. For example, we can declare and define an array of characters, and initialize it with a string constant:

```
char string[] = "Hello, world!";
```

In this case, we can leave out the dimension of the array, since the compiler can compute it for us based on the size of the initializer (14, including the terminating \0). This is the only case where the compiler sizes a string array for us, however; in other cases, it will be necessary that *we* decide how big the arrays and other data structures we use to hold strings are. To do anything else with strings, we must typically call functions. The C library contains a few basic string manipulation functions, and to learn more about strings, we'll be looking at how these functions might be implemented.

Since C never lets us assign entire arrays, we use the strcpy function to copy one string to another:

```
#include <string.h>
char string1[] = "Hello, world!";
char string2[20];
strcpy(string2, string1);
```

The destination string is strcpy's first argument, so that a call to strcpy mimics an assignment expression (with the destination on the left-hand side). Notice that we had to allocate string2 big enough to hold the string that would be copied to it. Also, at the top of any source file where we're using the standard library's string-handling functions (such as strcpy) we must include the line

```
#include <string.h>
```

which contains external declarations for these functions. Since C won't let us compare entire arrays, either, we must call a function to do that, too. The standard library's strcmp function compares two strings, and returns 0 if they are identical, or a negative number if the first string is alphabetically "less than" the second string, or a positive number if the first string is "greater."

(Roughly speaking, what it means for one string to be "less than" another is that it would come first in a dictionary or telephone book, although there are a few anomalies.)

Here is an example:

```
char string3[] = "this is";
char string4[] = "a test";
if(strcmp(string3, string4) == 0)
printf("strings are equal\n");
elseprintf("strings are different\n");
```

This code fragment will print "strings are different". Notice that strcmp does *not* return a Boolean, true/false, zero/nonzero answer, so it's not a good idea to write something like

```
if(strcmp(string3, string4))
...
```

because it will behave backwards from what you might reasonably expect. (Nevertheless, if you start reading other people's code, you're likely to come across conditionals like if(strcmp(a, b)) or even if(!strcmp(a, b)). The first does something if the strings are unequal; the second does something if they're equal. You can read these more easily if you pretend for a moment that strcmp's name were strdiff, instead.) Another standard library function is strcat, which concatenates strings. It does *not* concatenate two strings together and give you a third, new string; what it really does is append one string onto the end of another. (If it gave you a new string, it would have to allocate memory for it somewhere, and the standard library string functions generally never do that for you automatically.)

Here's an example:

```
char string5[20] = "Hello, ";
char string6[] = "world!";
printf("%s\n", string5);
strcat(string5, string6);
printf("%s\n", string5);
```

The first call to printf prints "Hello, ", and the second one prints "Hello, world!", indicating that the contents of string6 have been tacked on to the end ofstring5. Notice that we declared string5 with extra space, to make room for the appended characters. If you have a string and you want to know its length (perhaps so that you can check whether it will fit in some other array you've allocated for it), you can callstrlen, which returns the length of the string (i.e. the number of characters in it), not including the \0:

```
char string7[] = "abc";
int len = strlen(string7);
printf("%d\n", len);
```

Finally, you can print strings out with printf using the %s format specifier, as we've been doing in these examples already (e.g. printf("%s\n", string5);).

Since a string is just an array of characters, all of the string-handling functions we've just seen can be written quite simply, using no techniques more complicated than the ones we already know. In fact, it's quite instructive to look at how these functions might be implemented.

```
Here is a version of strcpy:
mystrcpy(char dest[], char src[])
{
  int i = 0;
  while(src[i] != '\0')
{
dest[i] = src[i];
i++;
```

```
}
dest[i] = '\0';
}
```

We've called it mystrcpy instead of strcpy so that it won't clash with the version that's already in the standard library. Its operation is simple: it looks at characters in the src string one at a time, and as long as they're not \0, assigns them, one by one, to the corresponding positions in the dest string. When it's done, it terminates the dest string by appending a \0. (After exiting the while loop, i is guaranteed to have a value one greater than the subscript of the last character in src.) For comparison, here's a way of writing the same code, using a for loop:

```
for(i = 0; src[i] != '\0'; i++)
dest[i] = src[i];
dest[i] = '\0';
```

Yet a third possibility is to move the test for the terminating \0 character out of the for loop header and into the body of the loop, using an explicit if and breakstatement, so that we can perform the test after the assignment and therefore use the assignment inside the loop to copy the \0 to dest, too:

```
for(i = 0; ; i++)
{
  dest[i] = src[i];
  if(src[i] == '\0')
  break;
}
```

Here is a version of strcmp:

mystrcmp(char str1[], char str2[])

```
{
int i = 0;
while(1)
{
  if(str1[i] != str2[i])
  return str1[i] - str2[i];
  if(str1[i] == '\0' || str2[i] == '\0')
  return 0;
```

```
        i++;
    }
    }
```

Characters are compared one at a time. If two characters in one position differ, the strings are different, and we are supposed to return a value less than zero if the first string (str1) is alphabetically less than the second string. Since characters in C are represented by their numeric character set values, and since most reasonable character sets assign values to characters in alphabetical order, we can simply subtract the two differing characters from each other: the expression str1[i] - str2[i] will yield a negative result if the i'th character of str1 is less than the corresponding character in str2.

(As it turns out, this will behave a bit strangely when comparing upper- and lower-case letters, but it's the traditional approach, which the standard versions of strcmp tend to use.) If the characters are the same, we continue around the loop, *unless* the characters we just compared were (both) \0, in which case we've reached the end of both strings, and they were both equal. Notice that we used what may at first appear to be an infinite loop—the controlling expression is the constant 1, which is always true. What actually happens is that the loop runs until one of the two return statements breaks out of it (and the entire function). Note also that when one string is longer than the other, the first test will notice this (because one string will contain a real character at the [i] location, while the other will contain \0, and these are not equal) and the return value will be computed by subtracting the real character's value from 0, or vice versa. (Thus the shorter string will be treated as "less than" the longer.)

Finally, here is a version of strlen:

```
int mystrlen(char str[])
{
    int i;
    for(i = 0; str[i] != '\0'; i++)
{}
    return i;
}
```

In this case, all we have to do is find the \0 that terminates the string, and it turns out that the three control expressions of the for loop do all the work; there's nothing left to do in the body. Therefore, we use an empty pair of braces {} as the loop body. Equivalently, we could use a *null statement*, which is simply a semicolon:

```
for(i = 0; str[i] != '\0'; i++)
;
```

Empty loop bodies can be a bit startling at first, but they're not unheard of. Everything we've looked at so far has come out of C's standard libraries. As one last example, let's write a substr function, for extracting a substring out of a larger string. We might call it like this:

```
char string8[] = "this is a test";
char string9[10];
substr(string9, string8, 5, 4);
printf("%s\n", string9);
```

The idea is that we'll extract a substring of length 4, starting at character 5 (0-based) of string8, and copy the substring to string9. Just as with strcpy, it's our responsibility to declare the destination string (string9) big enough. Here is an implementation of substr. Not surprisingly, it's quite similar to strcpy:

```
substr(char dest[], char src[], int offset,
int len)
{
  int i;
  for(i = 0; i < len && src[offset + i] !=
  '\0'; i++)
  dest[i] = src[i + offset];
  dest[i] = '\0';
}
```

If you compare this code to the code for mystrcpy, you'll see that the only differences are that characters are fetched from src[offset + i] instead of src[i], and that the loop stops when len characters have been copied (or when the src string runs out of characters, whichever comes first). In this chapter, we've been careless about declaring the return types of the string functions, and (with the exception of mystrlen) they haven't returned values. The real string functions do return values, but they're of type "pointer to character," which we haven't discussed yet.

When working with strings, it's important to keep firmly in mind the differences between characters and strings. We must also occasionally remember the way characters are represented, and about the relation between character values and integers.

As we have had several occasions to mention, a character is represented internally as a small integer, with a value depending on the character set in use. For example, we might find that 'A' had the value 65, that 'a' had the value 97, and that '+' had the value 43. (These are, in fact, the values in the ASCII character set, which most computers use. However, you don't need to learn these values, because the vast majority of the time, you use character constants to refer to characters, and the compiler worries about the values for you. Using character constants in preference to raw numeric values also makes your programmes more portable.) As we may also have mentioned, there is a big difference between a character and a string, even a string which contains only one character (other than the \0). For example, 'A' is *not* the same as "A". To drive home this point, let's illustrate it with a few examples.

If you have a string:

```
char string[] = "hello, world!";
you can modify its first character by saying
string[0] = 'H';
```

(Of course, there's nothing magic about the first character; you can modify any character in the string in this way. Be aware, though, that it is not always safe to modify strings in-place like this; we'll say more about the modifiability of strings in a later chapter on pointers.) Since you're replacing a character, you want a character constant, 'H'. It would *not* be right to write

```
string[0] = "H"; /* WRONG */
```

because "H" is a string (an array of characters), not a single character. (The destination of the assignment, string[0], is a char, but the right-hand side is a string; these types don't match.) On the other hand, when you need a string, you must use a string. To print a single newline, you could call

```
printf("\n");
It would not be correct to call
printf('\n');        /* WRONG */
```

printf always wants a string as its first argument. (As one final example, putchar wants a single character, so putchar ('\n') would be correct, andputchar("\n") would be incorrect.) We must also remember the difference between strings and integers. If we treat the character '1' as an integer, perhaps by saying

```
int i = '1';
```

we will probably *not* get the value 1 in i; we'll get the value of the character '1' in the machine's character set. (In ASCII, it's 49.) When we do need to find the numeric value of a digit character (or to go the other way, to get the digit character with a particular value) we can make use of the fact that, in any character set used by C, the values for the digit characters, whatever they are, are contiguous. In other words, no matter what values '0' and '1' have, '1' - '0' will be 1 (and, obviously, '0' - '0' will be 0). So, for a variable c holding some digit character, the expression

```
c - '0'
```

gives us its value. (Similarly, for an integer value i, i + '0' gives us the corresponding digit character, as long as 0 <= i <= 9.)

Just as the character '1' is not the integer 1, the string "123" is not the integer 123. When we have a string of digits, we can convert it to the corresponding integer by calling the standard function atoi:

```
char string[] = "123";
int i = atoi(string);
int j = atoi("456");
```

PREPROCESSOR

Conceptually, the "preprocessor" is a translation phase that is applied to your source code before the compiler proper gets its hands on it. (Once upon a time, the preprocessor was a separate programme, much as the compiler and linker may still be separate programmes today.) Generally, the preprocessor performs textual substitutions on your source code, in three sorts of ways:

- *File inclusion*: Inserting the contents of another file into your source file, as if you had typed it all in there.
- *Macro substitution*: Replacing instances of one piece of text with another.
- *Conditional compilation*: Arranging that, depending on various circumstances, certain parts of your source code are seen or not seen by the compiler at all.

The syntax of the preprocessor is different from the syntax of the rest of C in several respects. First of all, the preprocessor is "line based." Each of the preprocessor directives we're going to learn about (all of which begin with the # character) must begin at the beginning of a line, and each ends at the end of the line. (The rest of C treats line ends as just another whitespace character, and doesn't care how your programme text is arranged into lines.) Secondly, the preprocessor does not know about the structure of C—about functions, statements, or expressions. It is possible to play strange tricks with the preprocessor to turn something which does not look like C into C (or vice versa). It's also possible to run into problems when a preprocessor substitution does not do what you expected it to, because the preprocessor does not respect the structure of C statements and expressions (but you expected it to). For the simple uses of the preprocessor we'll be discussing, you shouldn't have any of these problems, but you'll want to be careful before doing anything tricky or outrageous with the preprocessor. (As it happens, playing tricky and outrageous games with the preprocessor is considered sporting in some circles, but it rapidly gets out of hand, and can lead to bewilderingly impenetrable programmes.)

WORKING OF PREPROCESSOR

Although the preprocessor is probably going to be

implemented as an integral part of an Standard C compiler, it can equally well be though of as a separate programme which transforms C source code containing preprocessor directives into source code with the directives removed.

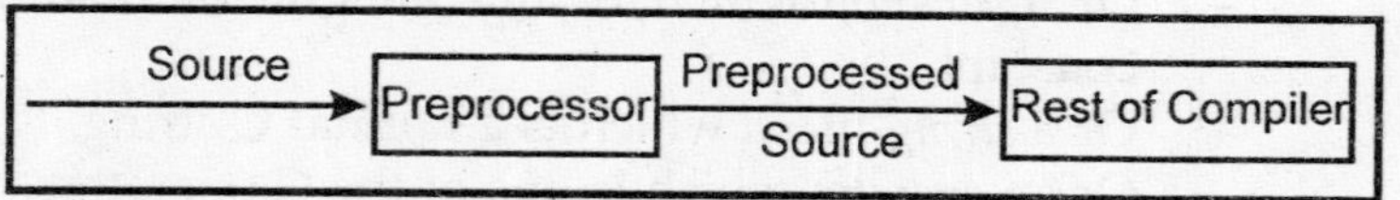

Fig. The Preprocessor.

It's important to remember that the preprocessor is not working to the same rules as the rest of C. It works on a line-by-line basis, so the end of a line means something special to it. The rest of C thinks that end-of-line is little different from a space or tab character.

The preprocessor doesn't know about the scope rules of C. Preprocessor directives like #define take effect as soon as they are seen and remain in effect until the end of the file that contains them; the program's block structure is irrelevant. This is one of the reasons why it's a good idea to make sparing use of these directives. The less you have in your programme that doesn't obey the 'normal' scope rules, the less likely you are to make mistakes. This is mainly what gives rise to our comments about the poor level of integration between the preprocessor and the rest of C.

The Standard gives some complicated rules for the syntax of the preprocessor, especially with respect to *tokens*. To understand the operation of the preprocessor you need to know a little about them. The text that is being processed is not considered to be a uniform stream of characters, but is separated into tokens then processed piecemeal.

For a full definition of the process, it is best to refer to the Standard, but an informal description follows. Each of the terms used to head the list below is used later in descriptions of the rules.

- Header-name
  - '<' almost any character '>'
- Preprocessing-token
  - A header-name as above but only when the

subject of #include,
- Or an *identifier* which is any C identifier or keyword,
- Or a *constant* which is any integral or floating constant,
- Or a *string-literal* which is a normal C string,
- Or an *operator* which is one of the C operators,
- Or one of *[ ] ( ) { }* * ,: = ;... # (punctuators)
- Or any non-white-space character not covered by the list above.

The *'almost any character'* above means any character except '>' or newline.

FILE INCLUSION

```
A line of the form
#include <filename.h>
or
#include "filename.h"
```

causes the contents of the file filenamc.h to be read, parsed, and compiled at that point. (After filename.h is processed, compilation continues on the line following the #include line.)

For example, suppose you got tired of retyping external function prototypes such as

```
extern int getline(char [], int);
```

at the top of each source file. You could instead place the prototype in a header file, perhaps getline.h, and then simply place

```
#include "getline.h"
```

at the top of each source file where you called getline. (You might not find it worthwhile to create an entire header file for a single function, but if you had a package of several related function, it might be very useful to place all of their declarations in one header file.)

As we may have mentioned, that's exactly what the Standard header files such as stdio.hare—collections of declarations (including external function prototype declarations) having to do with various sets of Standard library functions. When you use #include to read in a header file, you automatically get the prototypes and other declarations it contains, and you *should* use header files, precisely so that you will get the prototypes and other declarations they contain.

The difference between the <> and "" forms is where the preprocessor searches for filename.h. As a general rule, it searches for files enclosed in <> in central, standard directories, and it searches for files enclosed in "" in the "current directory," or the directory containing the source file that's doing the including. Therefore, "" is usually used for header files you've written, and <> is usually used for headers which are provided for you (which someone else has written).

The extension ".h", by the way, simply stands for "header," and reflects the fact that #include directives usually sit at the top (head) of your source files, and contain global declarations and definitions which you would otherwise put there. (That extension is not mandatory—you can theoretically name your own header files anything you wish—but .h is traditional, and recommended.)

As we've already begun to see, the reason for putting something in a header file, and then using #include to pull that header file into several different source files, is when the something (whatever it is) must be declared or defined consistently in all of the source files. If, instead of using a header file, you typed the something in to each of the source files directly, and the something ever changed, you'd have to edit all those source files, and if you missed one, your programme could fail in subtle (or serious) ways due to the mismatched declarations (i.e. due to the incompatibility between the new declaration in one source file and the old one in a source file you forgot to change). Placing common declarations and definitions into header files means that if they ever change, they only have to be changed in one place, which is a much more workable system.

What should you put in header files?

- External declarations of global variables and functions. We said that a global variable must have exactly one*defining instance*, but that it can have *external declarations* in many places. We said that it was a grave error to issue an external declaration in one place saying that a variable or function has one type, when the defining instance in some other place actually defines it with another type. (If the two places are two source files, separately compiled, the compiler will probably not even catch the discrepancy.) If you put the external declarations in a header file, however, and include the header wherever it's needed, the declarations are virtually guaranteed to be consistent. It's a good idea to include the header in the source file where the defining instance appears, too, so that the compiler can check that the declaration and definition match. (That is, if you ever change the type, you do still have to change it in two places: in the source file where the defining instance occurs, and in the header file where the external declaration appears. But at least you don't have to change it in an arbitrary number of places, and, if you've set things up correctly, the compiler can catch any remaining mistakes.)

- Preprocessor macro definitions (which we'll meet in the next section).
- Structure definitions (which we haven't seen yet).
- Typedef declarations (which we haven't seen yet).

However, there are a few things not to put in header files:

- Defining instances of global variables. If you put these in a header file, and include the header file in more than one source file, the variable will end up multiply defined.
- Function bodies (which are also defining instances). You don't want to put these in headers for the same reason—it's likely that you'll end up with multiple copies of the function and hence "multiply defined" errors. People sometimes put commonly-used functions in header files and then use #include to bring them (once) into each programme where they

use that function, or use #include to bring together the several source files making up a programme, but both of these are poor ideas. It's much better to learn how to use your compiler or linker to combine together separately-compiled object files.

Since header files typically contain only external declarations, and should *not* contain function bodies, you have to understand just what does and doesn't happen when you #include a header file. The header file may provide the declarations for some functions, so that the compiler can generate correct code when you call them (and so that it can make sure that you're calling them correctly), but the header file does *not* give the compiler the functions themselves. The actual functions will be combined into your programme at the end of compilation, by the part of the compiler called the *linker*. The linker may have to get the functions out of libraries, or you may have to tell the compiler/linker where to find them. In particular, if you are trying to use a third-party library containing some useful functions, the library will often come with a header file describing those functions. Using the library is therefore a two-step process: you must #include the header in the files where you call the library functions, *and* you must tell the linker to read in the functions from the library itself.

FILE INCLUSION

A line of the form

```
#include <filename.h>
or
#include "filename.h"
```

causes the contents of the file filename.h to be read, parsed, and compiled at that point. (After filename.h is processed, compilation continues on the line following the #include line.) For example, suppose you got tired of retyping external function prototypes such as

```
extern int getline(char [], int);
```

at the top of each source file. You could instead place the prototype in a header file, perhaps getline.h, and then simply place

```
#include "getline.h"
```

at the top of each source file where you called getline. (You might not find it worthwhile to create an entire header file for a single function, but if you had a package of several related function, it might be very useful to place all of their declarations in one header file.) As we may have mentioned, that's exactly what the Standard header files such as stdio.hare—collections of declarations (including external function prototype declarations) having to do with various sets of Standard library functions. When you use #include to read in a header file, you automatically get the prototypes and other declarations it contains, and you *should* use header files, precisely so that you will get the prototypes and other declarations they contain.

The difference between the <> and "" forms is where the preprocessor searches for filename.h. As a general rule, it searches for files enclosed in <> in central, standard directories, and it searches for files enclosed in "" in the "current directory," or the directory containing the source file that's doing the including. Therefore, "" is usually used for header files you've written, and <> is usually used for headers which are provided for you (which someone else has written).

The extension ".h", by the way, simply stands for "header," and reflects the fact that #include directives usually sit at the top (head) of your source files, and contain global declarations and definitions which you would otherwise put there. (That extension is not mandatory—you can theoretically name your own header files anything you wish—but .h is traditional, and recommended.)

As we've already begun to see, the reason for putting something in a header file, and then using #include to pull that header file into several different source files, is when the something (whatever it is) must be declared or defined consistently in all of the source files. If, instead of using a header file, you typed the something in to each of the source files directly, and the something ever changed, you'd have to edit all those source files, and if you missed one, your programme could fail in subtle (or serious) ways due to the mismatched declarations (i.e. due to the incompatibility between the new declaration in one source file and the old one in a source file you forgot to change). Placing common declarations and definitions into header files means that if they ever change, they only have to be changed in one place, which is a much more workable system.

What should you put in header files?

- External declarations of global variables and functions. We said that a global variable must have exactly one*defining instance*, but that it can have *external declarations* in many places. We said that it was a grave error to issue an external declaration in one place saying that a variable or function has one type, when the defining instance in some other place actually defines it with another type. (If the two places are two source files, separately compiled, the compiler will probably not even catch the discrepancy.) If you put the external declarations in a header file, however, and include the header wherever it's needed, the declarations are virtually guaranteed to be consistent. It's a good idea to include the header in the source file where the defining instance appears, too, so that the compiler can check that the declaration and definition match. (That is, if you ever change the type, you do still have to change it in two places: in the source file where the defining instance occurs, and in the header file where the external declaration appears. But at least you don't have to change it in an arbitrary number of places, and, if you've set things up correctly, the compiler can catch any remaining mistakes.)
- Preprocessor macro definitions (which we'll meet in the next section).
- Structure definitions (which we haven't seen yet).
- Typedef declarations (which we haven't seen yet).

However, there are a few things not to put in header files:

- Defining instances of global variables. If you put these in a header file, and include the header file in more than one source file, the variable will end up multiply defined.

- Function bodies (which are also defining instances). You don't want to put these in headers for the same reason—it's likely that you'll end up with multiple copies of the function and hence "multiply defined" errors. People sometimes put commonly-used functions in header files and then use #include to bring them (once) into each programme where they use that function, or use #include to bring together the several source files making up a programme, but both of these are poor ideas. It's much better to learn how to use your compiler or linker to combine together separately-compiled object files.

Since header files typically contain only external declarations, and should *not* contain function bodies, you have to understand just what does and doesn't happen when you #include a header file. The header file may provide the declarations for some functions, so that the compiler can generate correct code when you call them (and so that it can make sure that you're calling them correctly), but the header file does *not* give the compiler the functions themselves.

The actual functions will be combined into your programme at the end of compilation, by the part of the compiler called the *linker*. The linker may have to get the functions out of libraries, or you may have to tell the compiler/linker where to find them. In particular, if you are trying to use a third-party library containing some useful functions, the library will often come with a header file describing those functions. Using the library is therefore a two-step process: you must #include the header in the files where you call the library functions, *and* you must tell the linker to read in the functions from the library itself.

MACRO AND SUBSTITUTION

A preprocessor line of the form

```
#define name text
```

defines a *macro* with the given name, having as

its *value* the given replacement text. After that (for the rest of the current source file), wherever the preprocessor sees that name, it will replace it with the replacement text.

The name follows the same rules as ordinary identifiers (it can contain only letters, digits, and underscores, and may not begin with a digit). Since macros behave quite differently from normal variables (or functions), it is customary to give them names which are all capital letters (or at least which begin with a capital letter). The replacement text can be absolutely anything—it's not restricted to numbers, or simple strings, or anything.

The most common use for macros is to propagate various constants around and to make them more self-documenting.

We say:

```
char line[100];
...
getline(line, 100);
```

but this is neither readable nor reliable; it's not necessarily obvious what all those 100's scattered around the programme are, and if we ever decide that 100 is too small for the size of the array to hold lines, we'll have to remember to change the number in two (or more) places. A much better solution is to use a macro:

```
#define MAXLINE 100
char line[MAXLINE];
...
getline(line, MAXLINE);
```

Now, if we ever want to change the size, we only have to do it in one place, and it's more obvious what the wordsMAXLINE sprinkled through the programme mean than the magic numbers 100 did.

Since the replacement text of a preprocessor macro can be anything, it can also be an expression, although you have to realise that, as always, the text is substituted (and perhaps evaluated) later. No evaluation is performed when the macro is defined. For example, suppose that you write something like

```
#define A 2
#define B 3
```

```
#define C A + B
```

(this is a pretty meaningless example, but the situation does come up in practice). Then, later, suppose that you write

```
int x = C * 2;
```

If A, B, and C were ordinary variables, you'd expect x to end up with the value 10. But let's see what happens. The preprocessor always substitutes text for macros exactly as you have written it. So it first substitites the replacement text for the macro C, resulting in

```
int x = A + B * 2;
```

Then it substitutes the macros A and B, resulting in

```
int x = 2 + 3 * 2;
```

Only when the preprocessor is done doing all this substituting does the compiler get into the act. But when it evaluates that expression (using the normal precedence of multiplication over addition), it ends up initializing x with the value 8!

To guard against this sort of problem, it is always a good idea to include explicit parentheses in the definitions of macros which contain expressions. If we were to define the macro C as

```
#define C (A + B)
```

then the declaration of x would ultimately expand to

```
int x = (2 + 3) * 2;
```

and x would be initialized to 10, as we probably expected.

Notice that there does not have to be (and in fact there usually is *not*) a semicolon at the end of a #define line. (This is just one of the ways that the syntax of the preprocessor is different from the rest of C.) If you type

```
#define MAXLINE 100;   /* WRONG */
```

then when you later declare

```
char line[MAXLINE];
```

the preprocessor will expand it to

```
char line[100;]; /* WRONG */
```

which is a syntax error. This is what we mean when we say that the preprocessor doesn't know much of anything about the syntax of C—in this last example, the *value* or replacement text for the macro MAXLINE was the 4 characters 1 0 0 ;, and that's exactly what the preprocessor substituted (even though it didn't make any sense). Simple macros like MAXLINE act sort of like little variables, whose values are constant (or constant expressions).

It's also possible to have macros which look like little functions (that is, you invoke them with what looks like function call syntax, and they expand to replacement text which is a function of the actual arguments they are invoked with) but we won't be looking at these yet.

CONDITIONAL COMPILATION

The last preprocessor directive we're going to look at is #ifdef. If you have the sequence

```
#ifdef name
programme text
#else
more programme text
#endif
```

in your programme, the code that gets compiled depends on whether a preprocessor macro by that *name* is defined or not. If it is (that is, if there has been a #define line for a macro called *name*), then *"programme text"* is compiled and *"more programme text"* is ignored.

If the macro is not defined, *"more programme text"* is compiled and *"programme text"* is ignored. This looks a lot like an if statement, but it behaves completely differently: an if statement controls which statements of your programme are executed at run time, but #ifdef controls which parts of your programme actually get compiled.

Just as for the if statement, the #else in an #ifdef is optional. There is a companion directive #ifndef, which compiles code if the macro is *not* defined (although the "#else clause" of an #ifndef directive will then be compiled if the macro*is* defined).

There is also an #if directive which compiles code depending on whether a compile-time expression is true or false. (The expressions which are allowed in an #if directive are somewhat restricted, however, so we won't talk much about #if here.)

Conditional compilation is useful in two general classes of situations:

- You are trying to write a portable programme, but the way you do something is different depending on what compiler, operating system, or computer you're using. You place different versions of your code, one for each situation, between suitable #ifdef directives, and when you compile the progam in a particular environment, you arrange to have the macro names defined which select the variants you need in that environment. (For this reason, compilers usually have ways of letting you define macros from the invocation command line or in a configuration file, and many also predefine certain macro names related to the operating system, processor, or compiler in use. That way, you don't have to change the code to change the #define lines each time you compile it in a different environment.)

For example, in ANSI C, the function to delete a file is remove. On older Unix systems, however, the function was called unlink. So if filename is a variable containing the name of a file you want to delete, and if you want to be able to compile the programme under these older Unix systems, we write

- #ifdef unix
- unlink(filename);
- #else
- remove(filename);
- #endif

Then, you could place the line

```
#define unix
```

at the top of the file when compiling under an old Unix system. (Since all you're using the macro unix for is to control the #ifdef, you don't need to give it any replacement text at all. *Any* definition for a macro, even if the replacement text is empty, causes an #ifdef to succeed.). (In fact, in this example, you wouldn't even need to define the macro unix at all, because C compilers on old Unix systems tend to predefine it for you, precisely so you can make tests like these.)

- You want to compile several different versions of your programme, with different features present in the different versions. You bracket the code for each feature with #ifdef directives, and (as for the previous case) arrange to have the right macros defined or not to build the version you want to build at any given time. This way, you can build the several different versions from the same source code. (One common example is whether you turn debugging statements on or off. You can bracket each debugging printout with #ifdef DEBUG and #endif, and then turn on debugging only when you need it.)

For example, you might use lines like this:

- #ifdef DEBUG
- printf("x is %d\n", x);
- #endif

to print out the value of the variable x at some point in your programme to see if it's what you expect. To enable debugging printouts, you insert the line

```
#define DEBUG
```

at the top of the file, and to turn them off, you delete that line, but the debugging printouts quietly remain in your code, temporarily deactivated, but ready to reactivate if you find yourself needing them again later. (Also, instead of inserting and deleting the #define line, you might use a compiler flag such as -DDEBUG to define the macro DEBUGfrom the compiler invocatin line.)

Conditional compilation can be very handy, but it can also get out of hand. When large chunks of the programme are completely different depending on, say, what operating system the programme is being compiled for, it's often better to place the different versions in separate source files, and then only use one of the files (corresponding to one of the versions) to build the programme on any given system. Also, if you are using an ANSI Standard compiler and you are writing ANSI-compatible code, you usually won't need so much conditional compilation, because the Standard specifies exactly how the compiler must do certain things, and exactly which library functions it much provide, so you don't have to work so hard to accommodate the old variations among compilers and libraries.

DIRECTIVES

Directives are always introduced by a line that starts with a # character, optionally preceded by white space characters (although it isn't common practice to indent the #). Table below is a list of the directives defined in the Standard.

Table. Preprocessor directives

Directive	Meaning
# include	Include a source file
# define	Define a macro
# undef	Undefine a macro
# if	Conditional compilation
# ifdef	Conditional compilation
# ifndef	Conditional compilation
# elif	Conditional compilation
# else	Conditional compilation
# endif	Conditional compilation
# line	Control error reporting
# error	Force an error message
# pragma	Used for implementation-dependent control
#	Null directive; no effect

The meanings and use of these features are described in the following sections. Make a note that the # and the following keyword, if any, are individual items. They may be separated by white space.

DEFINE

There are two ways of defining *macros*, one of which looks like a function and one which does not.

Here is an example of each:

```
#define FMAC(a,b) a here, then b
#define NONFMAC some text here
```

Both definitions define a macro and some *replacement text*, which will be used to replace later occurrences of the macro name in the rest of the programme. After those definitions, they can be used as follows, with the effect of the macro replacement shown in comments:

```
NONFMAC
/* some text here */
FMAC(first text, some more)
/* first text here, then some more */
```

For the non-function macro, its name is simply replaced by its replacement text. The function macro is also replaced by its replacement text; wherever the replacement text contains an identifier which is the name of one of the macro's 'formal parameters', the actual text given as the argument is used in place of the identifier in the replacement text. The scope of the names of the formal parameters is limited to the body of the #define directive.

For both forms of macro, leading or trailing white space around the replacement text is discarded. A curious ambiguity arises with macros: how do you define a non-function macro whose replacement text happens to start with the opening parenthesis character (? The answer is simple. If the definition of the macro has a space in front of the (, then it isn't the definition of a function macro, but a simple replacement macro instead. When you use function-like macros, there's no equivalent restriction.

The Standard allows either type of macro to be redefined at any time, using another # define, provided that there isn't any attempt to change the type of the macro and that the tokens making up both the original definition and the redefinition are identical in number, ordering, spelling and use of white space.

In this context all white space is considered equal, so this would be correct:

```
# define XXX abc/*comment*/def hij
# define XXX abc def hij
```

because comment is a form of white space. The token sequence for both cases (*w-s* stands for a white-space token) is:

```
# w-s define w-s XXX w-s abc w-s def w-s hij
w-s
```

MACRO SUBSTITUTION

Where will occurrences of the macro name cause the replacement text to be substituted in its place? Practically anywhere in a programme that the identifier is recognized as a separate token, except as the identifier following the # of a preprocessor directive. You can't do this:

```
#define define XXX
#define YYY ZZZ
```

and expect the second #define to be replaced by #XXX, causing an error. When the identifier associated with a non-function macro is seen, it is replaced by the macro replacement tokens, then *rescanned* (see later) for further replacements to make. Function macros can be used like real functions; white space around the macro name, the argument list and so on, may include the newline character:

```
#define FMAC(a, b) printf("%s %s\n", a, b)
FMAC ("hello",
"sailor"
);
/* results in */
printf("%s %s\n", "hello", "sailor")
```

The 'arguments' of a function macro can be almost any arbitrary token sequence. Commas are used to separate the arguments from each other but can be hidden by enclosing them within parentheses, (and). Matched pairs of (and) inside the argument list balance each other out, so a) only ends the invocation of the macro if the corresponding (is the one that started the macro invocation.

```
#define CALL(a, b) a b
CALL(printf, ("%d %d %s\n",1, 24, "urgh"));
/* results in */
printf ("%d %d %s\n",1, 24, "urgh");
```

Note very carefully that the parentheses around the second argument to CALL were preserved in the replacement: they were not stripped from the text.

If you want to use macros like printt, taking a variable number of arguments, the Standard is no help to you. They are not supported. If any argument contains no preprocessor tokens then the behaviour is undefined. The same is true if the sequence of preprocessor tokens that forms the argument would otherwise have been another preprocessor directive:

```
#define CALL(a, b) a b
/* undefined behaviour in each case.... */
CALL(,hello)
CALL(xyz,
#define abc def)
```

In our opinion, the second of the erroneous uses of CALL should result in defined behaviour—anyone capable of writing that would clearly benefit from the attentions of a champion weightlifter wielding a heavy leather bullwhip.

When a function macro is being processed, the steps are as follows:

- All of its arguments are identified.
- Except in the cases listed in item 3 below, if any of the tokens in an argument are themselves candidates for macro replacement, the replacement is done until no further replacement is possible. If this introduces commas into the argument list, there is no danger of the macro suddenly seeming to have a different number of arguments; the arguments are *only* determined in the step above.
- In the macro replacement text, identifiers naming one of the macro formal arguments are replaced by the (by now expanded) token sequence supplied as the actual argument. The replacement is suppressed only if the identifier is preceded by one of # or ##, or followed by ##.

STRINGIZING

There is special treatment for places in the macro replacement text where one of the macro formal parameters is found preceded by #. The token list for the actual argument has any leading or trailing white space discarded, then the #

and the token list are turned into a single string literal. Spaces between the tokens are treated as space characters in the string. To prevent 'unexpected' results, any " or \ characters within the new string literal are preceded by \.

This example demonstrates the feature:

```
#define MESSAGE(x) printf("Message: %s\n",
#x)
MESSAGE (Text with "quotes");
/*
* Result is
* printf("Message: %s\n", "Text with
\"quotes\"");
*/
```

TOKEN PASTING

A ## operator may occur anywhere in the replacement text for a macro except at the beginning or end. If a parameter name of a function macro occurs in the replacement text preceded or followed by one of these operators, the actual token sequence for the corresponding macro argument is used to replace it. Then, for both function and non-function macros, the tokens surrounding the ## operator are joined together. If they don't form a valid token, the behaviour is undefined. Then rescanning occurs.

As an example of token pasting, here is a multi-stage operation, involving rescanning (which is described next).

```
#define REPLACE some replacement text
#define JOIN(a, b) a ## b
JOIN(REP, LACE)
becomes, after token pasting,
REPLACE
becomes, after rescanning
some replacement text
```

RESCANNING

Once the processing described above has occurred, the replacement text plus the following tokens of the source file is rescanned, looking for more macro names to replace. The one exception is that, within a macro's replacement text, the name of the macro itself is not expanded. Because macro replacement can be nested, it is possible for several macros to be in the process of being replaced at any one point: none of their names is a candidate for further replacement in the 'inner' levels of this process.

This allows redefinition of existing functions as macros:

```
#define exit(x)  exit((x)+1)
```

These macro names which were not replaced now become tokens which are immune from future replacement, even if later processing might have meant that they had become available for replacement. This prevents the danger of infinite recursion occurring in the preprocessor. The suppression of replacement is only if the macro name results directly from *replacement* text, not the other source text of the programme.

Here we mean:

```
#define m(x) m((x)+1)
/* so */
m(abc);
/* expands to */
m((abc)+1);
/*
*  even though the m((abc)+1) above looks
  like a macro,
* the rules say it is not to be re-replaced
*/
m(m(abc));
/*
* the outer m( starts a macro invocation,
* but the inner one is replaced first (as
  above)
* with m((abc)+1), which becomes the argument
  to the outer call,
* giving us effectively
*/
m(m((abc+1));
/*
```

```
* which expands to
*/
m((m((abc+1))+1);
```

If that doesn't make your brain hurt, then go and read what the Standard says about it, which will.

NOTES

There is a subtle problem when using arguments to function macros.

```
/* warning - subtle problem in this example
*/
#define SQR(x) ( x * x )
/*
* Wherever the formal parameters occur in
* the replacement text, they are replaced
* by the actual parameters to the macro.
*/
printf("sqr of %d is %d\n", 2, SQR(2));
```

The formal parameter of SQR is x; the actual argument is 2. The replacement text results in

```
printf("sqr of %d is %d\n", 2, ( 2 * 2 ));
```

The use of the parentheses should be noticed. The following example is likely to give trouble:

```
/* bad example */
#define DOUBLE(y) y+y
printf("twice %d is %d\n", 2, DOUBLE(2));
printf("six times %d is %d\n", 2,
3*DOUBLE(2));
```

The problem is that the last expression in the second printf is replaced by

```
3*2+2
```

which results in 8, not 12! The rule is that when using macros to build expressions, careful parenthesizing is necessary. Here's another example:

```
SQR(3+4)
/* expands to */
( 3+4 * 3+4 )
/* oh dear, still wrong! */
```

so, when formal parameters occur in the replacement text, you should look carefully at them too. Correct versions of SQR and DOUBLE are these:

```
#define SQR(x) ((x)*(x))
#define DOUBLE(x) ((x)+(x))
```

Macros have a last little trick to surprise you with, as this shows:

```
#include <stdio.h>
#include <stdlib.h>
#define DOUBLE(x) ((x)+(x))
main(){
int a[20], *ip;
ip = a;
a[0] = 1;
a[1] = 2;
printf("%d\n", DOUBLE(*ip++));
exit(EXIT_SUCCESS);
}
```

Example: Why is this going to cause problems? Because the replacement text of the macro refers to *ip++ twice, so ip gets incremented twice.

Macros should never be used with expressions that involve side effects, unless you check very carefully that they are safe. Despite these warnings, they provide a very useful feature, and one which will be used a lot from now on.

UNDEF

The name of any #defined identifier can be forcibly forgotten by saying

```
#undef NAME
```

It isn't an error to #undef a name which isn't currently defined.

INCLUDE

This comes in two flavours:

```
#include <filename>
#include "filename"
```

both of which cause a new file to be read at the point where they occur. It's as if the single line containing the directive is replaced by the contents of the specified file. If that file contains erroneous statements, you can reasonably expect that the errors will be reported with a correct file name and line number. It's the compiler writer's job to get that right. The Standard specifies that at least eight nested levels of # include must be supported.

The effect of using brackets <> or quotes " " around the filename is to change the places searched to find the specified file. The brackets cause a search of a number of implementation defined places, the quotes cause a search of somewhere associated with the original source file. Your implementation notes must tell you the specific details of what is meant by 'place'. If the form using quotes can't find the file, it tries again as if you had used brackets.

In general, brackets are used when you specify standard library header files, quotes are used for private header files—often specific to one programme only. Although the Standard doesn't define what constitutes a valid file name, it does specify that there must be an implementation-defined unique way of translating file names of the form xxx x (where x represents a 'letter'), into source file names. Distinctions of upper and lower case may be ignored and the implementation may choose only to use six significant characters before the '.' character.

You can also write this:

```
# define NAME <stdio.h>
# include NAME
```

to get the same effect as

```
# include <stdio.h>
```

but it's a rather roundabout way of doing it, and unfortunately it's subject to implementation defined rules about how the text between < and > is treated. It's simpler if the replacement text for NAME comes out to be a string, for example

```
#define NAME "stdio.h"
#include NAME
```

There is no problem with implementation defined behaviour here, but the paths searched are different, as explained above. For the first case, what happens is that the token sequence which replaces NAME is (by the rules already given)

```
<
stdio
.
h
>
```

and for the second case

```
"stdio.h"
```

The second case is easy, since it's just a *string-literal* which is a legal token for a# include directive. It is implementation defined how the first case is treated, and whether or not the sequence of tokens forms a legal *header-name*. Finally, the last character of a file which is being included must be a plain newline. Failure to include a file successfully is treated as an error.

PREDEFINED NAMES

The following names are predefined within the preprocessor:

`__LINE__`

The current source file line number, a decimal integer constant.

`__FILE__`

The 'name' of the current source code file, a string literal.

`__DATE__`

The current date, a string literal. The form is

```
Apr 21 1990
```

where the month name is as defined in the library function asctime and the first digit of the date is a space if the date is less than 10.

`__TIME__`

The time of the translation; again a string literal in the form produced by asctime, which has the form "hh:mm:ss".

`__STDC__`

The integer constant 1. This is used to test if the compiler is Standard-conforming, the intention being that it will have different values for different releases of the Standard. A common way of using these predefined names is the following.

```
#define TEST(x) if(!(x))\
printf("test failed, line %d file %s\n",\
__LINE__, __FILE__)
/**/
TEST(a != 23);
/**/
```

Example:

If the argument to TEST gives a false result, the message is printed, including the filename and line number in the message.

There's only one minor caveat: the use of the if statement can cause confusion in a case like this:

```
if(expression)
TEST(expr2);
else
statement_n;
```

The else will get associated with the hidden if generated by expanding the TESTmacro. This is most unlikely to happen in practice, but will be a thorough pain to track down if it ever does sneak up on you. It's good style to make the bodies of every control of flow statement compound anyway; then the problem goes away.

None of the names__LINE__, __FILE__, __DATE__, __TIME__, __STDC__ or defined may be used in #define or #undef directives.

The Standard specifies that any other reserved names will either start with an underscore followed by an upper case letter or another underscore, so you know that you are free to use any other names for your own purposes (but watch out for additional names reserved in Library header files that you may have included).

#LINE

This is used to set the value of the built in names __LINE__ and __FILE__. Why do this? Because a lot of tools nowadays actually generate C as their output. This directive allows them to control the current line number. It is of very limited interest to the 'ordinary' C programmer.

Its form is:

line number optional-string-literal newline. The number sets the value of __LINE__, the string literal, if present, sets the value of __FILE__. In fact, the sequence of tokens following #line will be macro expanded. After expansion, they are expected to provide a valid directive of the right form.

CONDITIONAL COMPILATION

A number of the directives control conditional compilation, which allows certain portions of a programme to be selectively compiled or ignored depending upon specified conditions.

The directives concerned are: #if, #ifdef, #ifndef, #elif, #else, #end if together with the preprocessor unary operator defined.

The way that they are used is like this:

```
#ifdef NAME
/* compile these lines if NAME is defined */
#endif
#ifndef NAME
/* compile these lines if NAME is not defined
*/
#else
/* compile these lines if NAME is defined */
#endif
```

So, #ifdef and #endif can be used to test the definition or otherwise of a given macro name. Of course the #else can be used with #ifdef (and #if or #elif) too. There is no ambiguity about what a given #else binds to, because the use of#endif to delimit the scope of these directives eliminates any possible ambiguity. The Standard specifies that at least eight levels of nesting of conditional directives must be supported, but in practice there is not likely to be any real limit.

These directives are most commonly used to select small fragments of C that are machine specific (when it is not possible to make the whole programme completely machine independent), or sometimes to select different algorithms depending on the need to make trade-offs. The #if and #elif constructs take a single integral constant expression as their arguments. Preprocessor integral constant expressions are the same as other integral constant expressions except that they must not contain cast operators.

The token sequence that makes up the constant expression undergoes macro replacement, except that names prefixed by defined are not expanded. In this context, the expression defined NAME or defined (NAME) evaluates to 1 if NAMEis currently defined, 0 if it is not. Any other identifiers in the expression *including those that are C keywords* are replaced with the value 0. Then the expression is evaluated. The replacement even of keywords means that sizeof can't be used in these expressions to get the result that you would normally expect.

As with the other conditional statements in C, a resulting value of zero is used to represent 'false', anything else is 'true'. The preprocessor always must use arithmetic with at least the ranges defined in the <limits.h> file and treats int expressions as long int and unsigned int as unsigned long int. Character constants do not necessarily have the same values as they do at execution time, so for highly portable programmes, it's best to avoid using them in preprocessor expressions. Overall, the rules mean that it is possible to get arithmetic results from the preprocessor which are different from the results at run time; although presumably only if the translation and execution are done on different machines. Here's an example.

```
#include <limits.h>
#if ULONG_MAX+1 != 0
printf("Preprocessor: ULONG_MAX+1 != 0\n");
#endif
if(ULONG_MAX+1 != 0)
printf("Runtime: ULONG_MAX+1 != 0\n");
```

Example: It is conceivable that the preprocessor might perform arithmetic with a greater range than that used in the target environment. In that case, the preprocessor expression ULONG_MAX+1 might not 'overflow' to give the result of 0, whereas in the execution environment, it *must*. The following skeleton example illustrates the use of such constants and also the 'conditional else', #elif.

```
#define NAME 100
#if ((NAME > 50) && (defined __STDC__))
/* do something */
#elif NAME > 25
/* do something else*/
#elif NAME > 10
/* do something else */
#else
/* last possibility */
#endif
```

A word of warning. These conditional compilation directives do not obey the same scope rules as the rest of C. They should be used sparingly, unless your programme is rapidly to become unreadable. It is impossible to read C when it is laced with these things every few lines. The urge to maim the author of a piece of code becomes very strong when you suddenly come across

```
#else
}
#endif
```

with no #if or whatever immediately visible above. They should be treated like chilli sauce; essential at times, but more than a tiny sprinkle is too much.

#PRAGMA

This was the Standard Committee's way of 'opening the back door'. It allows implementation-defined things to take place. If the implementation was not expecting what you wrote (i.e. doesn't recognize it), it is ignored.

Here is a possible example:

```
#pragma byte_align
```

Which could be used to tell the implementation that all structure members should be aligned on byte addresses - some processor architectures are able to cope with word-sized structure members aligned on byte addresses, but with a penalty in access speed being incurred.

It could, of course, mean anything else that the implementation chooses it to mean. If your implementation doesn't have any special meaning for this, then it will have no effect. It will *not* count as an error.

#ERROR

This directive is followed by one or more tokens at the end of the line. A diagnostic message is produced by the compiler, which includes those tokens, but no further detail is given in the Standard. It might be used like this to abort a compilation on unsuitable hardware:

```
#include <limits.h>
#if CHAR_MIN > -128
#error character range smaller than required
#endif
```

which would be expected to produce some sort of meaningful compilation error and message.

Chapter 9

Structure of Programme

PROGRAMMING LANGUAGE

Probably the best way to start learning a programming language is by writing a programme.

Therefore, here is our first programme:

```
// my first programme in C++
#include <iostream>
using namespace std;
int main ()
{
  cout << "Hello World!";
  return 0;
} Hello World!
```

The first panel shows the source code for our first programme. The second one shows the result of the programme once compiled and executed. The way to edit and compile a programme depends on the compiler you are using. Depending on whether it has a Development Interface or not and on its version.

Consult the compilers section and the manual or help included with your compiler if you have doubts on how to compile a C++ console programme. The previous programme is the typical programme that programmer apprentices write for the first time, and its result is the printing on screen of the "Hello World!" sentence.

It is one of the simplest programmes that can be written in C++, but it already contains the fundamental components that every C++ programme has.

We are going to look line by line at the code we have just written:

```
// my first programme in C++
```

This is a comment line. All lines beginning with two slash signs (//) are considered comments and do not have any effect on the behaviour of the programme. The programmer can use them to include short explanations or observations within the source code itself. In this case, the line is a brief description of what our programme is.

```
#include <iostream>
```

Lines beginning with a pound sign (#) are directives for the preprocessor. They are not regular code lines with expressions but indications for the compiler's preprocessor. In this case the directive #include <iostream> tells the preprocessor to include the iostream standard file. This specific file (iostream) includes the declarations of the basic standard input-output library in C++, and it is included because its functionality is going to be used later in the programme.

```
using namespace std;
```

All the elements of the standard C++ library are declared within what is called a namespace, the namespace with the name *std*. So in order to access its functionality we declare with this expression that we will be using these entities. This line is very frequent in C++ programmes that use the standard library, and in fact it will be included in most of the source codes included in these tutorials.

```
int main ()
```

This line corresponds to the beginning of the definition of the main function. The main function is the point by where all C++ programmes start their execution, independently of its location within the source code. It does not matter whether there are other functions with other names defined before or after it - the instructions contained within this function's definition will always be the first ones to be executed in any C++ programme. For that same reason, it is essential that all C++ programmes have a main function.

The word main is followed in the code by a pair of parentheses (()). That is because it is a function declaration: In C++, what differentiates a function declaration from other types of expressions are these parentheses that follow its name. Optionally, these parentheses may enclose a list of parameters within them. Right after these parentheses we can find the body of the main function enclosed in braces ({}). What is contained within these braces is what the function does when it is executed.

```
cout << "Hello World";
```

This line is a C++ statement. A statement is a simple or compound expression that can actually produce some effect. In fact, this statement performs the only action that generates a visible effect in our first programme.

cout represents the standard output stream in C++, and the meaning of the entire statement is to insert a sequence of characters (in this case the Hello World sequence of characters) into the standard output stream (which usually is the screen).

cout is declared in the iostream standard file within the std namespace, so that's why we needed to include that specific file and to declare that we were going to use this specific namespace earlier in our code.

Notice that the statement ends with a semicolon character (;). This character is used to mark the end of the statement and in fact it must be included at the end of all expression statements in all C++ programmes (one of the most common syntax errors is indeed to forget to include some semicolon after a statement).

```
return 0;
```

The return statement causes the main function to finish. return may be followed by a return code (in our example is followed by the return code 0). A return code of 0 for the main function is generally interpreted as the programme worked as expected without any errors during its execution. This is the most usual way to end a C++ console programme.

You may have noticed that not all the lines of this programme perform actions when the code is executed. There were lines containing only comments (those beginning by //). There were lines with directives for the compiler's preprocessor (those beginning by #). Then there were lines that began the declaration of a function (in this case, the main function) and, finally lines with statements (like the insertion into cout), which were all included within the block delimited by the braces ({}) of the main function. The programme has been structured in different lines in order to be more readable, but in C++, we do not have strict rules on how to separate instructions in different lines. For example, instead of

```
int main ()
{
  cout << " Hello World ";
  return 0;
}
```

We could have written:

```
int main () { cout << "Hello World"; return
0; }
```

All in just one line and this would have had exactly the same meaning as the previous code. In C++, the separation between statements is specified with an ending semicolon (;) at the end of each one, so the separation in different code lines does not matter at all for this purpose.

We can write many statements per line or write a single statement that takes many code lines. The division of code in different lines serves only to make it more legible and schematic for the humans that may read it.

Let us add an additional instruction to our first programme:

```
// my second programme in C++
#include <iostream>
using namespace std;
int main ()
{
  cout << "Hello World! ";
  cout << "I'm a C++ programme";
  return 0;
}
```

Hello World! I'm a C++ programme

In this case, we performed two insertions into cout in two different statements. Once again, the separation in different lines of code has been done just to give greater readability to the programme, since main could have been perfectly valid defined this way.

```
int main () { cout << " Hello World! "; cout
<< " I'm a C++ programme "; return 0; }
```

We were also free to divide the code into more lines if we considered it more convenient:

```
int main ()
{
  cout <<
  "Hello World!";
  cout
  << "I'm a C++ programme";
  return 0;
}
```

And the result would again have been exactly the same as in the previous examples. Preprocessor directives (those that begin by #) are out of this general rule since they are not statements. They are lines read and processed by the preprocessor and do not produce any code by themselves. Preprocessor directives must be specified in their own line and do not have to end with a semicolon (;).

COMMENTS

Comments are parts of the source code disregarded by the compiler. They simply do nothing. Their purpose is only to allow the programmer to insert notes or descriptions embedded within the source code.

C++ supports two ways to insert comments:

```
// line comment
/* block comment */
```

The first of them, known as line comment, discards everything from where the pair of slash signs (//) is found up to the end of that same line. The second one, known as block comment, discards everything between the /* characters and the first appearance of the */ characters, with the possibility of including more than one line.

We are going to add comments to our second programme:

```
/* my second programme in C++
with more comments */
#include <iostream>
```

```
using namespace std;
int main ()
{
  cout << "Hello World! "; // prints Hello
  World!
  cout << "I'm a C++ programme"; // prints
  I'm a C++ programme
  return 0;
} Hello World! I'm a C++ programme
```

If you include comments within the source code of your programmes without using the comment characters combinations //, /* or */, the compiler will take them as if they were C++ expressions, most likely causing one or several error messages when you compile it.

VARIABLES. DATA TYPES.

The usefulness of the "Hello World" programmes shown in the previous section is quite questionable. We had to write several lines of code, compile them, and then execute the resulting programme just to obtain a simple sentence written on the screen as result.

It certainly would have been much faster to type the output sentence by ourselves. However, programming is not limited only to printing simple texts on the screen. In order to go a little further on and to become able to write programmes that perform useful tasks that really save us work we need to introduce the concept of variable.

Let us think that I ask you to retain the number 5 in your mental memory, and then I ask you to memorize also the number 2 at the same time. You have just stored two different values in your memory. Now, if I ask you to add 1 to the first number I said, you should be retaining the numbers 6 (that is 5+1) and 2 in your memory.

Values that we could now for example subtract and obtain 4 as result. The whole process that you have just done with your mental memory is a simile of what a computer can do with two variables. The same process can be expressed in C++ with the following instruction set:

```
a = 5;
b = 2;
a = a + 1;
result = a - b;
```

Obviously, this is a very simple example since we have only used two small integer values, but consider that your computer can store millions of numbers like these at the same time and conduct sophisticated mathematical operations with them. Therefore, we can define a variable as a portion of memory to store a determined value.

Each variable needs an identifier that distinguishes it from the others, for example, in the previous code the variable identifiers were a, b and result, but we could have called the variables any names we wanted to invent, as long as they were valid identifiers.

IDENTIFIERS

A valid identifier is a sequence of one or more letters, digits or underscore characters (_). Neither spaces nor punctuation marks or symbols can be part of an identifier. Only letters, digits and single underscore characters are valid. In addition, variable identifiers always have to begin with a letter. They can also begin with an underline character (_), but in some cases these may be reserved for compiler specific keywords or external identifiers, as well as identifiers containing two successive underscore characters anywhere. In no case they can begin with a digit.

Another rule that you have to consider when inventing your own identifiers is that they cannot match any keyword of the C++ language nor your compiler's specific ones, which are *reserved keywords*. The standard reserved keywords are: asm, auto, bool, break, case, catch, char, class, const, const_cast, continue, default, delete, do, double, dynamic_cast, else, enum, explicit, export, extern, false, float, for, friend, goto, if, inline, int, long, mutable, namespace, new, operator, private, protected, public, register, reinterpret_cast, return, short, signed, sizeof, static, static_cast, struct, switch, template, this, throw, true, try, typedef, typeid, typename, union, unsigned, using, virtual, void, volatile, wchar_t, while. Additionally, alternative representations for some operators cannot be used as identifiers since they are reserved words under some circumstances:

```
and, and_eq, bitand, bitor, compl, not,
not_eq, or, or_eq, xor, xor_eq
```

Your compiler may also include some additional specific reserved keywords. Very important: The C++ language is a "case sensitive" language. That means that an identifier written in capital letters is not equivalent to another one with the same name but written in small letters. Thus, for example, the RESULT variable is not the same as the result variable or the Result variable. These are three different variable identifiers.

FUNDAMENTAL DATA TYPES

When programming, we store the variables in our computer's memory, but the computer has to know what kind of data we want to store in them, since it is not going to occupy the same amount of memory to store a simple number than to store a single letter or a large number, and they are not going to be interpreted the same way.

The memory in our computers is organized in bytes. A byte is the minimum amount of memory that we can manage in C++. A byte can store a relatively small amount of data: one single character or a small integer (generally an integer between 0 and 255). In addition, the computer can manipulate more complex data types that come from grouping several bytes, such as long numbers or non-integer numbers.

Next you have a summary of the basic fundamental data types in C++, as well as the range of values that can be represented with each one.

Name	Description	Size*	Range*
char	Character or small integer.	1byte	signed: -128 to 127 unsigned: 0 to 255
short int	Short Integer. (short)	2bytes	signed: -32768 to 32767 unsigned: 0 to 65535
int	Integer.	4bytes	signed: -2147483648 to 2147483647

			unsigned: 0 to 4294967295
long int (long)	Long integer.	4bytes	signed: -2147483648 to 2147483647
			unsigned: 0 to 4294967295
bool	Boolean value. It can take one of two values: true or false.	1byte	true or false
float	Floating point number.	4bytes	3.4e +/- 38 (7 digits)
double	Double precision floating point number.	8bytes	1.7e +/- 308 (15 digits)
long double	Long double precision floating point number.	8bytes	1.7e +/- 308 (15 digits)
wchar_t	Wide character.	2bytes	1 wide character

* The values of the columns Size and Range depend on the system the programme is compiled for. The values shown above are those found on most 32-bit systems. But for other systems, the general specification is that int has the natural size suggested by the system architecture (one *"word"*) and the four integer types char, short, int and long must each one be at least as large as the one preceding it, with char being always 1 byte in size. The same applies to the floating point types float, double and long double, where each one must provide at least as much precision as the preceding one.

DECLARATION OF VARIABLES

In order to use a variable in C++, we must first declare it specifying which data type we want it to be. The syntax to declare a new variable is to write the specifier of the desired data type (like int, bool, float...) followed by a valid variable identifier. For example:

```
int a;b
float mynumber;
```

These are two valid declarations of variables. The first one declares a variable of type int with the identifier a. The second one declares a variable of type float with the identifier my number. Once declared, the variables a and mynumber can be used within the rest of their scope in the programme.

If you are going to declare more than one variable of the same type, you can declare all of them in a single statement by separating their identifiers with commas. For example:

```
int a, b, c;
```

This declares three variables (a, b and c), all of them of type int, and has exactly the same meaning as:

```
int a;
int b;
int c;
```

The integer data types char, short, long and int can be either signed or unsigned depending on the range of numbers needed to be represented. Signed types can represent both positive and negative values, whereas unsigned types can only represent positive values (and zero). This can be specified by using either the specifier signed or the specifier unsigned before the type name. For example:

```
unsigned short int NumberOfSisters;
signed int MyAccountBalance;
```

By default, if we do not specify either signed or unsigned most compiler settings will assume the type to be signed, therefore instead of the second declaration above we could have written:

```
int MyAccountBalance;
```

with exactly the same meaning (with or without the keyword signed) An exception to this general rule is the char type, which exists by itself and is considered a different fundamental data type from signed char and unsigned char, thought to store characters. You should use either signed or unsigned if you intend to store numerical values in a char-sized variable. short and long can be used alone as type specifiers. In this case, they refer to their respective integer fundamental types: short is equivalent to short int and long is equivalent to long int. The following two variable declarations are equivalent:

```
short Year;
short int Year;
```

Finally, signed and unsigned may also be used as standalone type specifiers, meaning the same as signed int and unsigned int respectively. The following two declarations are equivalent:

```
unsigned NextYear;
unsigned int NextYear;
```

To see what variable declarations look like in action within a programme, we are going to see the C++ code of the example about your mental memory proposed at the beginning of this section:

```
// operating with variables
#include <iostream>
using namespace std;
int main ()
{
  // declaring variables:
  int a, b;
  int result;
  // process:
  a = 5;
  b = 2;
  a = a + 1;
  result = a - b;
  // print out the result:
  cout << result;
  // terminate the programme:
  return 0;
} 4
```

Do not worry if something else than the variable declarations themselves looks a bit strange to you. You will see the rest in detail in coming sections.

SCOPE OF VARIABLES

All the variables that we intend to use in a programme must have been declared with its type specifier in an earlier point in the code, like we did in the previous code at the beginning of the body of the function main when we declared that a, b, and result were of type int. A variable can be either of global or local scope. A global variable is a variable declared in the main body of the source code, outside all functions, while a local variable is one declared within the body of a function or a block.

```
#Include <iostream>
using namespace std;

int Integer;
char aCharacter;
char string [20];                    ——— Global vabialbles
unsigned int NumberOfSons;

int main()
{

unsigned short Age;                  ——— Local variables
float Anumber, AnotherOne;

count << "Enter your age:"
cin >> Age;                          ——— Instructions
...
}
```

Global variables can be referred from anywhere in the code, even inside functions, whenever it is after its declaration. The scope of local variables is limited to the block enclosed in braces ({}) where they are declared.

For example, if they are declared at the beginning of the body of a function (like in function main) their scope is between its declaration point and the end of that function. In the example above, this means that if another function existed in addition to main, the local variables declared in main could not be accessed from the other function and vice versa.

INITIALIZATION OF VARIABLES

When declaring a regular local variable, its value is by default undetermined. But you may want a variable to store a concrete value at the same moment that it is declared. In order to do that, you can initialize the variable.

There are two ways to do this in C++:

The first one, known as c-like, is done by appending an equal sign followed by the value to which the variable will be initialized.

```
type identifier = initial_value ;
```

For example, if we want to declare an int variable called a initialized with a value of 0 at the moment in which it is declared, we could write:

```
int a = 0;
```

The other way to initialize variables, known as constructor initialization, is done by enclosing the initial value between parentheses (()):

```
type identifier (initial_value) ;
```

For example:

```
int a (0);
```

Both ways of initializing variables are valid and equivalent in C++.

```
// initialization of variables
#include <iostream>
using namespace std;
int main ()
{
  int a=5; // initial value = 5
  int b(2); // initial value = 2
  int result; // initial value undetermined
  a = a + 3;
  result = a - b;
  cout << result;
  return 0;
} 6
```

STRINGS

Variables that can store non-numerical values that are longer than one single character are known as strings. The C++ language library provides support for strings through the standard string class. This is not a fundamental type, but it behaves in a similar way as fundamental types do in its most basic usage.

A first difference with fundamental data types is that in order to declare and use objects (variables) of this type we need to include an additional header file in our source code: <string> and have access to the std namespace (which we already had in all our previous programmes thanks to the using namespace statement).

```
// my first string
#include <iostream>
#include <string>
using namespace std;
int main ()
{
  string mystring = "This is a string";
  cout << mystring;
  return 0;
}
```

output

```
This is a string
```

As you may see in the previous example, strings can be initialized with any valid string literal just like numerical type variables can be initialized to any valid numerical literal. Both initialization formats are valid with strings:

```
string mystring = "This is a string";
string mystring ("This is a string");
```

Strings can also perform all the other basic operations that fundamental data types can, like being declared without an initial value and being assigned values during execution:

```
// my first string
#include <iostream>
#include <string>
using namespace std;
int main ()
{
  string mystring;
  mystring = "This is the initial string
  content";
  cout << mystring << endl;
  mystring = "This is a different string
  content";
  cout << mystring << endl;
  sreturn 0;
}
```

```
output
This is the initial string content
This is a different string content
```

For more details on C++ strings, you can have a look at the string class reference.

Constants: Constants are expressions with a fixed value.

LITERALS

Literals are used to express particular values within the source code of a programme. We have already used these previously to give concrete values to variables or to express messages we wanted our programmes to print out, for example, when we wrote:

```
a = 5;
```

the 5 in this piece of code was a literal constant.

Literal constants can be divided in Integer Numerals, Floating-Point Numerals, Characters, Strings and Boolean Values.

INTEGER NUMERALS

```
1776
707
-273
```

They are numerical constants that identify integer decimal values. Notice that to express a numerical constant we do not have to write quotes (") nor any special character. There is no doubt that it is a constant: whenever we write 1776 in a programme, we will be referring to the value 1776.

In addition to decimal numbers (those that all of us are used to use every day) C++ allows the use as literal constants of octal numbers (base 8) and hexadecimal numbers (base 16). If we want to express an octal number we have to precede it with a 0 (zero character). And in order to express a hexadecimal number we have to precede it with the characters 0x (zero, x). For example, the following literal constants are all equivalent to each other:

```
75 // decimal
0113 // octal
```

```
0x4b  // hexadecimal
```

All of these represent the same number: 75 (seventy-five) expressed as a base-10 numeral, octal numeral and hexadecimal numeral, respectively.

Literal constants, like variables, are considered to have a specific data type. By default, integer literals are of type int. However, we can force them to either be unsigned by appending the u character to it, or long by appending l:

```
75  // int
75u  // unsigned int
75l  // long
75ul  // unsigned long
```

In both cases, the suffix can be specified using either upper or lowercase letters.

FLOATING POINT NUMBERS

They express numbers with decimals and/or exponents. They can include either a decimal point, an e character (that expresses "by ten at the Xth height", where X is an integer value that follows the e character), or both a decimal point and an e character:

```
3.14159   // 3.14159
6.02e23   // 6.02 x 10^23
1.6e-19  // 1.6 x 10-19
3.0  // 3.0
```

These are four valid numbers with decimals expressed in C++. The first number is PI, the second one is the number of Avogadro, the third is the electric charge of an electron (an extremely small number) -all of them approximated- and the last one is the number three expressed as a floating-point numeric literal. The default type for floating point literals is double. If you explicitly want to express a float or long double numerical literal, you can use the f or l suffixes respectively:

```
3.14159L  // long double
6.02e23f  // float
```

Any of the letters than can be part of a floating-point numerical constant (e, f, l) can be written using either lower or uppercase letters without any difference in their meanings.

Character and string literals.

There also exist non-numerical constants, like:

```
'z'
'p'
"Hello world"
"How do you do?"
```

The first two expressions represent single character constants, and the following two represent string literals composed of several characters. Notice that to represent a single character we enclose it between single quotes (') and to express a string (which generally consists of more than one character) we enclose it between double quotes (").

When writing both single character and string literals, it is necessary to put the quotation marks surrounding them to distinguish them from possible variable identifiers or reserved keywords. Notice the difference between these two expressions:

```
x
'x'
```

x alone would refer to a variable whose identifier is x, whereas 'x' (enclosed within single quotation marks) would refer to the character constant 'x'.

Character and string literals have certain peculiarities, like the escape codes. These are special characters that are difficult or impossible to express otherwise in the source code of a programme, like newline (\n) or tab (\t). All of them are preceded by a backslash (\). Here you have a list of some of such escape codes:

```
\n newline
\r carriage return
\t tab
\v vertical tab
\b backspace
\f form feed (page feed)
\a alert (beep)
\' single quote (')
\" double quote (")
\? question mark (?)
```

```
\\ backslash (\)
```

For example:

```
'\n'
'\t'
"Left \t Right"
"one\ntwo\nthree"
```

Additionally, you can express any character by its numerical ASCII code by writing a backslash character (\) followed by the ASCII code expressed as an octal (base-8) or hexadecimal (base-16) number. In the first case (octal) the digits must immediately follow the backslash (for example \23 or \40), in the second case (hexadecimal), an x character must be written before the digits themselves (for example \x20 or \x4A). String literals can extend to more than a single line of code by putting a backslash sign (\) at the end of each unfinished line.

```
"string expressed in \
two lines"
```

You can also concatenate several string constants separating them by one or several blank spaces, tabulators, newline or any other valid blank character:

```
"this forms" "a single" "string" "of
characters"
```

Finally, if we want the string literal to be explicitly made of wide characters (wchar_t), instead of narrow characters (char), we can precede the constant with the L prefix:

```
L"This is a wide character string"
```

Wide characters are used mainly to represent non-English or exotic character sets.

BOOLEAN LITERALS

There are only two valid Boolean values: true and false. These can be expressed in C++ as values of type bool by using the Boolean literals true and false.

Defined constants (#define): You can define your own names for constants that you use very often without having to resort to memory-consuming variables, simply by using the #define preprocessor directive. Its format is.

```
#define identifier value
For example:
#define PI 3.14159265
#define NEWLINE '\n'
```

This defines two new constants: PI and NEWLINE. Once they are defined, you can use them in the rest of the code as if they were any other regular constant, For example

```
// defined constants: calculate circumference
#include <iostream>
using namespace std;
#define PI 3.14159
#define NEWLINE '\n'
int main ()
{
  double r=5.0; // radius
  double circle;
  circle = 2 * PI * r;
  cout << circle;
  cout << NEWLINE;
  return 0;
}
output
31.4159
```

In fact the only thing that the compiler preprocessor does when it encounters #define directives is to literally replace any occurrence of their identifier (in the previous example, these were PI and NEWLINE) by the code to which they have been defined (3.14159265 and '\n' respectively).

The #define directive is not a C++ statement but a directive for the preprocessor; therefore it assumes the entire line as the directive and does not require a semicolon (;) at its end. If you append a semicolon character (;) at the end, it will also be appended in all occurrences within the body of the programme that the preprocessor replaces.

DECLARED CONSTANTS (CONST)

With the const prefix you can declare constants with a specific type in the same way as you would do with a variable.

```
const int pathwidth = 100;
const char tabulator = '\t';
```

Here, pathwidth and tabulator are two typed constants. They are treated just like regular variables except that their values cannot be modified after their definition.

OPERATORS

Once we know of the existence of variables and constants, we can begin to operate with them. For that purpose, C++ integrates operators. Unlike other languages whose operators are mainly keywords, operators in C++ are mostly made of signs that are not part of the alphabet but are available in all keyboards. This makes C++ code shorter and more international, since it relies less on English words, but requires a little of learning effort in the beginning. You do not have to memorize all the content of this page. Most details are only provided to serve as a later reference in case you need it.

Assignment (=)

The assignment operator assigns a value to a variable.

```
a = 5;
```

This statement assigns the integer value 5 to the variable a. The part at the left of the assignment operator (=) is known as the *lvalue* (left value) and the right one as the *rvalue* (right value). The lvalue has to be a variable whereas the rvalue can be either a constant, a variable, the result of an operation or any combination of these.

The most important rule when assigning is the *right-to-left* rule: The assignment operation always takes place from right to left, and never the other way:

```
a = b;
```

This statement assigns to variable a (the lvalue) the value contained in variable b (the rvalue). The value that was stored until this moment in a is not considered at all in this operation, and in fact that value is lost.

Consider also that we are only assigning the value of b to a at the moment of the assignment operation. Therefore a later change of b will not affect the new value of a.

For example, let us have a look at the following code - I have included the evolution of the content stored in the variables as comments:

```
// assignment operator
#include <iostream>
using namespace std;
int main ()
{
  int a, b; // a:?,  b:?
  a = 10; // a:10, b:?
  b = 4; // a:10, b:4
  a = b; // a:4,  b:4
  b = 7; // a:4,  b:7
  cout << "a:";
  cout << a;
  cout << " b:";
  cout << b;
  return 0;
}
output
a:4 b:7
```

This code will give us as result that the value contained in a is 4 and the one contained in b is 7. Notice how a was not affected by the final modification of b, even though we declared a = b earlier (that is because of the *right-to-left rule*).

A property that C++ has over other programming languages is that the assignment operation can be used as the rvalue (or part of an rvalue) for another assignment operation.

For example:

```
a = 2 + (b = 5);
```

is equivalent to:

```
b = 5;
a = 2 + b;
```

that means: first assign 5 to variable b and then assign to a the value 2 plus the result of the previous assignment of b (i.e. 5), leaving a with a final value of 7.

The following expression is also valid in C++:

```
a = b = c = 5;
```

It assigns 5 to the all the three variables: a, b and c.

Arithmetic operators (+, -, *, /,%)

The five arithmetical operations supported by the C++ language are:

```
+ addition
- subtraction
* multiplication
/ division
% modulo
```

Operations of addition, subtraction, multiplication and division literally correspond with their respective mathematical operators. The only one that you might not be so used to see may be *modulo*; whose operator is the percentage sign (%). Modulo is the operation that gives the remainder of a division of two values. For example, if we write:

```
a = 11 % 3;
```

the variable a will contain the value 2, since 2 is the remainder from dividing 11 between 3.

Compound assignment (+=, -=, *=, /=,%=, >>=, <<=, &=, ^=, |=)

When we want to modify the value of a variable by performing an operation on the value currently stored in that variable we can use compound assignment operators.

Expression	Is Equivalent to
`value += increase;`	`value = value + increase;`
`a -= 5;`	`a = a - 5;`
`a /= b;`	`a = a / b;`
`price *= units + 1;`	`price = price * (units + 1);`

and the same for all other operators. For example:

```
// compound assignment operators
#include <iostream>
using namespace std;
int main ()
{
  int a, b=3;
  a = b;
  a+=2; // equivalent to a=a+2
```

```
cout << a;
return 0;
} 5
```

Increase and decrease (++, —)

Shortening even more some expressions, the increase operator (++) and the decrease operator (—) increase or reduce by one the value stored in a variable. They are equivalent to +=1 and to -=1, respectively. Thus:

```
c++;
c+=1;
c=c+1;
```

are all equivalent in its functionality: the three of them increase by one the value of c. In the early C compilers, the three previous expressions probably produced different executable code depending on which one was used. Nowadays, this type of code optimization is generally done automatically by the compiler, thus the three expressions should produce exactly the same executable code.

A characteristic of this operator is that it can be used both as a prefix and as a suffix. That means that it can be written either before the variable identifier (++a) or after it (a++). Although in simple expressions like a++ or ++a both have exactly the same meaning, in other expressions in which the result of the increase or decrease operation is evaluated as a value in an outer expression they may have an important difference in their meaning: In the case that the increase operator is used as a prefix (++a) the value is increased before the result of the expression is evaluated and therefore the increased value is considered in the outer expression; in case that it is used as a suffix (a++) the value stored in a is increased after being evaluated and therefore the value stored before the increase operation is evaluated in the outer expression. Notice the difference:

Example 1	Example 2
B=3; A=++B; // A contains 4, B contains 4	B=3; A=B++; // A contains 3, B contains 4s

In Example 1, B is increased before its value is copied to A. While in Example 2, the value of B is copied to A and then B is increased.

Relational and equality operators (==, !=, >, <, >=, <=)

In order to evaluate a comparison between two expressions we can use the relational and equality operators. The result of a relational operation is a Boolean value that can only be true or false, according to its Boolean result.

We may want to compare two expressions, for example, to know if they are equal or if one is greater than the other is. Here is a list of the relational and equality operators that can be used in C++:

```
==  Equal to
!=  Not equal to
> Greater than
< Less than
>=  Greater than or equal to
<=  Less than or equal to
```

Here there are some examples:

```
(7 == 5) // evaluates to false.
(5 > 4) // evaluates to true.
(3 != 2) // evaluates to true.
(6 >= 6) // evaluates to true.
(5 < 5) // evaluates to false.
```

Of course, instead of using only numeric constants, we can use any valid expression, including variables. Suppose that a=2, b=3 and c=6,

```
(a == 5) // evaluates to false since a is not equal to 5.
(a*b >= c) // evaluates to true since (2*3 >= 6) is true.
(b+4 > a*c) // evaluates to false since (3+4 > 2*6) is false.
((b=2) == a) // evaluates to true.
```

Be careful! The operator = (one equal sign) is not the same as the operator == (two equal signs), the first one is an assignment operator (assigns the value at its right to the variable at its left) and the other one (==) is the equality operator that compares whether both expressions in the two sides of it are equal to each other. Thus, in the last expression ((b=2) == a), we first assigned the value 2 to b and then we compared it to a, that also stores the value 2, so the result of the operation is true.

Logical operators (!, &&, ||)

The Operator ! is the C++ operator to perform the Boolean operation NOT, it has only one operand, located at its right, and the only thing that it does is to inverse the value of it, producing false if its operand is true and true if its operand is false. Basically, it returns the opposite Boolean value of evaluating its operand. For example:

```
!(5 == 5) // evaluates to false because the
 expression at its right (5 == 5) is true.
!(6 <= 4) // evaluates to true because (6 <=
4) would be false.
!true   // evaluates to false
!false   // evaluates to true.
```

The logical operators && and || are used when evaluating two expressions to obtain a single relational result. The operator && corresponds with Boolean logical operation AND. This operation results true if both its two operands are true, and false otherwise. The following panel shows the result of operator && evaluating the expression a && b:

```
&& OPERATOR
a b a && b
true true true
true false false
false true false
false false false
```

The operator || corresponds with Boolean logical operation OR. This operation results true if either one of its two operands is true, thus being false only when both operands are false themselves. Here are the possible results of a || b:

```
|| OPERATOR
a b a || b
true true true
```

```
true false true
false true true
false false false
```

For example:

```
((5 == 5) && (3 > 6)) // evaluates to false
( true && false ).
((5 == 5) || (3 > 6)) // evaluates to true (
true || false ).
```

Conditional operator (?)

The conditional operator evaluates an expression returning a value if that expression is true and a different one if the expression is evaluated as false. Its format is:

```
condition ? result1 : result2
```

If condition is true the expression will return result1, if it is not it will return result2.

```
7==5 ? 4 : 3  // returns 3, since 7 is not
equal to 5.
7==5+2 ? 4 : 3  // returns 4, since 7 is
equal to 5+2.
5>3 ? a : b  // returns the value of a, since
5 is greater than 3.
a>b ? a : b  // returns whichever is greater,
a or b.
```

```
// conditional operator
#include <iostream>
using namespace std;
int main ()
{
   int a,b,c;
   a=2;
   b=7;
   c = (a>b) ? a : b;
cout << c;
   return 0;
} 7
```

In this example a was 2 and b was 7, so the expression being evaluated (a>b) was not true, thus the first value specified after the question mark was discarded in favour of the second value (the one after the colon) which was b, with a value of 7.

Comma Operator (,)

The comma operator (,) is used to separate two or more expressions that are included where only one expression is expected. When the set of expressions has to be evaluated for a value, only the rightmost expression is considered.

For example, the following code:

```
a = (b=3, b+2);
```

Would first assign the value 3 to b, and then assign b+2 to variable a. So, at the end, variable a would contain the value 5 while variable b would contain value 3.

`Bitwise Operators (&, |, ^, ~, <<, >>)`

Bitwise operators modify variables considering the bit patterns that represent the values they store.

Operator	Asm equivalent	Description
&	AND	Bitwise AND
|	OR	Bitwise Inclusive OR
^	XOR	Bitwise Exclusive OR
~	NOT	Unary complement (bit inversion)
<<	SHL	Shift Left
>>	SHR	Shift Right

Explicit Type Casting Operator

Type casting operators allow you to convert a datum of a given type to another. There are several ways to do this in C++. The simplest one, which has been inherited from the C language, is to precede the expression to be converted by the new type enclosed between parentheses (()):

```
int i;
float f = 3.14;
i = (int) f;
```

The previous code converts the float number 3.14 to an integer value (3), the remainder is lost. Here, the typecasting operator was (int). Another way to do the same thing in C++ is using the functional notation: preceding the expression to be converted by the type and enclosing the expression between parentheses.

```
i = int ( f );
```

Both ways of type casting are valid in C++.

```
sizeof()
```

This operator accepts one parameter, which can be either a type or a variable itself and returns the size in bytes of that type or object:

```
a = sizeof (char);
```

This will assign the value 1 to a because char is a one-byte long type. The value returned by sizeof is a constant, so it is always determined before programme execution.

Other Operators

Later in these tutorials, we will see a few more operators, like the ones referring to pointers or the specifics for object-oriented programming. Each one is treated in its respective section.

Precedence of Operators

When writing complex expressions with several operands, we may have some doubts about which operand is evaluated first and which later. For example, in this expression:

```
a = 5 + 7 % 2
```

we may doubt if it really means:

```
a = 5 + (7 % 2)  // with a result of 6, or
a = (5 + 7)% 2   // with a result of 0
```

The correct answer is the first of the two expressions, with a result of 6. There is an established order with the priority of each operator, and not only the arithmetic ones (those whose preference come from mathematics) but for all the operators which can appear in C++. From greatest to lowest priority, the priority order is as follows.

Level	Operator	Description	Grouping
1	::	Scope	Left-to-right
2	() []. -> ++ — dynamic_ cast static_cast reinterpret	Postfix	Left-to-right

<table>
<tr><td></td><td>_cast const_cast typeid</td><td></td><td></td></tr>
<tr><td>3</td><td>++ — ~ !sizeof new delete</td><td>Unary (prefix)</td><td>Right-to-left</td></tr>
<tr><td></td><td>* &</td><td>Indirection and Reference (pointers)</td><td>Right-to-left</td></tr>
<tr><td></td><td>+ -</td><td>Unary sign operator</td><td></td></tr>
<tr><td>4</td><td>(type)</td><td>Type casting</td><td>Right-to-left</td></tr>
<tr><td>5</td><td>.* ->*</td><td>Pointer-to-member</td><td>Left-to-right</td></tr>
<tr><td>6</td><td>* /%</td><td>Multiplicative</td><td>Left-to-right</td></tr>
<tr><td>7</td><td>+ -</td><td>Additive</td><td>Left-to-right</td></tr>
<tr><td>8</td><td><< >></td><td>Shift</td><td>Left-to-right</td></tr>
<tr><td>9</td><td>< > <= >=</td><td>Relational</td><td>Left-to-right</td></tr>
<tr><td>10</td><td>== !=</td><td>Equality</td><td>Left-to-right</td></tr>
<tr><td>11</td><td>&</td><td>Bitwise AND</td><td>Left-to-right</td></tr>
<tr><td>12</td><td>^</td><td>Bitwise XOR</td><td>Left-to-right</td></tr>
<tr><td>13</td><td>|</td><td>Bitwise OR</td><td>Left-to-right</td></tr>
<tr><td>14</td><td>&&</td><td>Logical AND</td><td>Left-to-right</td></tr>
<tr><td>15</td><td>||</td><td>Logical OR</td><td>Left-to-right</td></tr>
<tr><td>16</td><td>?:</td><td>Conditional</td><td>Right-to-left</td></tr>
<tr><td>17</td><td>= *= /=%= += -= >>= <<= &= ^= |=</td><td>Assignment</td><td>Right-to-left</td></tr>
<tr><td>18</td><td>,</td><td>Comma</td><td>Left-to-right</td></tr>
</table>

Grouping defines the precedence order in which operators are evaluated in the case that there are several operators of the same level in an expression. All these precedence levels for operators can be manipulated or become more legible by removing possible ambiguities using parentheses signs (and), as in this example:

```
a = 5 + 7 % 2;
```

might be written either as:

```
a = 5 + (7 % 2);
or
a = (5 + 7)% 2;
```

depending on the operation that we want to perform.

So if you want to write complicated expressions and you are not completely sure of the precedence levels, always include parentheses. It will also become a code easier to read.

Basic Input/Output: Until now, the example programmes of previous sections provided very little interaction with the user, if any at all. Using the standard input and output library, we will be able to interact with the user by printing messages on the screen and getting the user's input from the keyboard. C++ uses a convenient abstraction called *streams* to perform input and output operations in sequential media such as the screen or the keyboard.

A stream is an object where a programme can either insert or extract characters to/from it. We do not really need to care about many specifications about the physical media associated with the stream - we only need to know it will accept or provide characters sequentialy.

The standard C++ library includes the header file iostream, where the standard input and output stream objects are declared.

Standard Output (cout): By default, the standard output of a programme is the screen, and the C++ stream object defined to access it is cout. cout is used in conjunction with the *insertion operator*, which is written as << (two "less than" signs).

```
cout << "Output sentence"; // prints Output
sentence on screen
cout << 120; / prints number 120 on screen
cout << x; // prints the content of x on
screen
```

The << operator inserts the data that follows it into the stream preceding it. In the examples above it inserted the constant string Output sentence, the numerical constant 120 and variable x into the standard output stream cout. Notice that the sentence in the first instruction is enclosed between double quotes (") because it is a constant string of characters. Whenever we want to use constant strings of characters we must enclose them between double quotes (") so that they can be clearly distinguished from variable names.

For example, these two sentences have very different results:

```
cout << "Hello"; // prints Hello
cout << Hello; // prints the content of
Hello variable
```

The insertion operator (<<) may be used more than once in a single statement:

```
cout << "Hello, " << "I am " << "a C++
statement";
```

This last statement would print the message Hello, I am a C++ statement on the screen. The utility of repeating the insertion operator (<<) is demonstrated when we want to print out a combination of variables and constants or more than one variable:

```
cout << "Hello, I am " << age << " years old
and my zipcode is " << zipcode;
```

If we assume the age variable to contain the value 24 and the zipcode variable to contain 90064 the output of the previous statement would be:

```
Hello, I am 24 years old and my zipcode is
90064
```

It is important to notice that cout does not add a line break after its output unless we explicitly indicate it, therefore, the following statements:

```
cout << "This is a sentence.";
cout << "This is another sentence.";
```

will be shown on the screen one following the other without any line break between them:

This is a sentence.This is another sentence.

even though we had written them in two different insertions into cout. In order to perform a line break on the output we must explicitly insert a new-line character into cout. In C++ a new-line character can be specified as \n (backslash, n):

```
cout << "First sentence.\n ";
cout << "Second sentence.\nThird sentence.";
This produces the following output:
First sentence.
Second sentence.
Third sentence.
```

Additionally, to add a new-line, you may also use the endl manipulator. For example:

```
cout << "First sentence." << endl;
cout << "Second sentence." << endl;
```

```
would print out:
First sentence.
Second sentence.
```

The endl manipulator produces a newline character, exactly as the insertion of '\n' does, but it also has an additional behaviour when it is used with buffered streams: the buffer is flushed. Anyway, cout will be an unbuffered stream in most cases, so you can generally use both the \n escape character and the endl manipulator in order to specify a new line without any difference in its behaviour.

Standard Input (cin).

The standard input device is usually the keyboard. Handling the standard input in C++ is done by applying the overloaded operator of extraction (>>) on the cin stream. The operator must be followed by the variable that will store the data that is going to be extracted from the stream. For example:

```
int age;
cin >> age;
```

The first statement de ares a variable of type int called age, and the second one waits for an input from cin (the keyboard) in order to store it in this integer variable. cin can only process the input from the keyboard once the RETURN key has been pressed. Therefore, even if you request a single character, the extraction from cin will not process the input until the user presses RETURN after the character has been introduced.

You must always consider the type of the variable that you are using as a container with cin extractions. If you request an integer you will get an integer, if you request a character you will get a character and if you request a string of characters you will get a string of characters.

```
// i/o example
#include <iostream>
using namespace std;
int main ()
{
  int i;
  cout << "Please enter an integer value: ";
```

```
  cin >> i;
  cout << "The value you entered is " << i;
  cout << " and its double is " << i*2 <<
 ".\n";
  return 0;
} Please enter an integer value: 702
The value you entered is 702 and its double
is 1404.
```

The user of a programme may be one of the factors that generate errors even in the simplest programmes that use cin (like the one we have just seen). Since if you request an integer value and the user introduces a name (which generally is a string of characters), the result may cause your programme to misoperate since it is not what we were expecting from the user. So when you use the data input provided by cin extractions you will have to trust that the user of your programme will be cooperative and that he/she will not introduce his/her name or something similar when an integer value is requested. A little ahead, when we see the stringstream class we will see a possible solution for the errors that can be caused by this type of user input.

You can also use cin to request more than one datum input from the user:

```
cin >> a >> b;
```

is equivalent to:

```
cin >> a;
cin >> b;
```

In both cases the user must give two data, one for variable a and another one for variable b that may be separated by any valid blank separator: a space, a tab character or a newline.

cin and strings

We can use cin to get strings with the extraction operator (>>) as we do with fundamental data type variables:

```
cin >> mystring;
```

However, as it has been said, cin extraction stops reading as soon as if finds any blank space character, so in this case we will be able to get just one word for each extraction. This behaviour may or may not be what we want; for example if we want to get a sentence from the user, this extraction operation would not be useful. In order to get entire lines, we can use the function getline, which is the more recommendable way to get user input with cin:

```
// cin with strings
#include <iostream>
#include <string>
using namespace std;
int main ()
{
  string mystr;
  cout << "What's your name? ";
  getline (cin, mystr);
  cout << "Hello " << mystr << ".\n";
  cout << "What is your favourite team? ";
  getline (cin, mystr);
  cout << "I like " << mystr << " too!\n";
  return 0;
} What's your name? Juan Soulié
Hello Juan Soulié.
What is your favourite team? The Isotopes
I like The Isotopes too!
```

Notice how in both calls to getline we used the same string identifier (mystr). What the programme does in the second call is simply to replace the previous content by the new one that is introduced.

Stringstream:

The standard header file <sstream> defines a class called stringstream that allows a string-based object to be treated as a stream. This way we can perform extraction or insertion operations from/to strings, which is especially useful to convert strings to numerical values and vice versa. For example, if we want to extract an integer from a string we can write:

```
string mystr ("1204");
int myint;
stringstream(mystr) >> myint;
```

This declares a string object with a value of "1204", and an int object. Then we use stringstream's constructor to construct an object of this type from the string object. Because we can use stringstream objects as if they were streams, we can extract an integer from it as we would have done on cin by applying the extractor operator (>>) on it followed by a variable of type int.

After this piece of code, the variable myint will contain the numerical value 1204.

```
// stringstreams
#include <iostream>
#include <string>
#include <sstream>
using namespace std;
int main ()
{
  string mystr;
  float price=0;
  int quantity=0;
  cout << "Enter price: ";
  getline (cin,mystr);
  stringstream(mystr) >> price;
  cout << "Enter quantity: ";
  getline (cin,mystr);
  stringstream(mystr) >> quantity;
  cout << "Total price: " << price*quantity
 <<
  endl;
  return 0;
} Enter price: 22.25
Enter quantity: 7
Total price: 155.75
```

In this example, we acquire numeric values from the standard input indirectly. Instead of extracting numeric values directly from the standard input, we get lines from the standard input (cin) into a string object (mystr), and then we extract the integer values from this string into a variable of type int (myint).

Using this method, instead of direct extractions of integer values, we have more control over what happens with the input of numeric values from the user, since we are separating the process of obtaining input from the user (we now simply ask for lines) with the interpretation of that input. Therefore, this method is usually preferred to get numerical values from the user in all programmes that are intensive in user input.

CONTROL STRUCTURES

A programme is usually not limited to a linear sequence of instructions. During its process it may bifurcate, repeat code or take decisions. For that purpose, C++ provides control structures that serve to specify what has to be done by our programme, when and under which circumstances.

With the introduction of control structures we are going to have to introduce a new concept: the *compound-statement* or *block*. A block is a group of statements which are separated by semicolons (;) like all C++ statements, but grouped together in a block enclosed in braces: { }:

```
{ statement1; statement2; statement3; }
```

Most of the control structures that we will see in this section require a generic statement as part of its syntax. A statement can be either a simple statement (a simple instruction ending with a semicolon) or a compound statement (several instructions grouped in a block), like the one just described. In the case that we want the statement to be a simple statement, we do not need to enclose it in braces ({}). But in the case that we want the statement to be a compound statement it must be enclosed between braces ({}), forming a block.

Conditional Structure: If and Else

The if keyword is used to execute a statement or block only if a condition is fulfilled. Its form is.

if (condition) statement:

Where condition is the expression that is being evaluated. If this condition is true, statement is executed. If it is false, statement is ignored (not executed) and the programme continues right after this conditional structure.

For example, the following code fragment prints x is 100 only if the value stored in the x variable is indeed 100:

```
if (x == 100)
cout << "x is 100";
```

If we want more than a single statement to be executed in case that the condition is true we can specify a block using braces { }:

```
if (x == 100)
{
  cout << "x is ";
  cout << x;
}
```

We can additionally specify what we want to happen if the condition is not fulfilled by using the keyword else. Its form used in conjunction with if is.

if (condition) statement1 else statement2

For example:

```
if (x == 100)
cout << "x is 100";
else
cout << "x is not 100";
```

prints on the screen x is 100 if indeed x has a value of 100, but if it has not -and only if not- it prints out x is not 100.

The if + else structures can be concatenated with the intention of verifying a range of values. The following example shows its use telling if the value currently stored in x is positive, negative or none of them (i.e. zero):

```
if (x > 0)
cout << "x is positive";
else if (x < 0)
cout << "x is negative";
else
cout << "x is 0";
```

Remember that in case that we want more than a single statement to be executed, we must group them in a block by enclosing them in braces { }.

Iteration structures (loops)

Loops have as purpose to repeat a statement a certain number of times or while a condition is fulfilled.

The while loop

Its format is:

while (expression) statement, and its functionality is simply to repeat statement while the condition set in expression is true.

For example, we are going to make a programme to countdown using a while-loop:

```
// custom countdown using while
#include <iostream>
using namespace std;
int main ()
{
  int n;
  cout << "Enter the starting number > ";
  cin >> n;
  while (n>0) {
  cout << n << ", ";
  --n;
}
cout << "FIRE!\n";
return 0;
}
Output
Enter the starting number > 8
8, 7, 6, 5, 4, 3, 2, 1, FIRE!
```

When the programme starts the user is prompted to insert a starting number for the countdown. Then the while loop begins, if the value entered by the user fulfills the condition n>0 (that n is greater than zero) the block that follows the condition will be executed and repeated while the condition (n>0) remains being true.

The whole process of the previous programme can be interpreted according to the following script (beginning in main):

1. User assigns a value to n
2. The while condition is checked (n>0). At this point there are two posibilities:

   * *Condition is true*: Statement is executed (to step 3)

* *Condition is false*: Ignore statement and continue after it (to step 5)

3. *Execute statement*:

   cout << n << ", "; —n;

   (prints the value of n on the screen and decreases n by 1)

4. End of block. Return automatically to step 2
5. Continue the programme right after the block: print FIRE! and end programme.

When creating a while-loop, we must always consider that it has to end at some point, therefore we must provide within the block some method to force the condition to become false at some point, otherwise the loop will continue looping forever. In this case we have included —n; that decreases the value of the variable that is being evaluated in the condition (n) by one - this will eventually make the condition (n>0) to become false after a certain number of loop iterations: to be more specific, when n becomes 0, that is where our while-loop and our countdown end.

Of course this is such a simple action for our computer that the whole countdown is performed instantly without any practical delay between numbers.

The do-while loop

Its format is:

do statement while (condition); Its functionality is exactly the same as the while loop, except that condition in the do-while loop is evaluated after the execution of statement instead of before, granting at least one execution of statement even if condition is never fulfilled. For example, the following example programme echoes any number you enter until you enter 0.

```
// number echoer
#include <iostream>
using namespace std;
int main ()
{
  unsigned long n;
  do {
  cout << "Enter number (0 to end): ";
```

```
    cin >> n;
    cout << "You entered: " << n << "\n";
  } while (n != 0);
  return 0;
  } Enter number (0 to end): 12345
  You entered: 12345
  output
  Enter number (0 to end): 160277
  You entered: 160277
  Enter number (0 to end): 0
  You entered: 0
```

The do-while loop is usually used when the condition that has to determine the end of the loop is determined within the loop statement itself, like in the previous case, where the user input within the block is what is used to determine if the loop has to end. In fact if you never enter the value 0 in the previous example you can be prompted for more numbers forever.

The for loop

Its format is:

for (initialization; condition; increase) statement; and its main function is to repeat statement while condition remains true, like the while loop. But in addition, the for loop provides specific locations to contain an initialization statement and an increase statement. So this loop is specially designed to perform a repetitive action with a counter which is initialized and increased on each iteration.

It works in the following way:

1. *Initialization is executed*: Generally it is an initial value setting for a counter variable. This is executed only once.
2. *Condition is checked*: If it is true the loop continues, otherwise the loop ends and statement is skipped.
3. *Statement is executed*: As usual, it can be either a single statement or a block enclosed in braces { }.
4. Finally, whatever is specified in the increase field is executed and the loop gets back to step 2.

Here is an example of countdown using a for loop:

```
// countdown using a for loop
```

```
#include <iostream>
using namespace std;
int main ()
{
  for (int n=10; n>0; n--) {
  cout << n << ", ";
}
cout << "FIRE!\n";
return 0;
}
output
10, 9, 8, 7, 6, 5, 4, 3, 2, 1, FIRE!
```

The initialization and increase fields are optional. They can remain empty, but in all cases the semicolon signs between them must be written. For example we could write: for (;n<10;) if we wanted to specify no initialization and no increase; or for (;n<10;n++) if we wanted to include an increase field but no initialization (maybe because the variable was already initialized before).

Optionally, using the comma operator (,) we can specify more than one expression in any of the fields included in a for loop, like in initialization, for example. The comma operator (,) is an expression separator, it serves to separate more than one expression where only one is generally expected. For example, suppose that we wanted to initialize more than one variable in our loop.

```
for ( n=0, i=100 ; n!=i ; n++, i--)
{
  // whatever here...
}
```

This loop will execute for 50 times if neither n or i are modified within the loop:

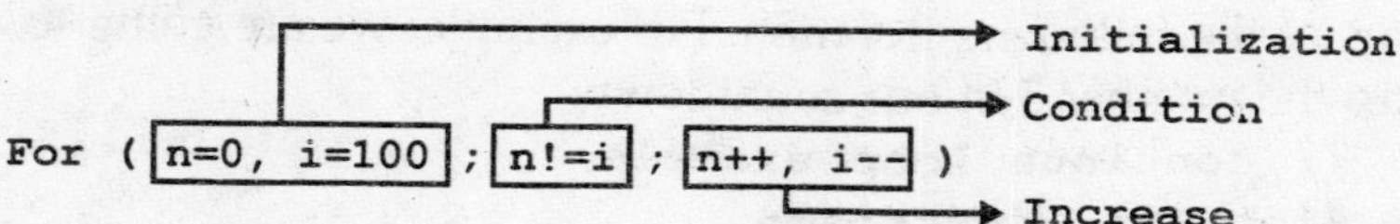

n starts with a value of 0, and i with 100, the condition is n!=i (that n is not equal to i). Because n is increased by one and i decreased by one, the loop's condition will become false after the 50th loop, when both n and i will be equal to 50.

Jump statements.

The break statement: Using break we can leave a loop even if the condition for its end is not fulfilled. It can be used to end an infinite loop, or to force it to end before its natural end. For example, we are going to stop the count down before its natural end (maybe because of an engine check failure?):

```
// break loop example
#include <iostream>
using namespace std;
int main ()
{
 int n;
 for (n=10; n>0; n--)
{
 cout << n << ", ";
 if (n==3)
{
 cout << "countdown aborted!";
 break;
 }
 }
return 0;
}
 output
 10, 9, 8, 7, 6, 5, 4, 3, countdown aborted!
```

THE CONTINUE STATEMENT

The continue statement causes the programme to skip the rest of the loop in the current iteration as if the end of the statement block had been reached, causing it to jump to the start of the following iteration. For example, we are going to skip the number 5 in our countdown:

```
// continue loop example
#include <iostream>
using namespace std;
int main ()
```

```
{
  for (int n=10; n>0; n-) {
  if (n==5) continue;
  cout << n << ", ";
}
cout << "FIRE!\n";
return 0;
}
output
10, 9, 8, 7, 6, 4, 3, 2, 1, FIRE!
```

THE GOTO STATEMENT

Goto allows to make an absolute jump to another point in the programme. You should use this feature with caution since its execution causes an unconditional jump ignoring any type of nesting limitations.

The destination point is identified by a label, which is then used as an argument for the goto statement. A label is made of a valid identifier followed by a colon (:).

Generally speaking, this instruction has no concrete use in structured or object oriented programming aside from those that low-level programming fans may find for it. For example, here is our countdown loop using goto:

```
// goto loop example
#include <iostream>
using namespace std;
int main ()
{
  int n=10;
  loop:
  cout << n << ", ";
  n-;
  if (n>0) goto loop;
  cout << "FIRE!\n";
  return 0;
}
output
10, 9, 8, 7, 6, 5, 4, 3, 2, 1, FIRE!
```

The exit function exit is a function defined in the cstdlib library. The purpose of exit is to terminate the current programme with a specific exit code. Its prototype is:

```
void exit (int exitcode);
```

The exitcode is used by some operating systems and may be used by calling programmes. By convention, an exit code of 0 means that the programme finished normally and any other value means that some error or unexpected results happened.

The selective structure: switch. The syntax of the switch statement is a bit peculiar. Its objective is to check several possible constant values for an expression. Something similar to what we did at the beginning of this section with the concatenation of several if and else if instructions. Its form is the following:

```
switch (expression)
{
  case constant1:
  group of statements 1;
  break;
  case constant2:
  group of statements 2;
  break;
.
.
.
  default:
  default group of statements
}
```

It works in the following way: switch evaluates expression and checks if it is equivalent to constant1, if it is, it executes group of statements 1 until it finds the break statement. When it finds this break statement the programme jumps to the end of the switch selective structure.

If expression was not equal to constant1 it will be checked against constant2. If it is equal to this, it will execute group of statements 2 until a break keyword is found, and then will jump to the end of the switch selective structure.

Finally, if the value of expression did not match any of the previously specified constants (you can include as many case labels as values you want to check), the programme will execute the statements included after the default: label, if it exists (since it is optional). Both of the following code fragments have the same behaviour: switch example if-else equivalent

```
switch (x) {
  case 1:
  cout << "x is 1";
  break;
  case 2:
  cout << "x is 2";
  break;
  default:
  cout << "value of x unknown";
  } if (x == 1) {
  cout << "x is 1";
  }
else if (x == 2) {
cout << "x is 2";
}
else {
cout << "value of x unknown";
}
```

The switch statement is a bit peculiar within the C++ language because it uses labels instead of blocks. This forces us to put break statements after the group of statements that we want to be executed for a specific condition. Otherwise the remainder statements -including those corresponding to other labels- will also be executed until the end of the switch selective block or a break statement is reached.

For example, if we did not include a break statement after the first group for case one, the programme will not automatically jump to the end of the switch selective block and it would continue executing the rest of statements until it reaches either a break instruction or the end of the switch selective block. This makes unnecessary to include braces { }

surrounding the statements for each of the cases, and it can also be useful to execute the same block of instructions for different possible values for the expression being evaluated.

For example:

```
switch (x) {
case 1:
case 2:
case 3:
cout << "x is 1, 2 or 3";
break;
default:
cout << "x is not 1, 2 nor 3";
}
```

Notice that switch can only be used to compare an expression against constants. Therefore we cannot put variables as labels (for example case n: where n is a variable) or ranges (case (1..3):) because they are not valid C++ constants.

If you need to check ranges or values that are not constants, use a concatenation of if and else if statements.

Functions (I): Using functions we can structure our programmes in a more modular way, accessing all the potential that structured programming can offer to us in C++.

A function is a group of statements that is executed when it is called from some point of the programme. The following is its format:

```
type name ( parameter1, parameter2,...) {
statements }
```

where:

- Type is the data type specifier of the data returned by the function.
- Name is the identifier by which it will be possible to call the function.
- Parameters (as many as needed): Each parameter consists of a data type specifier followed by an identifier, like any regular variable declaration (for example: int x) and which acts within the function as a regular local variable. They allow to pass arguments to the function when it is called. The

different parameters are separated by commas.

- Statements is the function's body. It is a block of statements surrounded by braces { }.

Here you have the first function example:

```
// function example
#include <iostream>
using namespace std;
int addition (int a, int b)
{
  int r;
  r=a+b;
  return (r);
}
int main ()
{
  int z;
  z = addition (5,3);
  cout << "The result is " << z;
  return 0;
} The result is 8
```

In order to examine this code, first of all remember something said at the beginning of this tutorial: a C++ programme always begins its execution by the main function. So we will begin there.

We can see how the main function begins by declaring the variable z of type int. Right after that, we see a call to a function called addition. Paying attention we will be able to see the similarity between the structure of the call to the function and the declaration of the function itself some code lines above.

```
Int addition (int a, int b)
              ↑       ↑
z = addition (5,      3);
```

The parameters and arguments have a clear correspondence. Within the main function we called to addition passing two values: 5 and 3, that correspond to the int a and int b parameters declared for function addition. At the point at which the function is called from within main, the control is lost by main and passed to function addition. The value of both arguments passed in the call (5 and 3) are copied to the local variables int a and int b within the function.

Function addition declares another local variable (int r), and by means of the expression r=a+b, it assigns to r the result of a plus b. Because the actual parameters passed for a and b are 5 and 3 respectively, the result is 8.

The following line of code:

```
return (r);
```

finalizes function addition, and returns the control back to the function that called it in the first place (in this case, main). At this moment the programme follows it regular course from the same point at which it was interrupted by the call to addition. But additionally, because the return statement in function addition specified a value: the content of variable r (return (r);), which at that moment had a value of 8. This value becomes the value of evaluating the function call.

```
Int addition (int a, int b)
 | 8
 ↓
z = addition (5,        3);
```

So being the value returned by a function the value given to the function call itself when it is evaluated, the variable z will be set to the value returned by addition (5, 3), that is 8. To explain it another way, you can imagine that the call to a function (addition (5,3)) is literally replaced by the value it returns (8).

The following line of code in main is:

```
cout << "The result is " << z;
```

That, as you may already expect, produces the printing of the result on the screen.

SCOPE OF VARIABLES

The scope of variables declared within a function or any other inner block is only their own function or their own block and cannot be used outside of them. For example, in the previous example it would have been impossible to use the variables a, b or r directly in function main since they were variables local to function addition. Also, it would have been impossible to use the variable z directly within function addition, since this was a variable local to the function main.

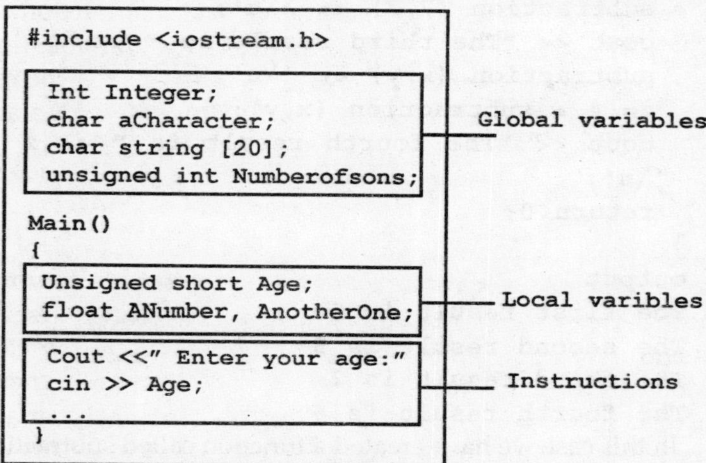

Therefore, the scope of local variables is limited to the same block level in which they are declared. Nevertheless, we also have the possibility to declare global variables; These are visible from any point of the code, inside and outside all functions. In order to declare global variables you simply have to declare the variable outside any function or block; that means, directly in the body of the programme.

And here is another example about functions:

```
// function example
#include <iostream>
using namespace std;
int subtraction (int a, int b)
{
  int r;
  r=a-b;
  return (r);
}
int main ()
{
  int x=5, y=3, z;
  z = subtraction (7,2);
  cout << "The first result is " << z <<
```

```
  '\n';
  cout << "The second result is " <<
  subtraction (7,2) << '\n';
  cout << "The third result is " <<
  subtraction (x,y) << '\n';
  z= 4 + subtraction (x,y);
  cout << "The fourth result is " << z <<
  '\n';
  return 0;
}
output
The first result is 5
The second result is 5
The third result is 2
The fourth result is 6
```

In this case we have created a function called subtraction. The only thing that this function does is to subtract both passed parameters and to return the result.

Nevertheless, if we examine function main we will see that we have made several calls to function subtraction. We have used some different calling methods so that you see other ways or moments when a function can be called.

In order to fully understand these examples you must consider once again that a call to a function could be replaced by the value that the function call itself is going to return. For example, the first case (that you should already know because it is the same pattern that we have used in previous examples):

```
z = subtraction (7,2);
cout << "The first result is " << z;
```

If we replace the function call by the value it returns (i.e., 5), we would have:

```
z = 5;
cout << "The first result is " << z;
```

As well as

```
cout << "The second result is " << subtraction
(7,2);
```

has the same result as the previous call, but in this case we made the call to subtraction directly as an insertion parameter for cout. Simply consider that the result is the same as if we had written:

```
cout << "The second result is " << 5;
```

since 5 is the value returned by subtraction (7,2).

In the case of:

```
cout << "The third result is " << subtraction
(x,y);
```

The only new thing that we introduced is that the parameters of subtraction are variables instead of constants. That is perfectly valid. In this case the values passed to function subtraction are the values of x and y, that are 5 and 3 respectively, giving 2 as result.

The fourth case is more of the same. Simply note that instead of:

```
z = 4 + subtraction (x,y);
```

we could have written:

```
z = subtraction (x,y) + 4;
```

with exactly the same result. I have switched places so you can see that the semicolon sign (;) goes at the end of the whole statement. It does not necessarily have to go right after the function call. The explanation might be once again that you imagine that a function can be replaced by its returned value:

```
z = 4 + 2;
z = 2 + 4;
```

Functions with no type. The use of void. If you remember the syntax of a function declaration:

type name (argument1, argument2 ...) statement you will see that the declaration begins with a type, that is the type of the function itself (i.e., the type of the datum that will be returned by the function with the return statement). But what if we want to return no value?

Imagine that we want to make a function just to show a message on the screen. We do not need it to return any value. In this case we should use the void type specifier for the function. This is a special specifier that indicates absence of type.

```
// void function example
#include <iostream>
using namespace std;
```

```
void printmessage ()
{
  cout << "I'm a function!";
}
int main ()
{
  printmessage ();
  return 0;
}
output
I'm a function!
```

void can also be used in the function's parameter list to explicitly specify that we want the function to take no actual parameters when it is called. For example, function printmessage could have been declared as:

```
void printmessage (void)
{
  cout << "I'm a function!";
}
```

Although it is optional to specify void in the parameter list. In C++, a parameter list can simply be left blank if we want a function with no parameters.

What you must always remember is that the format for calling a function includes specifying its name and enclosing its parameters between parentheses. The non-existence of parameters does not exempt us from the obligation to write the parentheses. For that reason the call to printmessage is:

```
printmessage ();
```

The parentheses clearly indicate that this is a call to a function and not the name of a variable or some other C++ statement. The following call would have been incorrect:

```
printmessage;
```

Functions (II): Arguments passed by value and by reference.

Until now, in all the functions we have seen, the arguments passed to the functions have been passed *by value*. This means that when calling a function with parameters, what we have passed to the function were copies of their values but never the variables themselves. For example, suppose that we called our first function addition using the following code:

```
int x=5, y=3, z;
z = addition ( x , y );
```

What we did in this case was to call to function addition passing the values of x and y, i.e. 5 and 3 respectively, but not the variables x and y themselves.

```
Int addition (int a, int b)
               ↑      ↑
z = addition (5,      3);
```

This way, when the function addition is called, the value of its local variables a and b become 5 and 3 respectively, but any modification to either a or b within the function addition will not have any effect in the values of x and y outside it, because variables x and y were not themselves passed to the function, but only copies of their values at the moment the function was called.

But there might be some cases where you need to manipulate from inside a function the value of an external variable. For that purpose we can use arguments passed by reference, as in the function duplicate of the following example:

```
// passing parameters by reference
#include <iostream>
using namespace std;
void duplicate (int& a, int& b, int& c)
{
  a*=2;
  b*=2;
  c*=2;
}
int main ()
{
  int x=1, y=3, z=7;
  duplicate (x, y, z);
  cout << "x=" << x << ", y=" << y << ", z="
 << z;
  return 0;
}
```

```
output
x=2, y=6, z=14
```

The first thing that should call your attention is that in the declaration of duplicate the type of each parameter was followed by an ampersand sign (&). This ampersand is what specifies that their corresponding arguments are to be passed *by reference* instead of *by value.*

When a variable is passed by reference we are not passing a copy of its value, but we are somehow passing the variable itself to the function and any modification that we do to the local variables will have an effect in their counterpart variables passed as arguments in the call to the function.

```
Void duplicate (int& a, int& b, int& c)
               ↕x       ↕       ↕z
     duplicate ( x,     y,      z);
```

To explain it in another way, we associate a, b and c with the arguments passed on the function call (x, y and z) and any change that we do on a within the function will affect the value of x outside it. Any change that we do on b will affect y, and the same with c and z.

That is why our program's output, that shows the values stored in x, y and z after the call to duplicate, shows the values of all the three variables of main doubled.

If when declaring the following function:

```
void duplicate (int& a, int& b, int& c)
```

we had declared it this way:

```
void duplicate (int a, int b, int c)
```

i.e., without the ampersand signs (&), we would have not passed the variables by reference, but a copy of their values instead, and therefore, the output on screen of our programme would have been the values of x, y and z without having been modified.

Passing by reference is also an effective way to allow a function to return more than one value. For example, here is a function that returns the previous and next numbers of the first parameter passed.

```
// more than one returning value
#include <iostream>
```

```
using namespace std;
void prevnext (int x, int& prev, int& next)
{
  prev = x-1;
  next = x+1;
}
int main ()
{
  int x=100, y, z;
  prevnext (x, y, z);
  cout << "Previous=" << y << ", Next=" <<
  z;
  return 0;
}
output
Previous=99, Next=101
```

Default values in parameters.

When declaring a function we can specify a default value for each parameter. This value will be used if the corresponding argument is left blank when calling to the function. To do that, we simply have to use the assignment operator and a value for the arguments in the function declaration. If a value for that parameter is not passed when the function is called, the default value is used, but if a value is specified this default value is ignored and the passed value is used instead. For example:

```
// default values in functions
#include <iostream>
using namespace std;
int divide (int a, int b=2)
{
  int r;
  r=a/b;
  return (r);
}
  int main ()
{
  cout << divide (12);
```

```
  cout << endl;
  cout << divide (20,4);
  return 0;
}
output
6
5
```

As we can see in the body of the programme there are two calls to function divide. In the first one:

```
divide (12)
```

we have only specified one argument, but the function divide allows up to two. So the function divide has assumed that the second parameter is 2 since that is what we have specified to happen if this parameter was not passed (notice the function declaration, which finishes with int b=2, not just int b). Therefore the result of this function call is 6 (12/2).

In the second call:

```
divide (20,4)
```

there are two parameters, so the default value for b (int b=2) is ignored and b takes the value passed as argument, that is 4, making the result returned equal to 5 (20/4).

Overloaded functions: In C++ two different functions can have the same name if their parameter types or number are different. That means that you can give the same name to more than one function if they have either a different number of parameters or different types in their parameters. For example:

```
// overloaded function
#include <iostream>
using namespace std;
int operate (int a, int b)
{
  return (a*b);
}
float operate (float a, float b)
{
  return (a/b);
}
int main ()
```

```
{
   int x=5,y=2;
   float n=5.0,m=2.0;
   cout << operate (x,y);
   cout << "\n";
   cout << operate (n,m);
   cout << "\n";
   return 0;
}
output
10 2.5
```

In this case we have defined two functions with the same name, operate, but one of them accepts two parameters of type int and the other one accepts them of type float. The compiler knows which one to call in each case by examining the types passed as arguments when the function is called. If it is called with two ints as its arguments it calls to the function that has two int parameters in its prototype and if it is called with two floats it will call to the one which has two float parameters in its prototype.

In the first call to operate the two arguments passed are of type int, therefore, the function with the first prototype is called; This function returns the result of multiplying both parameters. While the second call passes two arguments of type float, so the function with the second prototype is called. This one has a different behaviour: it divides one parameter by the other. So the behaviour of a call to operate depends on the type of the arguments passed because the function has been *overloaded*.

Notice that a function cannot be overloaded only by its return type. At least one of its parameters must have a different type.

INLINE FUNCTIONS

The inline specifier indicates the compiler that inline substitution is preferred to the usual function call mechanism for a specific function. This does not change the behaviour of a function itself, but is used to suggest to the compiler that the code generated by the function body is inserted at each point the function is called, instead of being inserted only once and perform a regular call to it, which generally involves some additional overhead in running time.

The format for its declaration is:

```
inline type name ( arguments ...) {
instructions ... }
```

and the call is just like the call to any other function. You do not have to include the inline keyword when calling the function, only in its declaration.

Most compilers already optimize code to generate inline functions when it is more convenient. This specifier only indicates the compiler that inline is preferred for this function.

Recursivity: Recursivity is the property that functions have to be called by themselves. It is useful for many tasks, like sorting or calculate the factorial of numbers. For example, to obtain the factorial of a number (n!) the mathematical formula would be:

```
n! = n * (n-1) * (n-2) * (n-3)... * 1
```

more concretely, 5! (factorial of 5) would be:

```
5! = 5 * 4 * 3 * 2 * 1 = 120
```

and a recursive function to calculate this in C++ could be:

```
// factorial calculator
#include <iostream>
using namespace std;
long factorial (long a)
{
  if (a > 1)
  return (a * factorial (a-1));
  else
  return (1);
}
int main ()
{
  long number;
  cout << "Please type a number: ";
  cin >> number;
  cout << number << "! = " << factorial
```

```
  (number);
  return 0;
}
output
Please type a number: 9
9! = 362880
```

Notice how in function factorial we included a call to itself, but only if the argument passed was greater than 1, since otherwise the function would perform an infinite recursive loop in which once it arrived to 0 it would continue multiplying by all the negative numbers (probably provoking a stack overflow error on runtime).

This function has a limitation because of the data type we used in its design (long) for more simplicity. The results given will not be valid for values much greater than 10! or 15!, depending on the system you compile it.

DECLARING FUNCTIONS.

Until now, we have defined all of the functions before the first appearance of calls to them in the source code. These calls were generally in function main which we have always left at the end of the source code. If you try to repeat some of the examples of functions described so far, but placing the function main before any of the other functions that were called from within it, you will most likely obtain compiling errors. The reason is that to be able to call a function it must have been declared in some earlier point of the code, like we have done in all our examples.

But there is an alternative way to avoid writing the whole code of a function before it can be used in main or in some other function. This can be achieved by declaring just a prototype of the function before it is used, instead of the entire definition. This declaration is shorter than the entire definition, but significant enough for the compiler to determine its return type and the types of its parameters.

Its form is:

```
type name ( argument_type1,
argument_type2,...);
```

It is identical to a function definition, except that it does not include the body of the function itself (i.e., the function statements that in normal definitions are enclosed in braces { }) and instead of that we end the prototype declaration with a mandatory semicolon (;).

The parameter enumeration does not need to include the identifiers, but only the type specifiers. The inclusion of a name for each parameter as in the function definition is optional in the prototype declaration. For example, we can declare a function called protofunction with two int parameters with any of the following declarations:

```
int protofunction (int first, int second);
int protofunction (int, int);
```

Anyway, including a name for each variable makes the prototype more legible.

```
// declaring functions prototypes
#include <iostream>
using namespace std;
void odd (int a);
void even (int a);
int main ()
{
  int i;
  do {
  cout << "Type a number (0 to exit): ";
  cin >> i;
  odd (i);
} while (i!=0);
  return 0;
}
  void odd (int a)
{
  if ((a%2)!=0) cout << "Number is odd.\n";
  else even (a);
}
  void even (int a)
{
  if ((a%2)==0) cout << "Number is even.\n";
```

```
  else odd (a);
}
output
Type a number (0 to exit): 9
Number is odd.
Type a number (0 to exit): 6
Number is even.
Type a number (0 to exit): 1030
Number is even.
Type a number (0 to exit): 0
Number is even.
```

This example is indeed not an example of efficiency. I am sure that at this point you can already make a programme with the same result, but using only half of the code lines that have been used in this example. Anyway this example illustrates how prototyping works. Moreover, in this concrete example the prototyping of at least one of the two functions is necessary in order to compile the code without errors.

The first things that we see are the declaration of functions odd and even:

```
void odd (int a);
void even (int a);
```

This allows these functions to be used before they are defined, for example, in main, which now is located where some people find it to be a more logical place for the start of a programme: the beginning of the source code.

Anyway, the reason why this programme needs at least one of the functions to be declared before it is defined is because in odd there is a call to even and in even there is a call to odd. If none of the two functions had been previously declared, a compilation error would happen, since either odd would not not be visible from even (because it has still not been declared), or even would not be visible from odd (for the same reason).

Having the prototype of all functions together in the same place within the source code is found practical by some programmers, and this can be easily achieved by declaring all functions prototypes at the beginning of a programme.

Arrays: An array is a series of elements of the same type placed in contiguous memory locations that can be individually referenced by adding an index to a unique identifier.

That means that, for example, we can store 5 values of type int in an array without having to declare 5 different variables, each one with a different identifier. Instead of that, using an array we can store 5 different values of the same type, int for example, with a unique identifier.

For example, an array to contain 5 integer values of type int called billy could be represented like this:

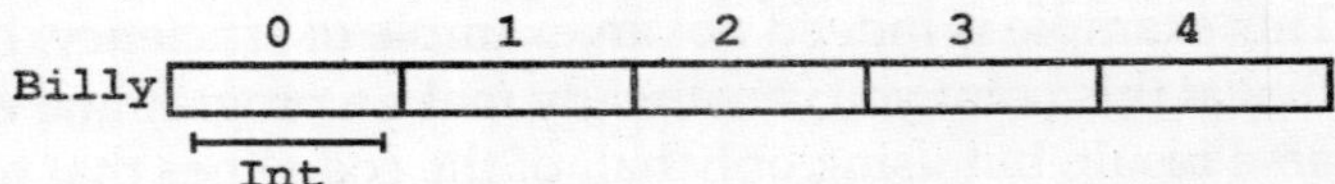

where each blank panel represents an element of the array, that in this case are integer values of type int. These elements are numbered from 0 to 4 since in arrays the first index is always 0, independently of its length.

Like a regular variable, an array must be declared before it is used. A typical declaration for an array in C++ is:

Type name [elements]; where type is a valid type (like int, float...), name is a valid identifier and the elements field (which is always enclosed in square brackets []), specifies how many of these elements the array has to contain.

Therefore, in order to declare an array called billy as the one shown in the above diagram it is as simple as:

```
int billy [5];
```

Note: The elements field within brackets [] which represents the number of elements the array is going to hold, must be a constant value, since arrays are blocks of non-dynamic memory whose size must be determined before execution. In order to create arrays with a variable length dynamic memory is needed, which is explained later in these tutorials.

Initializing arrays: When declaring a regular array of local scope (within a function, for example), if we do not specify otherwise, its elements will not be initialized to any value by default, so their content will be undetermined until we store some value in them. The elements of global and static arrays, on the other hand, are automatically initialized with their default values, which for all fundamental types this means they are filled with zeros.

In both cases, local and global, when we declare an array, we have the possibility to assign initial values to each one of its elements by enclosing the values in braces { }.

For example:

```
int billy [5] = { 16, 2, 77, 40, 12071 };
```

This declaration would have created an array like this:

	0	1	2	3	4
Billy	16	2	77	40	12071

The amount of values between braces { } must not be larger than the number of elements that we declare for the array between square brackets [ ]. For example, in the example of array billy we have declared that it has 5 elements and in the list of initial values within braces { } we have specified 5 values, one for each element.

When an initialization of values is provided for an array, C++ allows the possibility of leaving the square brackets empty [ ]. In this case, the compiler will assume a size for the array that matches the number of values included between braces { }:

```
int billy [] = { 16, 2, 77, 40, 12071 };
```

After this declaration, array billy would be 5 ints long, since we have provided 5 initialization values.

Accessing the values of an array.

In any point of a programme in which an array is visible, we can access the value of any of its elements individually as if it was a normal variable, thus being able to both read and modify its value. The format is as simple as:

name[index]

Following the previous examples in which billy had 5 elements and each of those elements was of type int, the name which we can use to refer to each element is the following:

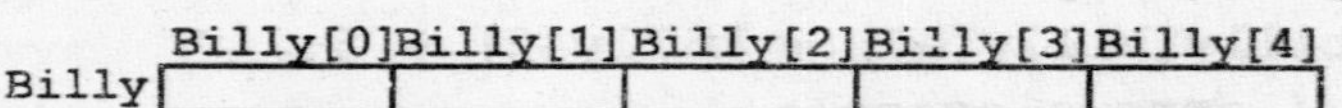

For example, to store the value 75 in the third element of billy, we could write the following statement:

```
billy[2] = 75;
```

and, for example, to pass the value of the third element of billy to a variable called a, we could write:

```
a = billy[2];
```

Therefore, the expression billy[2] is for all purposes like a variable of type int.

Notice that the third element of billy is specified billy[2], since the first one is billy[0], the second one is billy[1], and therefore, the third one is billy[2]. By this same reason, its last element is billy[4]. Therefore, if we write billy[5], we would be accessing the sixth element of billy and therefore exceeding the size of the array.

In C++ it is syntactically correct to exceed the valid range of indices for an array. This can create problems, since accessing out-of-range elements do not cause compilation errors but can cause runtime errors. The reason why this is allowed will be seen further ahead when we begin to use pointers.

At this point it is important to be able to clearly distinguish between the two uses that brackets [ ] have related to arrays. They perform two different tasks: one is to specify the size of arrays when they are declared; and the second one is to specify indices for concrete array elements. Do not confuse these two possible uses of brackets [ ] with arrays.

```
int billy[5]; // declaration of a new array
billy[2] = 75; // access to an element of
 the array.
```

If you read carefully, you will see that a type specifier always precedes a variable or array declaration, while it never precedes an access.

Some other valid operations with arrays:

```
billy[0] = a;
billy[a] = 75;
b = billy [a+2];
billy[billy[a]] = billy[2] + 5;
// arrays example
#include <iostream>
using namespace std;
```

```
int billy [] = {16, 2, 77, 40, 12071};
int n, result=0;
int main ()
{
  for ( n=0 ; n<5 ; n++)
{
  result += billy[n];
}
  cout << result;
  return 0;
}
output
12206
```

MULTIDIMENSIONAL ARRAYS

Multidimensional arrays can be described as "arrays of arrays". For example, a bidimensional array can be imagined as a bidimensional table made of elements, all of them of a same uniform data type.

Jimmy	0	1	2	3	4
0					
1					
2					

jimmy represents a bidimensional array of 3 per 5 elements of type int. The way to declare this array in C++ would be:

```
int jimmy [3][5];
```

and, for example, the way to reference the second element vertically and fourth horizontally in an expression would be:

```
jimmy[1][3]
```

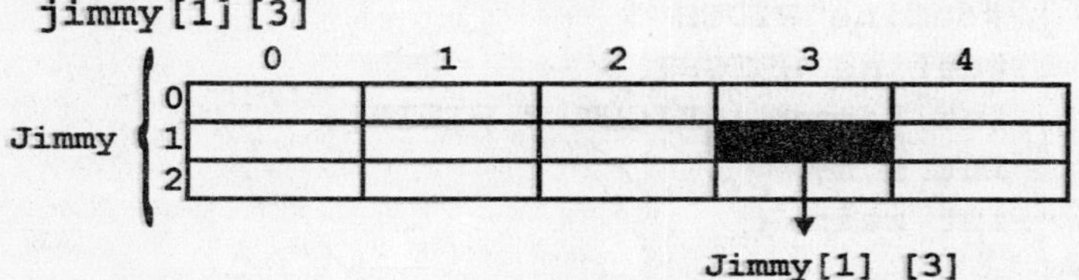

(remember that array indices always begin by zero).

Multidimensional arrays are not limited to two indices (i.e., two dimensions). They can contain as many indices as needed. But be careful! The amount of memory needed for an array rapidly increases with each dimension. For example:

```
char century [100][365][24][60][60];
```

declares an array with a char element for each second in a century, that is more than 3 billion chars. So this declaration would consume more than 3 gigabytes of memory!

Multidimensional arrays are just an abstraction for programmers, since we can obtain the same results with a simple array just by putting a factor between its indices:

```
int jimmy [3][5]; // is equivalent to
int jimmy [15]; // (3 * 5 = 15)
```

With the only difference that with multidimensional arrays the compiler remembers the depth of each imaginary dimension for us. Take as example these two pieces of code, with both exactly the same result. One uses a bidimensional array and the other one uses a simple array:

multidimensional array pseudo-multidimensional array

```
#define WIDTH 5
#define HEIGHT 3
int jimmy [HEIGHT][WIDTH];
int n,m;
int main ()
{
  for (n=0;n<HEIGHT;n++)
  for (m=0;m<WIDTH;m++)
{
  jimmy[n][m]=(n+1)*(m+1);
 }
  return 0;
} #define WIDTH 5
  #define HEIGHT 3
  int jimmy [HEIGHT * WIDTH];
  int n,m;
  int main ()
{
  for (n=0;n<HEIGHT;n++)
  for (m=0;m<WIDTH;m++)
{
```

```
    jimmy[n*WIDTH+m]=(n+1)*(m+1);
  }
  return 0;
}
```

None of the two source codes above produce any output on the screen, but both assign values to the memory block called jimmy in the following way:

Jimmy	0	1	2	3	4
0	1	2	3	4	5
1	2	4	6	8	10
2	3	6	9	12	15

We have used "defined constants" (#define) to simplify possible future modifications of the programme. For example, in case that we decided to enlarge the array to a height of 4 instead of 3 it could be done simply by changing the line:

```
#define HEIGHT 3
```

to:

```
#define HEIGHT 4
```

with no need to make any other modifications to the programme.

Arrays as parameters:

At some moment we may need to pass an array to a function as a parameter. In C++ it is not possible to pass a complete block of memory by value as a parameter to a function, but we are allowed to pass its address. In practice this has almost the same effect and it is a much faster and more efficient operation.

In order to accept arrays as parameters the only thing that we have to do when declaring the function is to specify in its parameters the element type of the array, an identifier and a pair of void brackets [].

For example, the following function:

```
void procedure (int arg[])
```

accepts a parameter of type "array of int" called arg. In order to pass to this function an array declared as:

```
int myarray [40];
```

it would be enough to write a call like this:

```
procedure (myarray);
```

Here you have a complete example:

```
// arrays as parameters
#include <iostream>
using namespace std;
void printarray (int arg[], int length) {
for (int n=0; n<length; n++)
cout << arg[n] << " ";
cout << "\n";
}
  int main ()
{
  int firstarray[] = {5, 10, 15};
  int secondarray[] = {2, 4, 6, 8, 10};
  printarray (firstarray,3);
  printarray (secondarray,5);
  return 0;
}
output
5 10 15 2 4 6 8 10
```

As you can see, the first parameter (int arg[]) accepts any array whose elements are of type int, whatever its length. For that reason we have included a second parameter that tells the function the length of each array that we pass to it as its first parameter. This allows the for loop that prints out the array to know the range to iterate in the passed array without going out of range.

In a function declaration it is also possible to include multidimensional arrays. The format for a tridimensional array parameter is:

```
base_type[][depth][depth]
```

for example, a function with a multidimensional array as argument could be:

```
void procedure (int myarray[][3][4])
```

Notice that the first brackets [] are left blank while the following ones are not. This is so because the compiler must be able to determine within the function which is the depth of each additional dimension. Arrays, both simple or multidimensional, passed as function parameters are a quite common source of errors for novice programmers. I recommend the reading of the chapter about Pointers for a better understanding on how arrays operate.

CHARACTER SEQUENCES

As you may already know, the C++ Standard Library implements a powerful string class, which is very useful to handle and manipulate strings of characters. However, because strings are in fact sequences of characters, we can represent them also as plain arrays of char elements.

For example, the following array:

```
char jenny [20];
```

is an array that can store up to 20 elements of type char. It can be represented as:

Therefore, in this array, in theory, we can store sequences of characters up to 20 characters long. But we can also store shorter sequences. For example, jenny could store at some point in a programme either the sequence "Hello" or the sequence "Merry christmas", since both are shorter than 20 characters.

Therefore, since the array of characters can store shorter sequences than its total length, a special character is used to signal the end of the valid sequence: the *null character*, whose literal constant can be written as '\0' (backslash, zero).

Our array of 20 elements of type char, called jenny, can be represented storing the characters sequences "Hello" and "Merry Christmas" as:

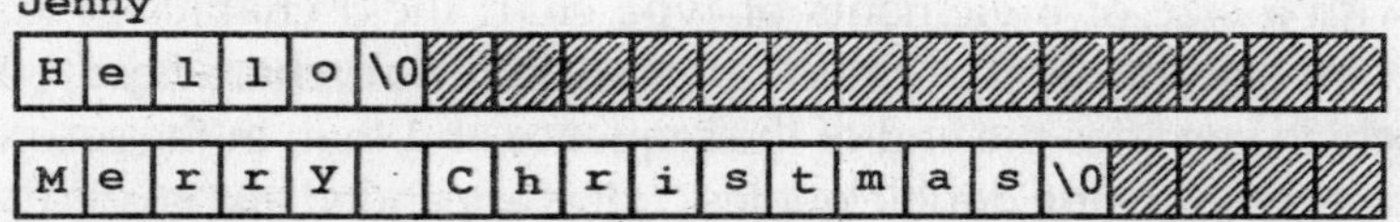

Notice how after the valid content a null character ('\0') has been included in order to indicate the end of the sequence. The panels in gray colour represent char elements with undetermined values. Initialization of null-terminated character sequences

Because arrays of characters are ordinary arrays they follow all their same rules. For example, if we want to initialize an array of characters with some predetermined sequence of characters we can do it just like any other array:

```
char myword[] = { 'H', 'e', 'l', 'l', 'o',
'\0' };
```

In this case we would have declared an array of 6 elements of type char initialized with the characters that form the word "Hello" plus a null character '\0' at the end.

But arrays of char elements have an additional method to initialize their values: using string literals. In the expressions we have used in some examples in previous chapters, constants that represent entire strings of characters have already showed up several times. These are specified enclosing the text to become a string literal between double quotes (").

For example:

```
"the result is: "
```

is a constant string literal that we have probably used already. Double quoted strings (") are literal constants whose type is in fact a null-terminated array of characters. So string literals enclosed between double quotes always have a null character ('\0') automatically appended at the end. Therefore we can initialize the array of char elements called myword with a null-terminated sequence of characters by either one of these two methods:

```
char myword [] = { 'H', 'e', 'l', 'l', 'o',
'\0' };
char myword [] = "Hello";
```

In both cases the array of characters myword is declared with a size of 6 elements of type char: the 5 characters that compose the word "Hello" plus a final null character ('\0') which specifies the end of the sequence and that, in the second case, when using double quotes (") it is appended automatically.

Please notice that we are talking about initializing an array of characters in the moment it is being declared, and not about assigning values to them once they have already been declared. In fact because this type of null-terminated arrays of characters are regular arrays we have the same restrictions that we have with any other array, so we are not able to copy blocks of data with an assignment operation.

Assuming mystext is a char[] variable, expressions within a source code like:

```
mystext = "Hello";
mystext[] = "Hello";
```

would not be valid, like neither would be:

```
mystext = { 'H', 'e', 'l', 'l', 'o', '\0' };
```

The reason for this may become more comprehensible once you know a bit more about pointers, since then it will be clarified that an array is in fact a constant pointer pointing to a block of memory.

Using null-terminated sequences of characters: Null-terminated sequences of characters are the natural way of treating strings in C++, so they can be used as such in many procedures. In fact, regular string literals have this type (char[]) and can also be used in most cases. For example, cin and cout support null-terminated sequences as valid containers for sequences of characters, so they can be used directly to extract strings of characters from cin or to insert them into cout.

For example:

```
// null-terminated sequences of characters
#include <iostream>
using namespace std;
int main ()
{
  char question[] = "Please, enter your first
  name: ";
  char greeting[] = "Hello, ";
  char yourname [80];
  cout << question;
  cin >> yourname;
  cout << greeting << yourname << "!";
  return 0;
}
output
Please, enter your first name: John
Hello, John!
```

As you can see, we have declared three arrays of char elements. The first two were initialized with string literal constants, while the third one was left uninitialized. In any case, we have to speficify the size of the array: in the first two (question and greeting) the size was implicitly defined by the length of the literal constant they were initialized to. While for yourname we have explicitly specified that it has a size of 80 chars. Finally, sequences of characters stored in char arrays can easily be converted into string objects just by using the assignment operator:

```
string mystring;
char myntcs[]="some text";
mystring = myntcs;
```

POINTERS

We have already seen how variables are seen as memory cells that can be accessed using their identifiers. This way we did not have to care about the physical location of our data within memory, we simply used its identifier whenever we wanted to refer to our variable. The memory of your computer can be imagined as a succession of memory cells, each one of the minimal size that computers manage (one byte).

These single-byte memory cells are numbered in a consecutive way, so as, within any block of memory, every cell has the same number as the previous one plus one. This way, each cell can be easily located in the memory because it has a unique address and all the memory cells follow a successive pattern. For example, if we are looking for cell 1776 we know that it is going to be right between cells 1775 and 1777, exactly one thousand cells after 776 and exactly one thousand cells before cell 2776.

REFERENCE OPERATOR (&)

As soon as we declare a variable, the amount of memory needed is assigned for it at a specific location in memory (its memory address). We generally do not actively decide the exact location of the variable within the panel of cells that we have imagined the memory to be - Fortunately, that is a task automatically performed by the operating system during runtime. However, in some cases we may be interested in knowing the address where our variable is being stored during runtime in order to operate with relative positions to it.

The address that locates a variable within memory is what we call a *reference* to that variable. This reference to a variable can be obtained by preceding the identifier of a variable with an ampersand sign (&), known as reference operator, and which can be literally translated as "address of". For example:

```
ted = &andy;
```

This would assign to ted the address of variable andy, since when preceding the name of the variable andy with the reference operator (&) we are no longer talking about the content of the variable itself, but about its reference (i.e., its address in memory). For now on we are going to assume that andy is placed during runtime in the memory address 1776. This number (1776) is just and arbitrary assumption we are inventing right now in order to help clarify some concepts in this tutorial, but in reality, we cannot know before runtime the real value the address of a variable will have in memory.

Consider the following code fragment:

```
andy = 25;
fred = andy;
ted = &andy;
```

The values contained in each variable after the execution of this, are shown in the following diagram:

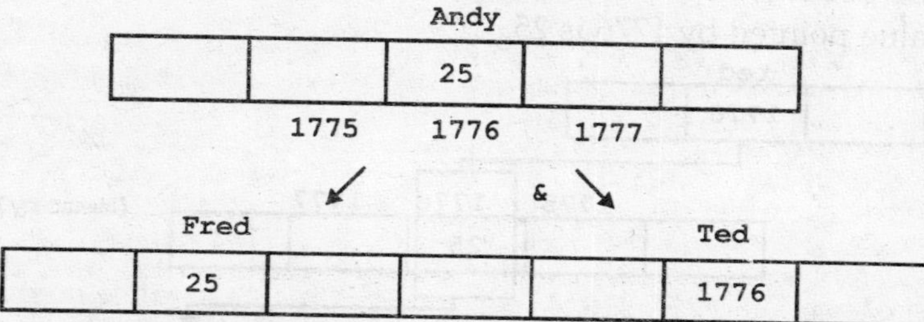

First, we have assigned the value 25 to andy (a variable whose address in memory we have assumed to be 1776). The second statement copied to fred the content of variable andy (which is 25). This is a standard assignment operation, as we have done so many times before. Finally, the third statement copies to ted not the value contained in andy but a reference to it (i.e., its address, which we have assumed to be 1776).

The reason is that in this third assignment operation we have preceded the identifier andy with the reference operator (&), so we were no longer referring to the value of andy but to its reference (its address in memory). The variable that stores the reference to another variable (like ted in the previous example) is what we call a *pointer*. Pointers are a very powerful feature of the C++ language that has many uses in advanced programming. Farther ahead, we will see how this type of variable is used and declared.

Dereference Operator (*)

We have just seen that a variable which stores a reference to another variable is called a pointer. Pointers are said to "point to" the variable whose reference they store.

Using a pointer we can directly access the value stored in the variable which it points to. To do this, we simply have to precede the pointer's identifier with an asterisk (*), which acts as dereference operator and that can be literally translated to "value pointed by". Therefore, following with the values of the previous example, if we write.

```
beth = *ted;
```

(that we could read as: "beth equal to value pointed by ted") beth would take the value 25, since ted is 1776, and the value pointed by 1776 is 25.

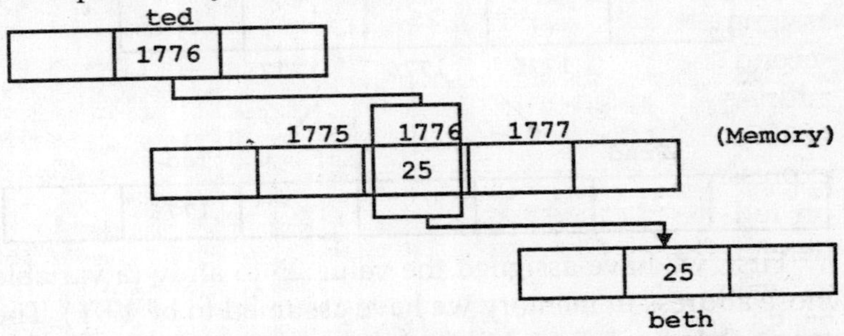

You must clearly differentiate that the expression ted refers to the value 1776, while *ted (with an asterisk * preceding the identifier) refers to the value stored at address 1776, which in this case is 25. Notice the difference of including or not including the dereference operator (I have included an explanatory commentary of how each of these two expressions could be read):

```
beth = ted; // beth equal to ted ( 1776 )
beth = *ted; // beth equal to value pointed
by ted ( 25 )
```

Notice the difference between the reference and dereference operators:

- & is the reference operator and can be read as "address of"
- * is the dereference operator and can be read as "value pointed by"

Thus, they have complementary (or opposite) meanings. A variable referenced with & can be dereferenced with *.

Earlier we performed the following two assignment operations:

```
andy = 25;
ted = &andy;
```

Right after these two statements, all of the following expressions would give true as result:

```
andy == 25
&andy == 1776
ted == 1776
*ted == 25
```

The first expression is quite clear considering that the assignment operation performed on andy was andy=25. The second one uses the reference operator (&), which returns the address of variable andy, which we assumed it to have a value of 1776. The third one is somewhat obvious since the second expression was true and the assignment operation performed on ted was ted=&andy. The fourth expression uses the dereference operator (*) that, as we have just seen, can be read as "value pointed by", and the value pointed by ted is indeed 25. So, after all that, you may also infer that for as long as the address pointed by ted remains unchanged the following expression will also be true.

```
*ted == andy
```

Declaring Variables of Pointer Types

Due to the ability of a pointer to directly refer to the value that it points to, it becomes necessary to specify in its declaration which data type a pointer is going point to. It is not the same thing to point to a char than to point to an int or a float.

The declaration of pointers follows this format:

type * name;

where type is the data type of the value that the pointer is intended to point to. This type is not the type of the pointer itself! but the type of the data the pointer points to. For example:

```
int * number;
char * character;
float * greatnumber;
```

These are three declarations of pointers. Each one is intended to point to a different data type, but in fact all of them are pointers and all of them will occupy the same amount of space in memory (the size in memory of a pointer depends on the platform where the code is going to run). Nevertheless, the data to which they point to do not occupy the same amount of space nor are of the same type: the first one points to an int, the second one to a char and the last one to a float. Therefore, although these three example variables are all of them pointers which occupy the same size in memory, they are said to have different types: int*, char* and float* respectively, depending on the type they point to.

I want to emphasize that the asterisk sign (*) that we use when declaring a pointer only means that it is a pointer (it is part of its type compound specifier), and should not be confused with the dereference operator that we have seen a bit earlier, but which is also written with an asterisk (*). They are simply two different things represented with the same sign.

Now have a look at this code:

```
// my first pointer
#include <iostream>
```

```
using namespace std;
int main ()
{
  int firstvalue, secondvalue;
  int * mypointer;
  mypointer = &firstvalue;
  *mypointer = 10;
  mypointer = &secondvalue;
  *mypointer = 20;
  cout << "firstvalue is " << firstvalue <<
 endl;
  cout << "secondvalue is " << secondvalue
 << endl;
  return 0;
}
firstvalue is 10
secondvalue is 20
```

Notice that even though we have never directly set a value to either firstvalue or secondvalue, both end up with a value set indirectly through the use of mypointer. This is the procedure:

First, we have assigned as value of mypointer a reference to firstvalue using the reference operator (&). And then we have assigned the value 10 to the memory location pointed by mypointer, that because at this moment is pointing to the memory location of firstvalue, this in fact modifies the value of firstvalue.

In order to demonstrate that a pointer may take several different values during the same programme I have repeated the process with secondvalue and that same pointer, mypointer.

Here is an example a little bit more elaborated:

```
// more pointers
#include <iostream>
using namespace std;
int main ()
{
  int firstvalue = 5, secondvalue = 15;
```

```
  int * p1, * p2;
  p1 = &firstvalue; // p1 = address of
  firstvalue
  p2 = &secondvalue; // p2 = address of
  secondvalue
  *p1 = 10; // value pointed by p1 = 10
  *p2 = *p1; // value pointed by p2 = value
  pointed by p1
  p1 = p2; // p1 = p2 (value of pointer is
  copied)
  *p1 = 20; // value pointed by p1 = 20
  cout << "firstvalue is " << firstvalue <<
  endl;
  cout << "secondvalue is " << secondvalue
 <<
  endl;
  return 0;
}
firstvalue is 10
secondvalue is 20
```

Notice that there are expressions with pointers p1 and p2, both with and without dereference operator (*). The meaning of an expression using the dereference operator (*) is very different from one that does not: When this operator precedes the pointer name, the expression refers to the value being pointed, while when a pointer name appears without this operator, it refers to the value of the pointer itself (i.e. the address of what the pointer is pointing to).

Another thing that may call your attention is the line:

```
int * p1, * p2;
```

This declares the two pointers used in the previous example. But notice that there is an asterisk (*) for each pointer, in order for both to have type int* (pointer to int).

Otherwise, the type for the second variable declared in that line would have been int (and not int*) because of precedence relationships. If we had written:

```
int * p1, p2;
```

p1 would indeed have int* type, but p2 would have type

int (spaces do not matter at all for this purpose). This is due to operator precedence rules. But anyway, simply remembering that you have to put one asterisk per pointer is enough for most pointer users.

Pointers and Arrays

The concept of array is very much bound to the one of pointer. In fact, the identifier of an array is equivalent to the address of its first element, as a pointer is equivalent to the address of the first element that it points to, so in fact they are the same concept. For example, supposing these two declarations:

```
int numbers [20];
int * p;
```

The following assignment operation would be valid:

```
p = numbers;
```

After that, p and numbers would be equivalent and would have the same properties. The only difference is that we could change the value of pointer p by another one, whereas numbers will always point to the first of the 20 elements of type int with which it was defined. Therefore, unlike p, which is an ordinary pointer, numbers is an array, and an array can be considered a *constant pointer*. Therefore, the following allocation would not be valid:

```
numbers = p;
```

Because numbers is an array, so it operates as a constant pointer, and we cannot assign values to constants. Due to the characteristics of variables, all expressions that include pointers in the following example are perfectly valid:

```
// more pointers
#include <iostream>
using namespace std;
int main ()
{
  int numbers[5];
  int * p;
  p = numbers; *p = 10;
  p++; *p = 20;
```

```
    p = &numbers[2]; *p = 30;
    p = numbers + 3; *p = 40;
    p = numbers; *(p+4) = 50;
    for (int n=0; n<5; n++)
    cout << numbers[n] << ", ";
    return 0;
  }
  10, 20, 30, 40, 50,
```

In the chapter about arrays we used brackets ([]) several times in order to specify the index of an element of the array to which we wanted to refer. Well, these bracket sign operators [] are also a dereference operator known as *offset operator*. They dereference the variable they follow just as * does, but they also add the number between brackets to the address being dereferenced. For example:

```
a[5] = 0; // a [offset of 5] = 0
*(a+5) = 0; // pointed by (a+5) = 0
```

These two expressions are equivalent and valid both if a is a pointer or if a is an array.

POINTER INITIALIZATION

When declaring pointers we may want to explicitly specify which variable we want them to point to:

```
int number;
int *tommy = &number;
```

The behaviour of this code is equivalent to:

```
int number;
int *tommy;
tommy = &number;
```

When a pointer initialization takes place we are always assigning the reference value to where the pointer points (tommy), never the value being pointed (*tommy). You must consider that at the moment of declaring a pointer, the asterisk (*) indicates only that it is a pointer, it is not the dereference operator (although both use the same sign: *). Remember, they are two different functions of one sign. Thus, we must take care not to confuse the previous code with.

```
int number;
```

```
int *tommy;
*tommy = &number;
```

that is incorrect, and anyway would not have much sense in this case if you think about it. As in the case of arrays, the compiler allows the special case that we want to initialize the content at which the pointer points with constants at the same moment the pointer is declared:

```
char * terry = "hello";
```

In this case, memory space is reserved to contain "hello" and then a pointer to the first character of this memory block is assigned to terry. If we imagine that "hello" is stored at the memory locations that start at addresses 1702, we can represent the previous declaration as:

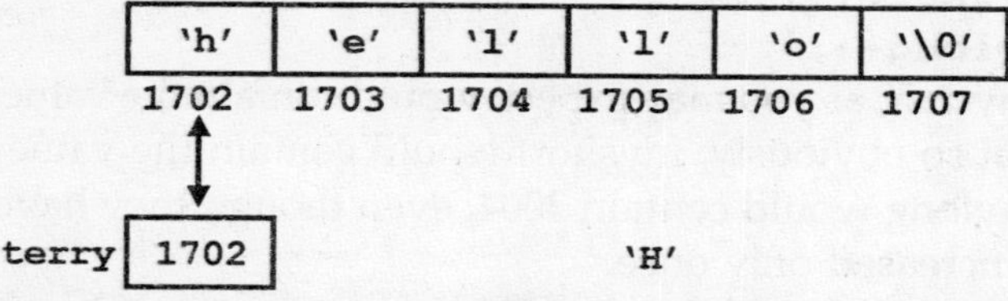

It is important to indicate that terry contains the value 1702, and not 'h' nor "hello", although 1702 indeed is the address of both of these.

The pointer terry points to a sequence of characters and can be read as if it was an array (remember that an array is just like a constant pointer). For example, we can access the fifth element of the array with any of these two expression:

```
*(terry+4)
terry[4]
```

Both expressions have a value of 'o' (the fifth element of the array).

POINTER ARITHMETICS

To conduct arithmetical operations on pointers is a little different than to conduct them on regular integer data types. To begin with, only addition and subtraction operations are allowed to be conducted with them, the others make no sense in the world of pointers. But both addition and subtraction have a different behaviour with pointers according to the size of the data type to which they point. When we saw the different fundamental data types, we saw that some occupy more or less space than others in the memory. For example, let's assume that in a given compiler for a specific machine, char takes 1 byte, short takes 2 bytes and long takes 4.

Suppose that we define three pointers in this compiler:

```
char *mychar;
short *myshort;
long *mylong;
```

and that we know that they point to memory locations 1000, 2000 and 3000 respectively.

So if we write:

```
mychar++;
myshort++;
mylong++;
```

mychar, as you may expect, would contain the value 1001. But not so obviously, myshort would contain the value 2002, and mylong would contain 3004, even though they have each been increased only once.

The reason is that when adding one to a pointer we are making it to point to the following element of the same type with which it has been defined, and therefore the size in bytes of the type pointed is added to the pointer.

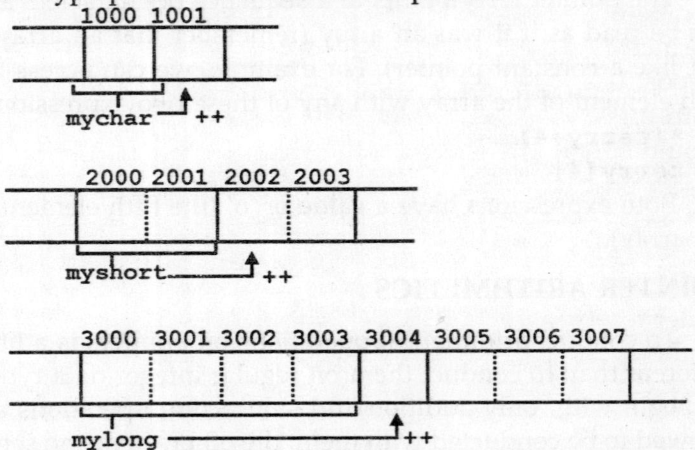

This is applicable both when adding and subtracting any number to a pointer. It would happen exactly the same if we write:

```
mychar = mychar + 1;
myshort = myshort + 1;
mylong = mylong + 1;
```

Both the increase (++) and decrease (—) operators have greater operator precedence than the dereference operator (*), but both have a special behaviour when used as suffix (the expression is evaluated with the value it had before being increased). Therefore, the following expression may lead to confusion:

```
*p++
```

Because ++ has greater precedence than *, this expression is equivalent to *(p++). Therefore, what it does is to increase the value of p (so it now points to the next element), but because ++ is used as postfix the whole expression is evaluated as the value pointed by the original reference (the address the pointer pointed to before being increased).

Notice the difference with:

```
(*p)++
```

Here, the expression would have been evaluated as the value pointed by p increased by one. The value of p (the pointer itself) would not be modified (what is being modified is what it is being pointed to by this pointer). If we write.

```
*p++ = *q++;
```

Because ++ has a higher precedence than *, both p and q are increased, but because both increase operators (++) are used as postfix and not prefix, the value assigned to *p is *q before both p and q are increased. And then both are increased. It would be roughly equivalent to:

```
*p = *q;
++p;
++q;
```

Like always, I recommend you to use parentheses () in order to avoid unexpected results and to give more legibility to the code.

POINTERS TO POINTERS

C++ allows the use of pointers that point to pointers, that these, in its turn, point to data (or even to other pointers). In order to do that, we only need to add an asterisk (*) for each level of reference in their declarations:

```
char a;
char * b;
char ** c;
a = 'z';
b = &a;
c = &b;
```

This, supposing the randomly chosen memory locations for each variable of 7230, 8092 and 10502, could be represented as:

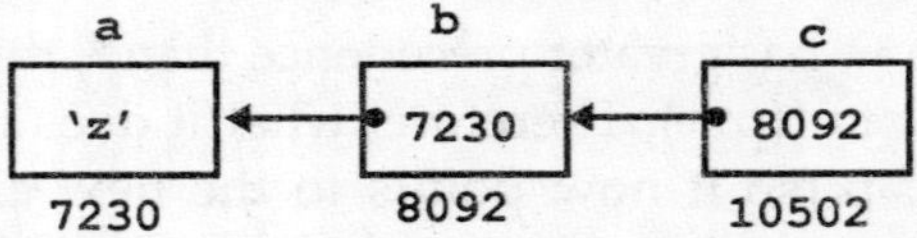

The value of each variable is written inside each cell; under the cells are their respective addresses in memory. The new thing in this example is variable c, which can be used in three different levels of indirection, each one of them would correspond to a different value:

- c has type char** and a value of 8092
- *c has type char* and a value of 7230
- **c has type char and a value of 'z'

VOID POINTERS

The void type of pointer is a special type of pointer. In C++, void represents the absence of type, so void pointers are pointers that point to a value that has no type (and thus also an undetermined length and undetermined dereference properties). This allows void pointers to point to any data type, from an integer value or a float to a string of characters. But in exchange they have a great limitation: the data pointed by them cannot be directly dereferenced (which is logical, since we have no type to dereference to), and for that reason we will always have to cast the address in the void pointer to some other pointer type that points to a concrete data type before dereferencing it.

One of its uses may be to pass generic parameters to a function:

```
// increaser
```

```
#include <iostream>
using namespace std;
void increase (void* data, int psize)
{
  if ( psize == sizeof(char))
  { char* pchar; pchar=(char*)data;
 ++(*pchar); }
  else if (psize == sizeof(int))
  { int* pint; pint=(int*)data; ++(*pint);
 }
}
  int main ()
{
  char a = 'x';
  int b = 1602;
  increase (&a,sizeof(a));
  increase (&b,sizeof(b));
  cout << a << ", " << b << endl;
  return 0;
}
output
y, 1603
```

sizeof is an operator integrated in the C++ language that returns the size in bytes of its parameter. For non-dynamic data types this value is a constant. Therefore, for example, sizeof(char) is 1, because char type is one byte long.

NULL POINTER

A null pointer is a regular pointer of any pointer type which has a special value that indicates that it is not pointing to any valid reference or memory address. This value is the result of type-casting the integer value zero to any pointer type.

```
int * p;
p = 0; // p has a null pointer value
```

Do not confuse null pointers with void pointers. A null pointer is a value that any pointer may take to represent that it is pointing to "nowhere", while a void pointer is a special type of pointer that can point to somewhere without a specific type. One refers to the value stored in the pointer itself and the other to the type of data it points to.

POINTERS TO FUNCTIONS

C++ allows operations with pointers to functions. The typical use of this is for passing a function as an argument to another function, since these cannot be passed dereferenced. In order to declare a pointer to a function we have to declare it like the prototype of the function except that the name of the function is enclosed between parentheses () and an asterisk (*) is inserted before the name:

```
// pointer to functions
#include <iostream>
using namespace std;
int addition (int a, int b)
{ return (a+b); }
int subtraction (int a, int b)
{ return (a-b); }
int operation (int x, int y, int
 (*functocall)(int,int))
{
  int g;
  g = (*functocall)(x,y);
  return (g);
}
int main ()
{
  int m,n;
  int (*minus)(int,int) = subtraction;
  m = operation (7, 5, addition);
  n = operation (20, m, minus);
  cout <<n;
  return 0;
}
output
8
```

In the example, minus is a pointer to a function that has two parameters of type int. It is immediately assigned to point to the function subtraction, all in a single line.

```
int (* minus)(int,int) = subtraction;
```

Dynamic Memory

Until now, in all our programmes, we have only had as much memory available as we declared for our variables, having the size of all of them to be determined in the source code, before the execution of the programme. But, what if we need a variable amount of memory that can only be determined during runtime? For example, in the case that we need some user input to determine the necessary amount of memory space. The answer is *dynamic memory*, for which C++ integrates the operators new and delete.

Operators new and new[]

In order to request dynamic memory we use the operator new. new is followed by a data type specifier and -if a sequence of more than one element is required- the number of these within brackets []. It returns a pointer to the beginning of the new block of memory allocated. Its form is:

```
pointer = new type
```

pointer = new type [number_of_elements]

The first expression is used to allocate memory to contain one single element of type type. The second one is used to assign a block (an array) of elements of type type, where number_of_elements is an integer value representing the amount of these. For example:

```
int * bobby;
bobby = new int [5];
```

In this case, the system dynamically assigns space for five elements of type int and returns a pointer to the first element of the sequence, which is assigned to bobby. Therefore, now, bobby points to a valid block of memory with space for five elements of type int.

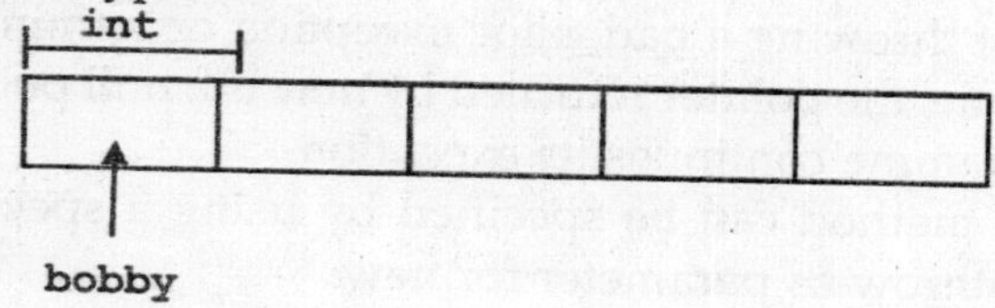

The first element pointed by bobby can be accessed either with the expression bobby[0] or the expression *bobby. Both are equivalent as has been explained in the section about pointers. The second element can be accessed either with bobby[1] or *(bobby+1) and so on...

You could be wondering the difference between declaring a normal array and assigning dynamic memory to a pointer, as we have just done. The most important difference is that the size of an array has to be a constant value, which limits its size to what we decide at the moment of designing the programme, before its execution, whereas the dynamic memory allocation allows us to assign memory during the execution of the programme (runtime) using any variable or constant value as its size.

The dynamic memory requested by our programme is allocated by the system from the memory heap. However, computer memory is a limited resource, and it can be exhausted. Therefore, it is important to have some mechanism to check if our request to allocate memory was successful or not.

C++ provides two standard methods to check if the allocation was successful: One is by handling exceptions. Using this method an exception of type bad_alloc is thrown when the allocation fails. Exceptions are a powerful C++ feature explained later in these tutorials. But for now you should know that if this exception is thrown and it is not handled by a specific handler, the programme execution is terminated.

This exception method is the default method used by new, and is the one used in a declaration like:

```
bobby = new int [5]; // if it fails an
exception is thrown
```

The other method is known as nothrow, and what happens when it is used is that when a memory allocation fails, instead of throwing a bad_alloc exception or terminating the programme, the pointer returned by new is a null pointer, and the programme continues its execution.

This method can be specified by using a special object called nothrow as parameter for new:

```
bobby = new (nothrow) int [5];
```

In this case, if the allocation of this block of memory failed, the failure could be detected by checking if bobby took a null pointer value:

```
int * bobby;
bobby = new (nothrow) int [5];
if (bobby == 0) {
// error assigning memory. Take measures.
};
```

This nothrow method requires more work than the exception method, since the value returned has to be checked after each and every memory allocation, but I will use it in our examples due to its simplicity. Anyway this method can become tedious for larger projects, where the exception method is generally preferred. The exception method will be explained in detail later in this tutorial.

Operator Delete

Since the necessity of dynamic memory is usually limited to specific moments within a programme, once it is no longer needed it should be freed so that the memory becomes available again for other requests of dynamic memory. This is the purpose of the operator delete, whose format is:

```
delete pointer;
delete [] pointer;
```

The first expression should be used to delete memory allocated for a single element, and the second one for memory allocated for arrays of elements.

The value passed as argument to delete must be either a pointer to a memory block previously allocated with new, or a null pointer (in the case of a null pointer, delete produces no effect).

```
// rememb-o-matic
#include <iostream>
using namespace std;
int main ()
{
  int i,n;
```

```
int * p;
cout << "How many numbers would you like
to type? ";
cin >> i;
p= new (nothrow) int[i];
if (p == 0)
cout << "Error: memory could not be
allocated";
else
{
for (n=0; n<i; n++)
{
cout << "Enter number: ";
cin >> p[n];
}
cout << "You have entered: ";
for (n=0; n<i; n++)
cout << p[n] << ", ";
delete[] p;
}
return 0;
}
output
How many numbers would you like to type? 5
Enter number : 75
Enter number : 436
Enter number : 1067
Enter number : 8
Enter number : 32
You have entered: 75, 436, 1067, 8, 32,
```

Notice how the value within brackets in the new statement is a variable value entered by the user (i), not a constant value:

```
p= new (nothrow) int[i];
```

But the user could have entered a value for i so big that our system could not handle it. For example, when I tried to give a value of 1 billion to the "How many numbers" question, my system could not allocate that much memory for the programme and I got the text message we prepared for this case (Error: memory could not be allocated). Remember that in the case that we tried to allocate the memory without specifying the nothrow parameter in the new expression, an exception would be thrown, which if it's not handled terminates the programme.

It is a good practice to always check if a dynamic memory block was successfully allocated. Therefore, if you use the nothrow method, you should always check the value of the pointer returned. Otherwise, use the exception method, even if you do not handle the exception. This way, the programme will terminate at that point without causing the unexpected results of continuing executing a code that assumes a block of memory to have been allocated when in fact it has not.

Chapter 10

Data Types

DEFINED DATA TYPES (TYPEDEF)

C++ allows the definition of our own types based on other existing data types. We can do this using the keyword typedef, whose fc mat is:

```
typedef existing_type new_type_name ;
```

where existing_type is a C++ fundamental or compound type and new_type_name is the name for the new type we are defining. For example:

```
typedef char C;
typedef unsigned int WORD;
typedef char * pChar;
typedef char field [50];
```

In this case we have defined four data types: C, WORD, pChar and field as char, unsigned int, char* and char[50] respectively, that we could perfectly use in declarations later as any other valid type:

```
C mychar, anotherchar, *ptc1;
WORD myword;
pChar ptc2;
field name;
```

typedef does not create different types. It only creates synonyms of existing types. That means that the type of myword can be considered to be either WORD or unsigned int, since both are in fact the same type.

typedef can be useful to define an alias for a type that is frequently used within a programme. It is also useful to define types when it is possible that we will need to change the type in later versions of our programme, or if a type you want to use has a name that is too long or confusing.

UNIONS

Unions allow one same portion of memory to be accessed as different data types, since all of them are in fact the same location in memory. Its declaration and use is similar to the one of structures but its functionality is totally different:

```
union union_name {
member_type1 member_name1;
member_type2 member_name2;
member_type3 member_name3;
.
.
} object_names;
```

All the elements of the union declaration occupy the same physical space in memory. Its size is the one of the greatest element of the declaration. For example:

```
union mytypes_t {
char c;
int i;
float f;
} mytypes;
```

defines three elements:

```
mytypes.c
mytypes.i
mytypes.f
```

each one with a different data type. Since all of them are referring to the same location in memory, the modification of one of the elements will affect the value of all of them. We cannot store different values in them independent from each other.

One of the uses a union may have is to unite an elementary type with an array or structures of smaller elements.

For example:

```
union mix_t {
long l;
struct {
```

```
    short hi;
    short lo;
  } s;
  char c[4];
  } mix;
```

defines three names that allow to access the same group of 4 bytes: mix.l, mix.s and mix.c and which we can use according to how we want to access these bytes, as if they were a single long-type data, as if they were two short elements or as an array of char elements, respectively. I have mixed types, arrays and structures in the union so that you can see the different ways that we can access the data.

For a little-endian system (most PC platforms), this union could be represented as:

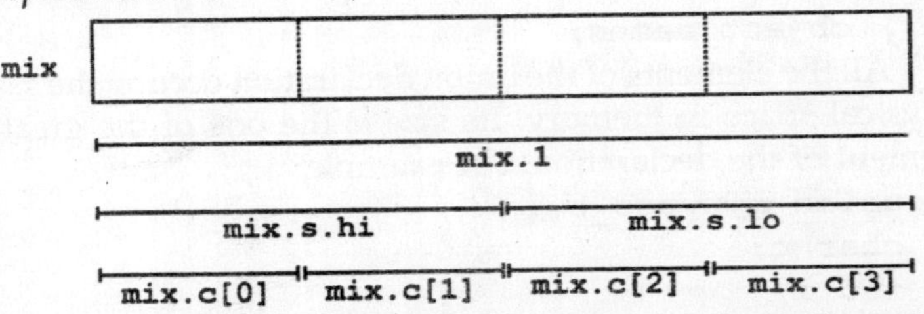

The exact alignment and order of the members of a union in memory is platform dependant. Therefore be aware of possible portability issues with this type of use.

ANONYMOUS UNIONS

In C++ we have the option to declare anonymous unions. If we declare a union without any name, the union will be anonymous and we will be able to access its members directly by their member names. For example, look at the difference between these two structure declarations: Structure with regular union structure with anonymous union

```
struct {
char title[50];
char author[50];
union {
float dollars;
int yens;
```

```
} price;
} book; struct {
char title[50];
char author[50];
union {
float dollars;
int yens;
};
} book;
```

The only difference between the two pieces of code is that in the first one we have given a name to the union (price) and in the second one we have not. The difference is seen when we access the members dollars and yens of an object of this type. For an object of the first type, it would be:

```
book.price.dollars
book.price.yens
```

whereas for an object of the second type, it would be:

```
book.dollars
book.yens
```

Once again I remind you that because it is a union and not a struct, the members dollars and yens occupy the same physical space in the memory so they cannot be used to store two different values simultaneously. You can set a value for price in dollars or in yens, but not in both.

ENUMERATIONS (ENUM)

Enumerations create new data types to contain something different that is not limited to the values fundamental data types may take. Its form is the following:

```
enum enumeration_name {
value1,
value2,
value3,
.
.
} object_names;
```

For example, we could create a new type of variable called colour to store colors with the following declaration:

```
enum colors_t {black, blue, green, cyan,
red, purple, yellow, white};
```

Notice that we do not include any fundamental data type in the declaration. To say it somehow, we have created a whole new data type from scratch without basing it on any other existing type. The possible values that variables of this new type color_t may take are the new constant values included within braces. For example, once the colors_t enumeration is declared the following expressions will be valid:

```
colors_t mycolor;
mycolor = blue;
if (mycolor == green) mycolor = red;
```

Enumerations are type compatible with numeric variables, so their constants are always assigned an integer numerical value internally. If it is not specified, the integer value equivalent to the first possible value is equivalent to 0 and the following ones follow a +1 progression. Thus, in our data type colors_t that we have defined above, black would be equivalent to 0, blue would be equivalent to 1, green to 2, and so on. We can explicitly specify an integer value for any of the constant values that our enumerated type can take. If the constant value that follows it is not given an integer value, it is automatically assumed the same value as the previous one plus one. For example:

```
enum months_t { january=1, february, march,
april,
may, june, july, august,
september, october, november, december}
y2k;
```

In this case, variable y2k of enumerated type months_t can contain any of the 12 possible values that go from january to december and that are equivalent to values between 1 and 12 (not between 0 and 11, since we have made january equal to 1).

CLASSES

CLASS HIERARCHY

The C++ class hierarchy which is used to represent the

basic repertoire of abstract data types is shown in Figure . Two kinds of classes are; *abstract* C++ *classes* , which look like this *Abstract Class,* and *concrete* C++ *classes* , which look like this *Concrete Class.* Lines in the figure indicate derivation; base classes always appear to the left of derived classes. An *abstract class* is a class which specifies an *interface* only. It is not possible create object instances of abstract classes. In C++ an abstract class typically has one or more *pure virtual member functions* . A *pure* virtual member function declares an interface only—there is no implementation defined. In effect, the interface specifies the set of operations without specifying the implementation. An abstract class is intended to be used a the *base class* from which other classes are *derived* . Declaring the member functions *virtual* makes it possible to access the implementations provided by the derived classes through the base-class interface. Consequently, we don't need to know how a particular object instance is implemented, nor do we need to know of which derived class it is an instance. This design pattern uses the idea of *polymorphism* . Polymorphism literally means "having many forms." The essential idea is that a single, common abstraction is used to define the set of values and the set of operations—the abstract data type. The remainder of this section presents the top levels of the class hierarchy which are shown in Figure . The top levels define those attributes of objects which are common to all of the classes in the hierarchy. The lower levels of the hierarchy (i.e., those derived from the Container class) are presented in subsequent chapters where the abstractions are defined and various implementations of those abstractions are elaborated.

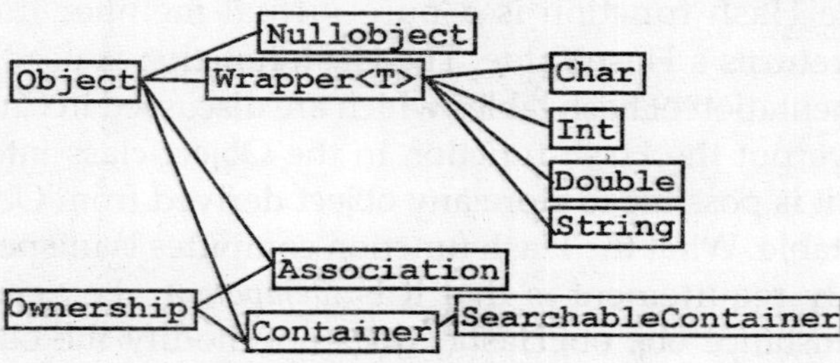

Fig. Object Class Hierarchy.

OBJECTS

The abstract class at the top of the class hierarchy is called Object. With the exception of the Ownership class, all the other classes in the hierarchy are derived from this class. Programme gives the declaration of the Object class. Altogether only six member functions are declared: the destructor, IsNull, Hash, Put, Compare and CompareTo.

PROGRAMME: OBJECT CLASS DEFINITION

The Object class destructor is declared virtual. It is essential to declare it so, because the Object is an abstract class, and instances of derived class objects are very likely to be accessed through the base class interface. In particular, it is necessary for the destructor of the derived class to be called through the base class interface—this is precisely what the virtual keyword achieves. The IsNull function is a pure virtual member function which returns a Boolean value. This function is used in conjunction with the NullObject concrete classes described below in Section. The IsNull function shall return false for all object instances derived from Object except if the object instance is the NullObject. We will see later that certain functions return object references. For example, a function which searches through a data structure for a particular object returns a reference to that object if it is found. If the object is not found, the search returns a reference to the NullObject instance. By using the IsNull function, the programmer can test whether the search was successful. This is analogous to the NULL pointer in the C programming language and to the pointer value 0 in C++.

The Hash function is a pure virtual member function which returns a HashValue. The Hash function is used in the implementation of hash tables which are discussed in Chapter . We have put the Hash function in the Object class interface, so that it is possible to store any object derived from Object in a hash table. What the Hash function computes is unspecified. The only requirement is that it is *idempotent* . I.e., given an object instance obj, obj.Hash() does not modify the object in any way, and as long as obj is not modified in the interim, repeated calls always give exactly the same result. Two functions for comparing objects are declared—Compare and CompareTo. Compare is a public member function. that takes a const reference to Object and returns an int. Given two objects obj1 and obj2, calling obj1.Compare (obj2) *compares* the value of obj1 with the value of obj2. The result is equal to zero if ; less than zero if ; and, greater than zero if .

It is not necessary that the two objects compared using Compare have the same type. As long as they are instances of classes derived from Object, they can be compared. The Compare function is used in the overloading of the comparison operators operator==, operator!=, operator<, operator<=, operator>, and operator>=, as shown in Programme. The second comparison function, CompareTo, is a pure virtual function. An implementation for this function must be given in every concrete class derived from Object. The purpose of this function is to compare two objects that are both instances of the same derived class. The purpose of the Put member function of the Object class is to output a human-readable representation of the object on the specified output stream.

The Put function is a pure virtual function. However, since it has the side-effect of output, it is not strictly idempotent. Nevertheless, it is a const member function which means that calling the Put member function does not modify the object in any way. The use of the Put in the overloading of the ostream insertion operator, operator<<, is shown in Programme .

PROGRAMME: OBJECT OPERATOR DEFINITIONS

The use of polymorphism in the way shown gives the programmer enormous leverage. The fact almost all objects will be derived from the Object base class, together with the fact that the Put and CompareTo member functions are virtual functions, ensures that the overloaded operators work as we expect for all derived class instances.

Implementation

Only three functions need to be implemented to complete the definition of the Object class. These are shown in Programme .

PROGRAMME: OBJECT CLASS MEMBER FUNCTION DEFINITIONS

The Object class destructor is trivial. Since there are no member variables, nothing remains to be cleaned up. It is necessary to define the destructor in any event. As explained above, the destructor needs to be virtual and because in C++ there is no such thing as a pure virtual destructor.

The implementation of the IsNull member function is trivial. It simply returns the Boolean value false. The Compare member function makes use of *run-time type information* to ensure that the CompareTo member function is only invoked for objects which are of the same class. For objects which are not instances of the same class, the before function is used to order those objects based on their types. The C++ run-time library provides an implementation for the before function which returns true if the left hand type precedes the right hand type in the implementation's collation order.

The NullObject Singleton Class

The declaration of the NullObject class is given in Programme . The NullObject class is a concrete class derived from the Object abstract base class. The NullObject class is also a *singleton* class. I.e., it is a class of which there will only ever be exactly one instance. The one instance is in fact a static member variable of the class itself. In order to ensure that no other instances can be created, the default constructor is declared to be a private member function. The static member function Instance returns a reference to the one and only NullObject instance.

PROGRAMME: NULLOBJECT CLASS DEFINITION

Implementation

Programme shows how the member functions of the NullObject class are defined. The most important characteristic of the NullObject class is that its IsNull member function returns the value true.

PROGRAMME: NULLOBJECT CLASS MEMBER FUNCTION DEFINITIONS

The remaining functions are trivial: The constructor does nothing; the two member functions Hash and CompareTo both return zero; and the Put function simply prints "NullObject". Finally, the Instance static member function returns a reference to the static member variable instance which is the one and only instance of the NullObject class.

Object Wrappers for the Built-In Types: One of the design goals of the C++ language is to treat user-defined data types and the built-in data types as equally as possible. However, the built-in data types of C++ do have one shortcoming with respect to user-defined ones—a built-in data type cannot be used as the base class from which other classes are derived. E.g., it is not possible to write:

```
class D : public int // Wrong!
```

Consequently, it is not possible to extend the functionality of a built-in type using inheritance. The usual design pattern for dealing with this deficiency is to put instances of the built-in types inside a *wrapper* class and to use the wrapped objects in place of the built-in types. Programme illustrates this idea. The class Wrapper<T> is a concrete class which is derived from the abstract base class Object. It is also a generic class, the purpose of which is to encapsulate an object of type T. Each instance of the Wrapper<T> class contains a single member variable of type T called datum.

PROGRAMME: WRAPPER<T> CLASS DEFINITION

A *class* is an expanded concept of a data structure: instead of holding only data, it can hold both data and functions. An *object* is an instantiation of a class. In terms of variables, a class would be the type, and an object would be the variable. Classes are generally declared using the keyword class, with the following format:

```
class class_name {
access_specifier_1:
member1;
access_specifier_2:
```

```
    member2;
  ...
  } object_names;
```

Where class_name is a valid identifier for the class, object_names is an optional list of names for objects of this class. The body of the declaration can contain members, that can be either data or function declarations, and optionally access specifiers.

All is very similar to the declaration on data structures, except that we can now include also functions and members, but also this new thing called *access specifier*. An access specifier is one of the following three keywords: private, public or protected. These specifiers modify the access rights that the members following them acquire:

- Private members of a class are accessible only from within other members of the same class or from their *friends*.
- Protected members are accessible from members of their same class and from their friends, but also from members of their derived classes.
- Finally, public members are accessible from anywhere where the object is visible.

By default, all members of a class declared with the class keyword have private access for all its members. Therefore, any member that is declared before one other class specifier automatically has private access. For example:

```
class CRectangle {
int x, y;
public:
void set_values (int,int);
int area (void);
} rect;
```

Declares a class (i.e., a type) called CRectangle and an object (i.e., a variable) of this class called rect. This class contains four members: two data members of type int (member x and member y) with private access (because private is the default access level) and two member functions with public access: set_values() and area(), of which for now we have only included their declaration, not their definition. Notice the difference between the class name and the object name: In the previous example, CRectangle was the class name (i.e., the type), whereas rect was an object of type CRectangle. It is the same relationship int and a have in the following declaration:

```
int a;
```

where int is the type name (the class) and a is the variable name (the object). After the previous declarations of CRectangle and rect, we can refer within the body of the programme to any of the public members of the object rect as if they were normal functions or normal variables, just by putting the object's name followed by a dot (.) and then the name of the member. All very similar to what we did with plain data structures before. For example:

```
rect.set_values (3,4);
myarea = rect.area();
```

The only members of rect that we cannot access from the body of our programme outside the class are x and y, since they have private access and they can only be referred from within other members of that same class.

Here is the complete example of class CRectangle:

```
// classes example
#include <iostream>
using namespace std;
class CRectangle {
int x, y;
public:
void set_values (int,int);
 int area () {return (x*y);}
};
void CRectangle::set_values (int a, int b)
{
  x = a;
  y = b;
}
int main () {
CRectangle rect;
rect.set_values (3,4);
```

```
cout << "area: " << rect.area();
return 0;
} area: 12
```

The most important new thing in this code is the operator of scope (::, two colons) included in the definition of set_values(). It is used to define a member of a class from outside the class declaration itself.

You may notice that the definition of the member function area() has been included directly within the definition of the CRectangle class given its extreme simplicity, whereas set_values() has only its prototype declared within the class, but its definition is outside it. In this outside declaration, we must use the operator of scope (::) to specify that we are defining a function that is a member of the class CRectangle and not a regular global function.

The scope operator (::) specifies the class to which the member being declared belongs, granting exactly the same scope properties as if this function definition was directly included within the class definition. For example, in the function set_values() of the previous code, we have been able to use the variables x and y, which are private members of class CRectangle, which means they are only accessible from other members of their class.

The only difference between defining a class member function completely within its class and to include only the prototype and later its definition, is that in the first case the function will automatically be considered an inline member function by the compiler, while in the second it will be a normal (not-inline) class member function, which in fact supposes no difference in behaviour.

Members x and y have private access (remember that if nothing else is said, all members of a class defined with keyword class have private access). By declaring them private we deny access to them from anywhere outside the class. This makes sense, since we have already defined a member function to set values for those members within the object: the member function set_values(). Therefore, the rest of the programme does not need to have direct access to them. Perhaps in a so simple example as this, it is difficult to see an utility in protecting those two variables, but in greater projects it may be very important that values cannot be modified in an unexpected way (unexpected from the point of view of the object).

One of the greater advantages of a class is that, as any other type, we can declare several objects of it. For example, following with the previous example of class CRectangle, we could have declared the object rectb in addition to the object rect:

```
// example: one class, two objects
#include <iostream>
using namespace std;
class CRectangle {
int x, y;
public:
void set_values (int,int);
int area () {return (x*y);}
};
void CRectangle::set_values (int a, int b)
{
 x = a;
 y = b;
}
int main () {
CRectangle rect, rectb;
rect.set_values (3,4);
rectb.set_values (5,6);
cout << "rect area: " << rect.area() <<
endl;
cout << "rectb area: " << rectb.area() <<
endl;
return 0;
} rect area: 12
rectb area: 30
```

In this concrete case, the class (type of the objects) to which we are talking about is CRectangle, of which there are two instances or objects: rect and rectb. Each one of them has its own member variables and member functions. Notice that the call to rect.area() does not give the same result as the call to rectb.area(). This is because each object of class CRectangle has its own variables x and y, as they, in some way, have also their own function members set_value() and area() that each uses its object's own variables to operate.

That is the basic concept of *object-oriented programming*: Data and functions are both members of the object. We no longer use sets of global variables that we pass from one function to another as parameters, but instead we handle objects that have their own data and functions embedded as members. Notice that we have not had to give any parameters in any of the calls to rect.area or rectb.area. Those member functions directly used the data members of their respective objects rect and rectb.

Constructors and Destructors

Objects generally need to initialize variables or assign dynamic memory during their process of creation to become operative and to avoid returning unexpected values during their execution. For example, what would happen if in the previous example we called the member function area() before having called function set_values()? Probably we would have gotten an undetermined result since the members x and y would have never been assigned a value.

In order to avoid that, a class can include a special function called constructor, which is automatically called whenever a new object of this class is created. This constructor function must have the same name as the class, and cannot have any return type; not even void. We are going to implement CRectangle including a constructor:

```
// example: class constructor
#include <iostream>
using namespace std;
class CRectangle {
int width, height;
public:
CRectangle (int,int);
```

```
int area () {return (width*height);}
};
CRectangle::CRectangle (int a, int b) {
width = a;
height = b;
}
  int main () {
  CRectangle rect (3,4);
CRectangle rectb (5,6);
cout << "rect area: " << rect.area() <<
endl;
cout << "rectb area: " << rectb.area() <<
endl;
return 0;
} rect area: 12
rectb area: 30
```

As you can see, the result of this example is identical to the previous one. But now we have removed the member function set_values(), and have included instead a constructor that performs a similar action: it initializes the values of x and y with the parameters that are passed to it. Notice how these arguments are passed to the constructor at the moment at which the objects of this class are created:

```
CRectangle rect (3,4);
CRectangle rectb (5,6);
```

Constructors cannot be called explicitly as if they were regular member functions. They are only executed when a new object of that class is created. You can also see how neither the constructor prototype declaration (within the class) nor the latter constructor definition include a return value; not even void. The *destructor* fulfills the opposite functionality. It is automatically called when an object is destroyed, either because its scope of existence has finished (for example, if it was defined as a local object within a function and the function ends) or because it is an object dynamically assigned and it is released using the operator delete.

The destructor must have the same name as the class, but preceded with a tilde sign (~) and it must also return no value.

The use of destructors is especially suitable when an object assigns dynamic memory during its lifetime and at the moment of being destroyed we want to release the memory that the object was allocated.

```
// example on constructors and destructors
#include <iostream>
using namespace std;
class CRectangle {
int *width, *height;
public:
CRectangle (int,int);
~CRectangle ();
int area () {return (*width * *height);}
};
  CRectangle::CRectangle (int a, int b) {
  width = new int;
  height = new int;
  *width = a;
  *height = b;
}
  CRectangle::~CRectangle () {
  delete width;
  delete height;
}
  int main () {
  CRectangle rect (3,4), rectb (5,6);
  cout << "rect area: " << rect.area() <<
  endl;
  cout << "rectb area: " << rectb.area() <<
  endl;
  return 0;
} rect area: 12
rectb area: 30
```

Overloading Constructors

Like any other function, a constructor can also be overloaded with more than one function that have the same name but different types or number of parameters. Remember that for overloaded functions the compiler will call the one whose parameters match the arguments used in the function call. In the case of constructors, which are automatically called when an object is created, the one executed is the one that matches the arguments passed on the object declaration:

```
// overloading class constructors
#include <iostream>
using namespace std;
class CRectangle {
int width, height;
public:
CRectangle ();
CRectangle (int,int);
int area (void) {return (width*height);}
};
CRectangle::CRectangle () {
width = 5;
height = 5;
}
  CRectangle::CRectangle (int a, int b) {
  width = a;
  height = b;
}
int main () {
CRectangle rect (3,4);
CRectangle rectb;
cout << "rect area: " << rect.area() <<
endl;
cout << "rectb area: " << rectb.area() <<
endl;
return 0;
} rect area: 12
rectb area: 25
```

In this case, rectb was declared without any arguments, so it has been initialized with the constructor that has no parameters, which initializes both width and height with a value of 5. Important: Notice how if we declare a new object and we want to use its default constructor (the one without parameters), we do not include parentheses ():

```
CRectangle rectb; // right
CRectangle rectb(); // wrong!
```

Default Constructor

If you do not declare any constructors in a class definition, the compiler assumes the class to have a default constructor with no arguments. Therefore, after declaring a class like this one:

```
class CExample {
public:
int a,b,c;
void multiply (int n, int m) { a=n; b=m;
c=a*b; };
};
```

The compiler assumes that CExample has a default constructor, so you can declare objects of this class by simply declaring them without any arguments:

```
CExample ex;
```

But as soon as you declare your own constructor for a class, the compiler no longer provides an implicit default constructor. So you have to declare all objects of that class according to the constructor prototypes you defined for the class:

```
class CExample {
public:
int a,b,c;
CExample (int n, int m) { a=n; b=m; };
void multiply () { c=a*b; };
};
```

Here we have declared a constructor that takes two parameters of type int. Therefore the following object declaration would be correct:

```
CExample ex (2,3);
```

But,

```
CExample ex;
```

Would not be correct, since we have declared the class to have an explicit constructor, thus replacing the default constructor. But the compiler not only creates a default constructor for you if you do not specify your own. It provides three special member functions in total that are implicitly declared if you do not declare your own. These are the *copy constructor*, the *copy assignment operator*, and the default destructor.

The copy constructor and the copy assignment operator copy all the data contained in another object to the data members of the current object. For CExample, the copy constructor implicitly declared by the compiler would be something similar to:

```
CExample::CExample (const CExample& rv) {
a=rv.a;  b=rv.b;  c=rv.c;
}
```

Therefore, the two following object declarations would be correct:

```
CExample ex (2,3);
CExample ex2 (ex); // copy constructor (data
copied from ex)
```

Pointers to Classes

It is perfectly valid to create pointers that point to classes. We simply have to consider that once declared, a class becomes a valid type, so we can use the class name as the type for the pointer. For example:

```
CRectangle * prect;
```

is a pointer to an object of class CRectangle.

As it happened with data structures, in order to refer directly to a member of an object pointed by a pointer we can use the arrow operator (->) of indirection. Here is an example with some possible combinations:

```
// pointer to classes example
#include <iostream>
using namespace std;
class CRectangle {
int width, height;
public:
void set_values (int, int);
```

```
int area (void) {return (width * height);}
};
  void CRectangle::set_values (int a, int
  b)
{
  width = a;
  height = b;
}
int main () {
CRectangle a, *b, *c;
CRectangle * d = new CRectangle[2];
b= new CRectangle;
c= &a;
a.set_values (1,2);
b->set_values (3,4);
d->set_values (5,6);
d[1].set_values (7,8);
cout << "a area: " << a.area() << endl;
cout << "*b area: " << b->area() << endl;
cout << "*c area: " << c->area() << endl;
cout << "d[0] area: " << d[0].area() <<
endl;
cout << "d[1] area: " << d[1].area() <
endl;
delete[] d;
delete b;
return 0;
} a area: 2
*b area: 12
*c area: 2
d[0] area: 30
d[1] area: 56
```

Next you have a summary on how can you read some pointer and class operators (*, &,., ->, [ ]) that appear in the previous example:

expression can be read as

```
*x pointed by x
&x address of x
```

```
x.y member y of object x
x->y member y of object pointed by x
(*x).y member y of object pointed by x
(equivalent to the        previous one)
x[0]  first object pointed by x
x[1]  second object pointed by x
x[n]  (n+1)th object pointed by x
```

Be sure that you understand the logic under all of these expressions before proceeding with the next sections. If you have doubts, read again this section and/or consult the previous sections about pointers and data structures.

CLASSES WITH STRUCT AND UNION

Classes can be defined not only with keyword class, but also with keywords struct and union. The concepts of class and data structure are so similar that both keywords have in C++ the exact same functionality except that the members of classes declared with keyword struct have public access by default, instead of private access, as classes declared with keyword class have. That is the only difference. For all other purposes both keywords are equivalent.

The concept under unions is different from than of struct and class, since unions only store one data member at a time, but they are also classes and thus can also hold function members. The default access in union classes is public.

Classes (II): Overloading Operators

C++ incorporates the option to use standard operators to perform operations with classes in addition to with fundamental types. For example:

```
int a, b, c;
a = b + c;
```

This is obviously valid code in C++, since the different variables of the addition are all fundamental types. Nevertheless, it is not so obvious that we could perform an operation similar to the following one:

```
struct {
string product;
float price;
```

```
} a, b, c;
a = b + c;
// vectors: overloading operators example
#include <iostream>
using namespace std;
class CVector {
public:
int x,y;
CVector () {};
CVector (int,int);
CVector operator + (CVector);
};
  CVector::CVector (int a, int b) {
  x = a;
  y = b;
}
  CVector CVector::operator+ (CVector param)
  {
  CVector temp;
  temp.x = x + param.x;
  temp.y = y + param.y;
  return (temp);
}
  int main () {
  CVector a (3,1);
  CVector b (1,2);
  CVector c;
  c = a + b;
  cout << c.x << "," << c.y;
  return 0;
} 4,3
```

It may be a little confusing to see so many times the CVector identifier. But, consider that some of them refer to the class name (type) CVector and some others are functions with that name (constructors must have the same name as the class). Do not confuse them:

```
CVector (int, int); // function name CVector
(constructor)
```

```
CVector operator+ (CVector); // function
returns a CVector
```

The function operator+ of class CVector is the one that is in charge of overloading the addition operator (+). This function can be called either implicitly using the operator, or explicitly using the function name:

```
c = a + b;
c = a.operator+ (b);
```

Both Expressions are Equivalent

Notice also that we have included the empty constructor (without parameters) and we have defined it with an empty block:

```
CVector () { };
```

This is necessary, since we have explicitly declared another constructor:

```
CVector (int, int);
```

And when we explicitly declare any constructor, with any number of parameters, the default constructor with no parameters that the compiler can declare automatically is not declared, so we need to declare it ourselves in order to be able to construct objects of this type without parameters. Otherwise, the declaration:

```
CVector c;
```

included in main() would not have been valid.

Anyway, I have to warn you that an empty block is a bad implementation for a constructor, since it does not fulfill the minimum functionality that is generally expected from a constructor, which is the initialization of all the member variables in its class. In our case this constructor leaves the variables x and y undefined. Therefore, a more advisable definition would have been something similar to this:

```
CVector () { x=0; y=0; };
```

which in order to simplify and show only the point of the code I have not included in the example. As well as a class includes a default constructor and a copy constructor even if they are not declared, it also includes a default definition for the assignment operator (=) with the class itself as parameter.

The behaviour which is defined by default is to copy the whole content of the data members of the object passed as argument (the one at the right side of the sign) to the one at the left side:

```
CVector d (2,3);
CVector e;
e = d; // copy assignment operator
```

The copy assignment operator function is the only operator member function implemented by default. Of course, you can redefine it to any other functionality that you want, like for example, copy only certain class members or perform additional initialization procedures.

The overload of operators does not force its operation to bear a relation to the mathematical or usual meaning of the operator, although it is recommended. For example, the code may not be very intuitive if you use operator + to subtract two classes or operator== to fill with zeros a class, although it is perfectly possible to do so.

Static Members

A class can contain *static* members, either data or functions. Static data members of a class are also known as "class variables", because there is only one unique value for all the objects of that same class. Their content is not different from one object of this class to another.

For example, it may be used for a variable within a class that can contain a counter with the number of objects of that class that are currently allocated, as in the following example:

```
// static members in classes
#include <iostream>
using namespace std;
class CDummy {
public:
static int n;
CDummy () { n++; };
~CDummy () { n-; };
};
int CDummy::n=0;
int main () {
```

```
CDummy a;
CDummy b[5];
CDummy * c = new CDummy;
cout << a.n << endl;
delete c;
cout << CDummy::n << endl;
return 0;
 } 7
```

Chapter 11

Object-Oriented Extensions

In this section we present how the object-oriented concepts of section 4 are used in C++.

CLASSES AND OBJECTS

C++ allows the declaration and definition of classes. Instances of classes are called *objects*. Recall the drawing programme example of section 5 again.

There we have developed a class Point. In C++ this would look like this:

```
class Point {
  int _x, _y; // point coordinates
public: // begin interface section
  void setX(const int val);
  void setY(const int val);
  int getX() { return _x; }
  int getY() { return _y; }
};
Point apoint;
```

This declares a class *Point* and defines an object *apoint*. You can think of a class definition as a structure definition with functions (or "methods").

Additionally, you can specify the *access rights* in more detail. For example, *_x* and *_y* are private, because elements of classes are private as default. Consequently, we explicitly must "switch" the access rights to declare the following to be public.

We do that by using the keyword public followed by a colon: Every element following this keyword are now accessible from outside of the class. We can switch back to private access rights by starting a private section with private:

This is possible as often as needed:

```
class Foo {
  // private as default...
public:
  // what follows is public until...
private:
  //... here, where we switch back to
private...
public:
  //... and back to public.
};
```

Recall that a structure struct is a combination of various data elements which are accessible from the outside. We are now able to express a structure with help of a class, where all elements are declared to be public:

```
class Struct {
public: // Structure elements are public by
default
    // elements, methods
};
```

This is exactly what C++ does with struct. Structures are handled like classes. Whereas elements of classes (defined with class) are private by default, elements of structures (defined with struct) are public. However, we can also use private: to switch to a private section in structures.

Let's come back to our class *Point*. Its interface starts with the public section where we define four methods. Two for each coordinate to set and get its value. The set methods are only declared. Their actual functionality is still to be defined. The get methods have a function body: They are defined *within* the class or, in other words, they are *inlined methods*.

This type of method definition is useful for small and simple bodies. It also improve performance, because bodies of inlined methods are "copied" into the code wherever a call to such a method takes place. On the contrary, calls to the set methods would result in a "real" function call. We define these methods outside of the class declaration. This makes it necessary, to indicate to which class a method definition belongs to.

For example, another class might just define a method *setX()* which is quite different from that of *Point*.

We must be able to define the scope of the definition; we therefore use the scope operator "::":

```
void Point::setX(const int val) {
_x = val;
}
void Point::setY(const int val) {
_y = val;
}
```

Here we define method *setX()* (*setY()*) within the scope of class *Point*.

The object apoint can use these methods to set and get information about itself:

```
Point apoint;
apoint.setX(1); // Initialization
apoint.setY(1);
//
// x is needed from here, hence, we define it
here and
// initialize it to the x-coordinate of apoint
//
int x = apoint.getX();
```

The question arises about how the methods "know" from which object they are invoked. This is done by implicitly passing a pointer to the invoking object to the method. We can access this pointer within the methods as this.

The definitions of methods *setX()* and *setY()* make use of class members *_x* and *_y*, respectively. If invoked by an object, these members are "automatically" mapped to the correct object.

We could use this to illustrate what actually happens:

```
void Point::setX(const int val) {
  this->_x = val; // Use this to reference
invoking
```

```
    // object
  }
  void Point::setY(const int val) {
    this->_y = val;
  }
```

Here we explicitly use the pointer this to explicitly dereference the invoking object. Fortunately, the compiler automatically "inserts" these dereferences for class members, hence, we really can use the first definitions of *setX()* and *setY()*. However, it sometimes make sense to know that there is a pointer this available which indicates the invoking object.

Currently, we need to call the set methods to initialize a point object [v]. However, we would like to initialize the point when we define it. We therefore use special methods called constructors.

CONSTRUCTORS

Constructors are methods which are used to initialize an object at its definition time. We extend our class *Point* such that it initializes a point to coordinates (0, 0):

```
class Point {
  int _x, _y;
public:
  Point() {
    _x = _y = 0;
  }
  void setX(const int val);
  void setY(const int val);
  int getX() { return _x; }
  int getY() { return _y; }
};
```

Constructors have the same name of the class (thus they are identified to be constructors). They have no return value. As other methods, they can take arguments. For example, we may want to initialize a point to other coordinates than (0, 0).

We therefore define a second constructor taking two integer arguments within the class:

```
  class Point {
```

```
  int _x, _y;
public:
  Point() {
    _x = _y = 0;
  }
  Point(const int x, const int y) {
    _x = x;
    _y = y;
  }
  void setX(const int val);
  void setY(const int val);
  int getX() { return _x; }
  int getY() { return _y; }
};
```

Constructors are implicitly called when we define objects of their classes:

```
Point apoint; // Point::Point()
Point bpoint(12, 34); // Point::Point(const
int, const int)
```

With constructors we are able to initialize our objects at definition time as we have requested it in section 2 for our singly linked list. We are now able to define a class *List* where the constructors take care of correctly initializing its objects.

If we want to create a point from another point, hence, copying the properties of one object to a newly created one, we sometimes have to take care of the copy process. For example, consider the class *List* which allocates dynamically memory for its elements. If we want to create a second list which is a copy of the first, we must allocate memory and copy the individual elements.

In our class Point we therefore add a third constructor which takes care of correctly copying values from one object to the newly created one:

```
class Point {
  int _x, _y;
public:
  Point() {
    _x = _y = 0;
```

```
  }
  Point(const int x, const int y) {
    _x = x;
    _y = y;
  }
  Point(const Point &from) {
    _x = from._x;
    _y = from._y;
  }
  void setX(const int val);
  void setY(const int val);
  int getX() { return _x; }
  int getY() { return _y; }
};
```

The third constructor takes a constant reference to an object of class *Point* as an argument and assigns *_x* and *_y* the corresponding values of the provided object.

This type of constructor is so important that it has its own name: copy constructor. It is highly recommended that you provide for each of your classes such a constructor, even if it is as simple as in our example.

The copy constructor is called in the following cases:

```
  Point apoint; // Point::Point()
  Point bpoint(apoint); // Point::Point(const
Point &)
  Point cpoint = apoint; // Point::Point(const
  Point &)
```

With help of constructors we have fulfilled one of our requirements of implementation of abstract data types: Initialization at definition time. We still need a mechanism which automatically "destroys" an object when it gets invalid (for example, because of leaving its scope). Therefore, classes can define *destructors*.

DESTRUCTORS

Consider a class List: Elements of the list are dynamically appended and removed. The constructor helps us in creating an initial empty list. However, when we leave the scope of the definition of a list object, we must ensure that the allocated memory is released.

We therefore define a special method called destructor which is called once for each object at its destruction time:

```
void foo() {
  List alist; // List::List() initializes to
              // empty list.
  ...         // add/remove elements
}             // Destructor call!
```

Destruction of objects take place when the object leaves its scope of definition or is explicitly destroyed. The latter happens, when we dynamically allocate an object and release it when it is no longer needed.

Destructors are declared similar to constructors. Thus, they also use the name prefixed by a tilde (~) of the defining class:

```
class Point {
  int _x, _y;
public:
  Point() {
    _x = _y = 0;
}
Point(const int x, const int y) {
  _x = xval;
  _y = yval;
}
Point(const Point &from) {
  _x = from._x;
  _y = from._y;
}
~Point() { /* Nothing to do! */ }
void setX(const int val);
void setY(const int val);
int getX() { return _x; }
int getY() { return _y; }
};
```

Destructors take no arguments. It is even invalid to define one, because destructors are implicitly called at destruction time: You have no chance to specify actual arguments.

INHERITANCE

In our pseudo language, we formulate inheritance with "inherits from". In C++ these words are replaced by a colon. As an example let's design a class for 3D points. Of course we want to reuse our already existing class *Point*.

We start designing our class as follows:

```
class Point3D: public Point {
  int _z;
public:
   Point3D() {
     setX(0);
     setY(0);
     _z = 0;
  }
  Point3D(const int x, const int y, const int
  z) {
    setX(x);
    setY(y);
    _z = z;
  }
  ~Point3D() { /* Nothing to do */ }
  int getZ() { return _z; }
  void setZ(const int val) { _z = val; }
};
```

TYPES OF INHERITANCE

You might notice again the keyword public used in the first line of the class definition (its *signature*). This is necessary because C++ distinguishes two types of inheritance. *public* and *private*. As a default, classes are privately derived from each other. Consequently, we must explicitly tell the compiler to use public inheritance.

The type of inheritance influences the access rights to elements of the various superclasses. Using public inheritance, everything which is declared private in a superclass remains private in the subclass. Similarly, everything which is public remains public. When using private inheritance the things are quite different as is shown in table.

Table. Access Rights and Inheritance

	Type of Inheritance	
	Private	**Public**
Private	Private	Private
Protected	Private	Protected
Public	Private	Public

The leftmost column lists possible access rights for elements of classes. It also includes a third type protected. This type is used for elements which should be directly usable in subclasses but which should not be accessible from the outside. Thus, one could say elements of this type are between private and public elements in that they can be used within the class hierarchy rooted by the corresponding class.

The second and third column show the resulting access right of the elements of a superclass when the subclass is privately and publically derived, respectively.

CONSTRUCTION

When we create an instance of class *Point3D* its constructor is called. Since *Point3D* is derived from *Point* the constructor of class *Point* is also called.

However, this constructor is called *before* the body of the constructor of class *Point3D* is executed. In general, prior to the execution of the particular constructor body, constructors of every superclass are called to initialize their part of the created object.

When we create an object with:

```
Point3D point(1, 2, 3);
```

the second constructor of *Point3D* is invoked. Prior to the execution of the constructor body, the constructor *Point()* is invoked, to initialize the *point* part of object *point*.

Fortunately, we have defined a constructor which takes no arguments. This constructor initializes the 2D coordinates *_x* and *_y* to 0 (zero).

As *Point3D* is only derived from *Point* there are no other constructor calls and the body of *Point3D(const int, const int, const int)* is executed. Here we invoke methods *setX()* and *setY()* to explicitly override the 2D coordinates. Subsequently, the value of the third coordinate *_z* is set.

This is very unsatisfactory as we have defined a constructor *Point()* which takes two arguments to initialize its coordinates to them.

Thus we must only be able to tell, that instead of using the *default constructor Point()* the parameterized *Point(const int, const int)* should be used.

We can do that by specifying the desired constructors after a single colon just before the body of constructor Point3D ():

```
class Point3D: public Point {
  ...
public:
  Point3D() {... }
  Point3D(
    const int x,
    const int y,
    const int z): Point(x, y) {
      _z = z;
  }
  ...
};
```

If we would have more super classes we simply provide their constructor calls as a comma separated list. We also use this mechanism to create contained objects. For example, suppose that class *Part* only defines a constructor with one argument.

Then to correctly create an object of class Compound we must invoke Part() with its argument:

```
class Compound {
  Part part;
  ...
public:
  Compound(const int part Parameter): part(part
  Parameter) {
    ...
  }
```

```
  ...
};
```

This dynamic initialization can also be used with built-in data types.

For example, the constructors of class Point could be written as:

```
Point(): _x(0), _y(0) {}
Point(const int x, const int y): _x(x), _y(y)
{}
```

You should use this initialization method as often as possible, because it allows the compiler to create variables and objects correctly initialized instead of creating them with a default value and to use an additional assignment (or other mechanism) to set its value.

DESTRUCTION

If an object is destroyed, for example by leaving its definition scope, the destructor of the corresponding class is invoked. If this class is derived from other classes their destructors are also called, leading to a recursive call chain.

MULTIPLE INHERITANCE

C++ allows a class to be derived from more than one superclass, as was already briefly mentioned in previous sections.

You can easily derive from more than one class by specifying the super classes in a comma separated list:

```
class DrawableString: public Point, public
DrawableObject {
  ...
public:
  DrawableString(...):
    Point(...),
    DrawableObject(...) {
      ...
  }
  ~DrawableString() {... }
  ...
```

```
};
```

We will not use this type of inheritance in the remainder of this tutorial. Therefore we will not go into further detail here.

POLYMORPHISM

In our pseudo language we are able to declare methods of classes to be virtual, to force their evaluation to be based on object content rather than object type.

We can also use this in C++:

```
class DrawableObject {
public:
  virtual void print();
};
```

Class *DrawableObject* defines a method *print()* which is virtual. We can derive from this class other classes:

```
class Point: public DrawableObject {
    ...
public:
    ...
    void print() {... }
};
```

Again, *print()* is a virtual method, because it inherits this property from *DrawableObject*. The function *display()* which is able to display any kind of drawable object, can then be defined as:

```
void display(const DrawableObject &obj) {
  // prepare anything necessary
  obj.print();
}
```

When using virtual methods some compilers complain if the corresponding class destructor is not declared virtual as well. This is necessary when using pointers to (virtual) subclasses when it is time to destroy them.

As the pointer is declared as superclass normally its destructor would be called. If the destructor is virtual, the destructor of the actual referenced object is called (and then, recursively, all destructors of its superclasses).

Here is an example adopted from:

```
  class Colour {
 public:
  virtual ~Colour();
 };
  class Red: public Colour {
  public:
   ~Red(); // Virtuality inherited from Colour
  };
  class LightRed: public Red {
  public:
   ~LightRed();
  };
```

Using these classes, we can define a palette as follows:

```
Colour *palette[3];
palette[0] = new Red; // Dynamically create a
new Red object
palette[1] = new LightRed;
palette[2] = new Colour;
```

The newly introduced operator new creates a new object of the specified type in dynamic memory and returns a pointer to it.

Thus, the first new returns a pointer to an allocated object of class *Red* and assigns it to the first element of array *palette.* The elements of *palette* are pointers to *Colour* and, because *Red* is-a *Colour* the assignment is valid.

The contrary operator to new is delete which explicitly destroys an object referenced by the provided pointer.

If we apply delete to the elements of palette the following destructor calls happen:

```
delete palette[0];
// Call destructor ~Red() followed by ~Colour()
delete palette[1];
// Call ~LightRed(), ~Red() and ~Colour()
delete palette[2];
// Call ~Colour()
```

The various destructor calls only happen, because of the use of virtual destructors. If we would have not declared them virtual, each delete would have only called ~ *Colour()* (because *palette[i]* is of type pointer to *Colour*).

ABSTRACT CLASSES

Abstract classes are defined just as ordinary classes. However, some of their methods are designated to be necessarily defined by subclasses. We just mention their *signature* including their return type, name and parameters but not a definition.

One could say, we omit the method body or, in other words, specify "nothing".

This is expressed by appending "= 0" after the method signatures:

```
class DrawableObject {
...
public:
...
virtual void print() = 0;
};
```

This class definition would force every derived class from which objects should be created to define a method *print()*. These method declarations are also called *pure methods*.

Pure methods must also be declared virtual, because we only want to use objects from derived classes.

Classes which define pure methods are called abstract classes.

OPERATOR OVERLOADING

If we recall the abstract data type for complex numbers, Complex, we could create a C++ class as follows:

```
class Complex {
  double _real,
         _imag;
public:
  Complex(): _real(0.0), _imag(0.0) {}
  Complex(const double real, const double
imag):
    _real(real), _imag(imag) {}
  Complex add(const Complex op);
```

```
  Complex mul(const Complex op);
  ...
};
```

We would then be able to use complex numbers and to "calculate" with them:

```
Complex a(1.0, 2.0), b(3.5, 1.2), c;
c = a.add(b);
```

Here we assign *c* the sum of *a* and *b*. Although absolutely correct, it does not provide a convenient way of expression. What we would rather like to use is the well-known "+" to express addition of two complex numbers. Fortunately, C++ allows us to *overload* almost all of its operators for newly created types.

For example, we could define a "+" operator for our class Complex:

```
class Complex {
    ...
public:
...
Complex operator +(const Complex &op) {
  double real = _real + op._real,
           imag = _imag + op._imag;
  return(Complex(real, imag));
}
  ...
};
```

In this case, we have made operator + a member of class *Complex*.

An expression of the form

```
c = a + b;
```

is translated into a method call

```
c = a.operator +(b);
```

Thus, the binary operator + only needs one argument. The first argument is implicitly provided by the invoking object (in this case *a*).

However, an operator call can also be interpreted as a usual function call, as in:

```
c = operator +(a, b);
```

In this case, the overloaded operator is not a member of a class. It is rather defined outside as a normal overloaded function.

For example, we could define operator + in this way:

```
class Complex {
  ...
public:
  ...
  double real() { return _real; }
  double imag() { return _imag; }
  // No need to define operator here!
};
Complex operator +(Complex &op1, Complex &op2)
{
  double real = op1.real() + op2.real(),
         imag = op1.imag() + op2.imag();
  return(Complex(real, imag));
}
```

In this case we must define access methods for the real and imaginary parts because the operator is defined outside of the class's scope. However, the operator is so closely related to the class, that it would make sense to allow the operator to access the private members. This can be done by declaring it to be a *friend* of class *Complex*.

CLASS OF FUNCTION

We can define functions or classes to be friends of a class to allow them direct access to its private data members. For example, in the previous section we would like to have the function for operator + to have access to the private data members *_real* and *_imag* of class *Complex*.

Therefore we declare operator + to be a friend of class Complex:

```
class Complex {
  ...
public:
  ...
friend Complex operator +(
  const Complex &,
```

```
    const Complex &
  );
};
  Complex operator +(const Complex &op1, const
  Complex &op2) {
    double real = op1._real + op2._real,
           imag = op1._imag + op2._imag;
    return(Complex(real, imag));
  }
```

CASE STUDY

GENERIC TYPES (TEMPLATES)

In C++ generic data types are called *class templates********* or just *templates* for short. A class template looks like a normal class definition, where some aspects are represented by *placeholders*.

In the forthcoming list example we use this mechanism to generate lists for various data types:

```
template <class T>
class List:... {
public:
  ...
  void append(const T data);
  ...
};
```

In the first line we introduce the keyword template which starts every template declaration. The arguments of a template are enclosed in angle brackets.

Each argument specifies a placeholder in the following class definition. In our example, we want class *List* to be defined for various data types. One could say, that we want to define a *class of lists*[v]. In this case the class of lists is defined by the type of objects they contain. We use the name *T* for the placeholder. We now use *T* at any place where normally the type of the actual objects are expected. For example, each list provides a method to append an element to it. We can now define this method as shown above with use of *T*.

An actual list *definition* must now specify the type of the list. If we stick to the class expression used before, we have to *create a class instance.*

From this class instance we can then create "real" object instances:

```
List<int> integerList;
```

Here we create a class instance of a *List* which takes integers as its data elements. We specify the type enclosed in angle brackets. The compiler now applies the provided argument "int" and automatically generates a class definition where the placeholder *T* is replaced by *int*, for example, it generates the following method declaration for *append()*:

```
void append(const int data);
```

Templates can take more than one argument to provide more placeholders. For example, to declare a dictionary class which provides access to its data elements by a key, one can think of the following declaration:

```
template <class K, class T>
class Dictionary {
  ...
public:
  ...
  K getKey(const T from);
  T getData(const K key);
  ...
};
```

Here we use two placeholders to be able to use dictionaries for various key and data types.

Template arguments can also be used to generate parameterized class definitions. For example, a stack might be implemented by an array of data elements.

The size of the array could be specified dynamically:

```
template <class T, int size>
class Stack {
  T _store[size];
public:
  ...
};
```

```
Stack<int,128> mystack;
```

In this example, *mystack* is a stack of integers using an array of 128 elements. However, in the following we will not use parameterized classes.

SHAPE AND TRAVERSAL

In the following discussion we distinguish between a data structure's *shape* and its *traversing strategies*. The first is the "look", which already provides plenty information about the *building blocks* of the data structure.

A traversing strategy defines the *order* in which elements of the data structure are to be visited. It makes sense to separate the shape from traversing strategies, because some data structures can be traversed using various strategies.

Traversing of a data structure is implemented using *iterators*. Iterators guarantee to visit each data item of their associated data structure in a well defined order.

They must provide at least the following properties:

- *Current element*: The iterator visits data elements one at a time. The element which is currently visited is called "current element".
- *Successor function*: The execution of the step to the next data element depends on the traversing strategy implemented by the iterator. The "successor function" is used to return the element which is next to be visited: It returns the successor of the current element.
- *Termination condition*: The iterator must provide a mechanism to check whether all elements are visited or not.

SHAPE IMPLEMENTATION

NODE TEMPLATES

The basic building block of a list is the *node*. Thus, let's first declare a class for it. A node has nothing more than a pointer to another node. Let's assume, that this neighbour is always on the right side.

Have a look at the following declaration of class *Node*.

```
class Node {
  Node *_right;
public:
  Node(Node *right = NULL): _right(right) {}
  Node(const Node &val): _right(val._right)
{}
  const Node *right() const { return _right;
  }
  Node *&right() { return _right; }
  Node &operator =(const Node &val) {
    _right = val._right;
    return *this;
  }
  const int operator ==(const Node &val) const
  {
    return _right == val._right;
  }
  const int operator !=(const Node &val) const
  {
    return !(*this == val);
  }
};
```

A look to the first version of method *right()* contains a const just before the method body. When used in this position, const declares the method to be constant regarding the elements of the invoking object. Consequently, you are only allowed to use this mechanism in method declarations or definitions, respectively.

This type of const modifier is also used to check for overloading. Thus,

```
class Foo {
  ...
  int foo() const;
  int foo();
};
```

declare two different methods. The former is used in constant contexts whereas the second is used in variable contexts.

Although template class *Node* implements a simple node it seems to define plenty of functionality.

We do this, because it is good practice to offer at least the following functionality for each defined data type:

- *Copy Constructor*: The copy constructor is needed to allow definition of objects which are initialized from already existing ones.
- *operator* =: Each object should know how to assign other objects (of the same type) to itself. In our example class, this is simply the pointer assignment.
- *operator* =: Each object should know how to compare itself with another object.

The unequality operator "!=" is implemented by using the definition of the equality operator. Recall, that this points to the invoking object, thus,

```
Node a, b;
...
if (a != b)...
```

would result in a call to *operator !=()* with this set to the address of *a*. We dereference this using the standard dereference operator "*". Now, *this is an object of class *Node* which is compared to another object using *operator ==()*. Consequently, the definition of *operator ==()* of class *Node* is used. Using the standard boolean NOT operator "!" we negate the result and obtain the truth value of *operator !=()*.

The above methods should be available for each class you define. This ensures that you can use your objects as you would use any other objects, for example integers. If some of these methods make no sense for whatever reason, you should declare them in a private section of the class to explicitly mark them as not for public use. Otherwise the C++ compiler would substitute standard operators.

Obviously, real applications require the nodes to carry data. As mentioned above, this means to specialize the nodes. Data can be of any type, hence, we are using the template construct.

```
template <class T>
class DataNode: public Node {
```

```
    T _data;
  public:
  DataNode(const T data, DataNode *right =
NULL):
    Node(right), _data(data) {}
  DataNode(const DataNode &val):
    Node(val), _data(val._data) {}
  const DataNode *right() const {
    return((DataNode *) Node::right());
  }
  DataNode *&right() { return((DataNode *&)
Node::right()); }
  const T &data() const { return _data; }
  T &data() { return _data; }
  DataNode &operator =(const DataNode &val) {
    Node::operator =(val);
    _data = val._data;
    return *this;
  }
  const int operator ==(const DataNode &val)
const {
    return(
      Node::operator ==(val) &&
      _data == val._data);
  }
  const int operator !=(const DataNode &val)
const {
      return !(*this == val);
    }
};
```

The above template *DataNode* simply specializes class *Node* to carry data of any type. It adds functionality to access its data element and also offers the same set of standard functionality: *Copy Constructor, operator =()* and *operator ==()*. Note, how we reuse functionality already defined by class *Node*.

List Templates

Now we are able to declare the list template. We also use

the template mechanism here, because we want the list to carry data of arbitrary type. For example, we want to be able to define a list of integers. We start with an abstract class template *ListBase* which functions as the base class of all other lists. For example, doubly linked lists obviously share the same properties like singly linked lists.

```
template <class T>
class ListBase {
public:
  virtual ~ListBase() {} // Force destructor
  to be
                         // virtual
virtual void flush() = 0;
virtual void putInFront(const T data) = 0;
virtual void append(const T data) = 0;
virtual void delFromFront() = 0;
virtual const T &getFirst() const = 0;
virtual T &getFirst() = 0;
virtual const T &getLast() const = 0;
virtual T &getLast() = 0;
virtual const int isEmpty() const = 0;
};
```

What we actually do is to describe the interface of every list by specifying the prototypes of required methods. We do that for every operation we have identified in section 10.3. Additionally, we also include a method *flush()* which allows us to delete all elements of a list.

For operations *get-first* and *get-last* we have declared two versions. One is for use in a constant context and the other in a variable context.

With this abstract class template we are able to actually define our list class template:

```
template <class T>
class List: public ListBase<T> {
  DataNode<T> *_head, *_tail;
public:
  List(): _head(NULL), _tail(NULL) {}
  List(const List &val): _head(NULL),
```

```
  _tail(NULL) {
      *this = val;
  }
  virtual ~List() { flush(); }
  virtual void flush();
  virtual void putInFront(const T data);
  virtual void append(const T data);
  virtual void delFromFront();
  virtual const T &getFirst() const { return
_head->data(); }
  virtual T &getFirst() { return _head->data();
  }
  virtual const T &getLast() const { return
 _tail->data(); }
  virtual T &getLast() { return _tail->data();
  }
  virtual const int isEmpty() const { return
_head == NULL; }
  List &operator =(const List &val) {
  flush();
    DataNode<T> *walkp = val._head;
    while (walkp) append(walkp->data());
    return *this;
  }
  const int operator ==(const List &val) const
  {
    if (isEmpty() && val.isEmpty()) return 1;
    DataNode<T> *thisp = _head,
                *valp = val._head;
    while (thisp && valp) {
      if (thisp->data() != valp->data()) return
      0;
      thisp = thisp->right();
      valp = valp->right();
    }
    return 1;
  }
  const int operator !=(const List &val) const
```

```
{
    return !(*this == val);
  }
    friend class ListIterator<T>;
  };
```

The constructors initialize the list's elements *_head* and *_tail* to NULL which is the NUL pointer in C and C++. You should know how to implement the other methods from your programming experience.

Here we only present the implementation of method putInFront():

```
template <class T> void
List<T>::putInFront(const T data) {
  _head = new DataNode<T>(data, _head);
  if (!_tail) _tail = _head;
} /* putInFront */
```

If we define methods of a class template outside of its declaration, we must also specify the template keyword. Again we use the new operator to create a new data node dynamically. This operator allows initialization of its created object with arguments enclosed in parenthesis. In the above example, new creates a new instance of class *DataNode<T>*. Consequently, the corresponding constructor is called.

Also notice how we use placeholder *T*. If we would create a class instance of class template *List*, say, *List<int>* this would also cause creation of a class instance of class template *DataNode*, viz *DataNode<int>*. The last line of the class template declaration declares class template *ListIterator* to be a friend of *List*. We want to separately define the list's iterator. However, it is closely related, thus, we allow it to be a friend.

ITERATOR IMPLEMENTATION

In this chapter we have introduced the concept of iterators to traverse through a data structure.

Iterators must implement three properties:

- Current element.
- Successor function.
- Termination condition.

Generally speaking, the iterator successively returns data associated with the current element. Obviously, there will be a method, say, *current()* which implements this functionality. The return type of this method depends on the type of data stored in the particular data structure. For example, when iterating over *List<int>* the return type should be int.

The successor function, say, *succ()*, uses additional information which is stored in structural elements of the data structure. In our list example, these are the nodes which carry the data *and* a pointer to their right neighbour. The type of the structural elements usually differs from that of the raw data. Consider again our *List<int>* where *succ()* must use *DataNode<int>* as structural elements.

The termination condition is implemented by a method, say, *terminate()*, which returns *TRUE* if (and only if) all data elements of the associated data structure have been visited. As long as *succ()* can find an element not yet visited, this method returns *FALSE*.

Again we want to specify an abstract iterator class which defines properties of every iterator.

The thoughts above lead to the following declaration:

```
template <class Data, class Element>
class Iterator {
protected:
    Element _start,
            _current;
public:
  Iterator(const Element start):
    _start(start), _current(start) {}
  Iterator(const Iterator &val):
    _start(val._start), _current(val._current)
    {}
virtual ~Iterator() {}
virtual const Data current() const = 0;
virtual void succ() = 0;
virtual const int terminate() const = 0;
virtual void rewind() { _current = _start; }
Iterator &operator =(const Iterator &val) {
```

```
    _start = val._start;
    _current = val._current;
    return *this;
  }
  const int operator ==(const Iterator &val)
const {
    return(_start == val._start && _current ==
    val._current);
  }
    const int operator !=(const Iterator &val)
    const {
      return !(*this == val);
  }
};
```

Again we use the template mechanism to allow the use of the iterator for any data structure which stores data of type *Data* and which uses structural elements of type *Element*. Each iterator "knows" a starting (structural) element and the current element.

We make both accessible from derived classes because derived iterators need access to them to implement the following iterator properties. You should already understand how the constructors operate and why we force the destructor to be virtual.

Subsequently we specify three methods which should implement the three properties of an iterator. We also add a method *rewind()* which simply sets the current element to the start element.

However, complex data structures (for example hash tables) might require more sophisticated rewind algorithms. For that reason we also specify this method to be virtual, allowing derived iterators to redefine it for their associated data structure.

The last step in the iterator implementation process is the declaration of the list iterator. This iterator is highly related to our class template *List*, for example, it is clear that the structural elements are class templates *DataNode*. The only "open" type is the one for the data.

Once again, we use the template mechanism to provide list iterators for the different list types:

```
  template <class T>
  class ListIterator: public Iterator<T,
 DataNode<T> *> {
  public:
    ListIterator(const List<T> &list):
      Iterator<T, DataNode<T> *>(list._head) {}
    ListIterator(const ListIterator &val):
      Iterator<T, DataNode<T> *>(val) {}
  virtual const T current() const { return
 _current->data(); }
  virtual void succ() { _current = _current-
>right(); }
  virtual const int terminate() const {
    return _current == NULL;
  }
  T &operator ++(int) {
    T &tmp = _current->data();
    succ();
    return tmp;
  }
  ListIterator &operator =(const ListIterator
 &val) {
    Iterator<T, DataNode<T> *>::operator =(val);
    return *this;
  }
 };
```

The class template *ListIterator* is derived from *Iterator*. The type of data is, of course, the type for which the list iterator is declared, hence, we insert placeholder *T* for the iterator's data type *Data*. The iteration process is achieved with help of the structural elements of type *DataNode*.

Obviously the starting element is the head of the list *_head* which is of type *DataNode<T> **. We choose this type for the element type *Element*.

Note that the list iterator actually hides the details about the structural elements. This type highly depends on the implementation of the list. For example, if we would have chosen an array implementation, we may have used integers as structural elements where the current element is indicated by an array index.

The first constructor takes the list to traverse as its argument and initializes its iterator portion accordingly. As each *ListIterator<T>* is a friend of *List<T>* it has access to the list's private members. We use this to initialize the iterator to point to the head of the list.

We omit the destructor because we do not have any additional data members for the list iterator. Consequently, we do nothing special for it. However, the destructor of class template *Iterator* is called. Recall that we have to define this destructor to force derived classes to also have a virtual one.

The next methods just define the required three properties.

*Now that we have structural elements defined as DataNode<T> * we use them as follows*:

- The current element is the data carried by the current structural element.
- The successor function is to set the current structural element to its right neighbour.
- The termination condition is to check the current structural element if it is the NULL pointer.

Note that this can happen only in two cases:

- The list is empty. In this case the current element is already NULL because the list's head *_head* is NULL.
- The current element reached the last element. In this case the previous successor function call set the current element to the right neighbour of the last element which is NULL.

We have also included an overloaded postincrement operator "++". To distinguish this operator from the preincrement operator, it takes an additional (anonymous) integer argument. As we only use this argument to declare a correct operator prototype and because we do not use the value of the argument, we omit the name of the argument.

The last method is the overloaded assignment operator for list iterators. Similar to previous assignment operators, we just reuse already defined assignments of superclasses; *IteratorM<T>::operator =()* in this case.

The other methods and operators, namely *rewind()*, *operator ==()* and *operator !=()* are all inherited from class template *Iterator*.

EXAMPLE USAGE

The list template as introduced in previous sections can be used as follows:

```
int
main() {
  List<int> list;
  int ix;
  for (ix = 0; ix < 10; ix++) list.append(ix);
  ListIterator<int> iter(list);
  while (!iter.terminate()) {
    printf("%d ", iter.current());
    iter.succ();
  }
  puts("");
  return 0;
}
```

As we have defined a postincrement operator for the list iterator, the loop can also be written as:

```
  while (!iter.terminate())
    print("%d ", iter++);
```

Index